THE
REASON
WHY

THE
REASON
WHY

by Cecil Woodham-Smith

With an Introduction by Gordon A. Craig

TIME Reading Program Special Edition
Time-Life Books Inc., Alexandria, Virginia

TIME®
LIFE
BOOKS

Time-Life Books Inc.
is a wholly owned subsidiary of
TIME INCORPORATED

Time Reading Program: *Editor,* Max Gissen

Library of Congress CIP data following page 312.

For information about any Time-Life book, please write:
Reader Information, Time-Life Books,
541 North Fairbanks Court, Chicago, Illinois 60611

Contents

Editors' Preface

Bravery and stupidity often go hand in hand in the same man, and military history is unhappily rich in examples. If Cecil Woodham-Smith had done nothing more in *The Reason Why* than document a classic instance during the Crimean War, hers would still be an excellent book. Certainly anyone familiar with Tennyson's *The Charge of the Light Brigade* would be unlikely to put it aside unfinished. Yet documenting the tragic follies of a few highly placed officers might not be enough to put her in that small pantheon of women who have written brilliantly about war. Historian Bruce Catton says of *The Reason Why:* "Here is battle writing as good as the best."

What she attempted, and succeeded in doing with faultless skill, was to show that consigning the Light Brigade to death was not an isolated instance of unintelligent leadership. It was, in fact, an end result of a system of social and political feeling about men at arms that all of England was guilty of perpetuating. If the witless sons of highborn men could buy—for enormous sums, to be sure—the high ranks for which they had not the slightest qualifications, then eventual disaster became certain.

Two such sons are the central actors in *The Reason Why.* Both dreamed of military glory, but under the system neither was required to win his spurs through experience and ability.

viii

Why should they? Even the Duke of Wellington, who happened to be a military genius, believed in the system of buying rank. Did it not protect the nation from possible domination by military professionals by putting the important commands into the hands of people who had a social and financial stake in the country? And so it came about that when the Crimean War started, 54-year-old George Charles Bingham, third Earl of Lucan, sailed for the Black Sea as major-general in command of the cavalry division; 57-year-old James Thomas Brudenell, seventh Earl of Cardigan, went as brigadier-general in command of the Light Brigade. Neither lord was competent to command, both had flaws of character so serious as to promise trouble from the first, and as brothers-in-law who detested each other, Lord Lucan and Lord Cardigan were soon absorbed in a personal wrangle that became fully as important to them as the war itself.

Possibly no one read an omen into the fact that Lord Cardigan was given command of the Light Brigade on April Fool's Day, 1854. He had never commanded troops in action. He had abused his men and officers so contemptuously that his was a hated name and he was repeatedly booed when he appeared in public. His love affairs were "legendary, and whole villages in Northamptonshire were said to have been populated by him with the children denied him in marriage." It was his habit when setting out for the hunt in his carriage to breakfast on pheasant and champagne, then throw the remains out the window ("That's the only way to enjoy a picnic in comfort, without any mess!").

Author Woodham-Smith was fascinated as she dug into the facts about Lord Cardigan: "I fell in love with him. He was so handsome, so brave, so stupid, so generous—and arrogant—that's what I adored about him." Unfortunately, a lot of other people including Queen Victoria and her consort, Prince Albert, felt the same way about him. What did not seem to matter to his admirers was the very thing that *The Reason Why* makes clear: "The melancholy truth was that his glorious golden head had nothing in it."

Lord Lucan did not suffer from the same degree of empty-headedness, but he was incompetent to command for other reasons. His cruelty to the starving peasants on his huge Irish estates brought him the ugly name of The Exterminator. He was a martinet, an unreasonable stickler for petty detail, and so far behind the times in military matters (he had been in retirement for the past 17 years) that he had not even mastered the contemporary words of command. When he gave an order during training exercises, he was simply not understood. Like Lord Cardigan, he neither knew nor had troubled to learn the most elementary lessons of military experience. Both men were brave, but there was one important difference between them: Lord Lucan shared the discomforts of his men; Cardigan lived luxuriously aboard his well-provisioned yacht anchored in Balaclava Harbor while his men died of cold, hunger and disease.

The Crimean War, as military historian Gordon A. Craig points out in his Introduction to this special edition of *The Reason Why*, was a war wanted by no one (unless one excepts public opinion inflamed by an irresponsible press) and blundered through to inconclusion. Small boys playing at soldiers might have given sounder orders in the same circumstances. When the ships sailed from England, women accompanied their men as if it were a holiday outing. Horses were smashed to death in the inadequate transports, supply lines were almost ingeniously unreliable and medical equipment was lacking. Disease, especially cholera, killed more Englishmen than the enemy. As if all this were not enough, Lord Raglan, the commander-in-chief of the British expeditionary forces, had no experience as a combat commander. He had been an aide to Wellington and had lost an arm at Waterloo, but now at 65, he was tragically incompetent on and off the battlefield.

Take it as biography, social history or the imperishable story of a military blunder, *The Reason Why* is a fine achievement. What is remarkable is that the book is the work of a frail, charming lady in her sixties who lived in London but might be said to have breathed the air of the 19th Century. After writing advertising and fiction, she was persuaded to direct her deep but informal knowledge of the time of Victoria toward a biography of Florence Nightingale. It took eight years to research and write, and when it appeared it was at once recognized by critics as the superior book it was: "passionately interesting" and "brilliantly illuminating."

The Reason Why is a sort of by-product of *Florence Nightingale,* for it was a chance letter found in doing research for her first book that led Cecil Woodham-Smith to unravel the lives of Lords Lucan and Cardigan, and so search out the truth of what happened and why on that bloody day at Balaclava in the Crimea. The book took five years to write.

Before her death in 1977, the author of *The Reason Why* had plans for one more book: "I should like for fun to write a military biography of my own great-great-uncle, that brave, foul-mouthed old devil, General Sir Thomas Picton, one of Wellington's generals. He used to lead troops into battle wearing a top hat and yelling 'Tally Ho.' He was killed at Waterloo, and when the news was brought to Wellington the Iron Duke wept."

—THE EDITORS

Introduction

Among the many distinguished writers who have dealt with the war in the Crimea, none has been as successful as Cecil Woodham-Smith in portraying the tragic mismanagement that characterized that foolish military speculation. In her masterful biography of Florence Nightingale, where she dealt with the failure to provide medical and sanitary facilities for an army that had to campaign in lands where cholera was endemic, there are pages from which the stench of misery and disease and despair assaults the nostrils of the reader, leaving him shaken and appalled. In *The Reason Why*, shifting the focus of her attention to the operational aspects of the British war effort, she has written a classic account of what can happen to a spirited and disciplined force of fighting men when it is commanded by officers who do not know their trade.

The Crimean War is an inglorious episode of the Victorian era, and it reflects credit neither on British statecraft nor on British arms. After the conflict had started, there were few Englishmen who could have explained why it had been necessary to go to war in the Near East, and after it was over, Lord Stanmore said sadly that the struggle had been "undertaken to resist an attack that was never threatened and probably never contemplated."

The beginning was an obscure dispute in the Holy Land that led the Russian government to intervene in Turkish affairs. Protests were made by the governments of France and Great Britain. Diplomatic negotiations that were intended to settle the original differences were badly handled and led to mutual recrimination and suspicion of bad faith. As tension mounted and fighting broke out between the Russians and the Turks, English public opinion, stimulated by jingoistic newspaper stories, began to clamor for war. Although there were opportunities that might have been exploited by a diplomacy bent upon settlement, the government yielded to pressure and dispatched to St. Petersburg an ultimatum that precipitated hostilities.

In view of the condition of the British army, this action bordered on irresponsibility. The army had been resting on the laurels it had won under Wellington's leadership in the Peninsula and at Waterloo, and it had done nothing to keep pace with military developments that had occurred in the intervening 40 years. Albert, the Prince Consort, who had resisted the drift toward war and been vilified by the newspapers for his pains, was among the few who were aware of the army's unpreparedness. In a careful memorandum written after the fighting had started, he pointed out: "We have no generals trained and practised in the duties of that rank; no general staff or corps; no field commissariat; no field army department; no ambulance corps; no baggage train; no corps of drivers; no corps of artisans; no practice, or possibility of acquiring it, in the combined use of the three arms—cavalry, infantry and artillery; no general qualified to handle more than one of these arms; and the artillery kept as distinct from the army as if it were a separate profession."

In these circumstances, to attempt to fight a war on a far-off peninsula in the Black Sea against a powerful empire that had defeated the genius of Bonaparte by its size alone was to invite disaster. The Crimean War was—as Lloyd George was to say later of another unfortunate British campaign—"a muddy and muddled enterprise" in which the total casualties were higher than those of any other European war between 1815 and 1914, and in which nearly every operational plan conceived by the British command revealed ignorance of the principles of modern war.

The system of command in any army is, of course, a reflection of the social organization and stratification of the country that raised it. Despite the political and social changes set in train by the Industrial Revolution, England, in the first half of the 19th Century, was still a country in which the aristocracy was regarded with deference and given privileges that were not open to other men. Lord Melbourne once said that what he liked about the Order of the Garter was that there was "no damned merit" in the selection of its membership. The same might have been said about other organizations and professions in which the sons of noble families interested themselves: the possession of talent was not a prerequisite for their preferment, and delinquencies that would have ruined lesser men went unpunished when committed by aristocrats. A glaring example was the British army, which practiced the traditional system of purchase, whereby a man first bought his commission and then paid for each subsequent step in rank.

How this system worked is revealed in the first part of Mrs. Woodham-Smith's book, which describes the early careers of George Bingham (later Lord Lucan) and his brother-in-law James Brudenell (later Lord Cardigan). Both these men advanced to the rank of lieutenant-colonel before they were 35 years old, and found themselves giving orders to officers with long years of garrison and overseas service. Lucan was a barely competent peacetime commander. But even for garrison duty, Cardigan proved to be impossible; he indulged in a neurotic campaign of persecution against those of his junior officers who had served in India, exposed them to public embarrassment, and denied them leaves and promotions. When these antics became a national scandal and led to the loss of his first command in 1834, his court connections were powerful enough to secure his reinstatement as colonel of another regiment.

The British commander-in-chief, Lord Raglan, a veteran of Waterloo with a tired mind and a disinclination to be bothered with matters of detail, proved incapable of imposing his own wavering will upon his headstrong subordinates and could not persuade himself to recommend the recall of either of them. The disastrous charge of the Light Brigade at Balaclava was the end result of this situation. Mrs. Woodham-Smith's brilliant account of the charge reveals the way in which Raglan's indecisiveness and Lucan's intentness on preserving his authority combined to send the gallant horsemen of the Light Brigade on their doomed mission against the Russian batteries.

Mrs. Woodham-Smith's skill as a social analyst, so ably demonstrated in her Nightingale biography, is also evident on every page of this book. In addition, she shows here a remarkable gift for describing battle engagements. In all the literature on the Crimean War, there is no more exciting and moving account of the Light Brigade's advance than the one given in the final chapters of *The Reason Why*. But this episode does not stand alone, and the reader will find himself remembering other vivid passages. There is, for example, the marvelous description of the uphill charge of the Heavy Brigade at Balaclava. Mrs. Woodham-Smith shows us this engagement as Raglan saw it from his command post on the heights above the battlefield: the "astonishing sight" of the Inniskillings and the Scots Greys being "swallowed up, lost and engulfed in the great grey Russian mass, and then suddenly they had not disappeared. Red coats were visible, bright specks of colour against the Russian grey: the men of the Heavy Brigade were alive, fighting, their sword arms moving like toys and . . . the great grey square heaved and upon the heights a roar like the roar of the sea could be heard, made up, said those who were near the battle, of the violent and ceaseless cursing of the British troopers hacking at the thick Russian uniforms."

Nathaniel Hawthorne once observed that the Crimean War gave Britain "a vast impulse toward democracy." The revelation of the criminal blunderings of men like Raglan, Lucan and Cardigan cast a cold, clear light on the inadequacies of a system based upon privilege. The resultant demand for reform not only revolutionized the administration of the British army but effected changes in many other areas in the years after the war. The tragic conflict in the Crimea was, therefore, not wholly without positive result, and the valor of the common soldier, so ably portrayed in this fine book, was not in vain.

—GORDON A. CRAIG

Acknowledgment

This curious story has never been told before—no biography of
Lord Lucan, Lord Cardigan, or Lord Raglan having, as yet, been
written. It has emerged piece by piece from private letters and
diaries, from dispatches and War Office correspondence, from
law reports, from files of newspapers, and from privately printed
pamphlets preserved in country houses.

I am above all indebted to the Earl of Lucan, M.C., who with
great generosity placed his family papers unreservedly at my
disposal. Without his support and information this book could
not have been written. I have received valuable assistance from
Mr. George Brudenell, the present owner of Deene Park, and
Miss Joan Wake, the Secretary of the Northamptonshire Record
Society. I was not only allowed to use the Brudenell papers at
Lamport Hall, but was also assisted with much private information. I should also like to thank the Earl of Cardigan for allowing me access to the Ailesbury Papers and for his kindness and
patience. I owe a special debt of gratitude to the Duke of Wellington, K.G., who gave me permission to see the Wellington
Papers at Apsley House and to quote unpublished extracts from
them, and I should like to thank His Grace's Librarian, Mr.
Francis Needham, for guiding me in my search through that
immense collection of papers. I was enabled to use Field Marshal

Lord Raglan's Military Papers, deposited at the library of the Royal United Service Institution, by the kind permission of Lord Raglan.

I have been singularly fortunate in the large number of letters and diaries which have been placed at my disposal, and I should like especially to thank Mrs. Monro for the exceptional collection of letters and notes written, as a young man serving in the 11th Hussars, by Gen. William Charles Forrest, C.B. I am also grateful to the Misses Paynter for the letters of Lieutenant Seager, 8th Hussars, later Lieutenant-General Seager, C.B. Among many privately printed letters I am particularly indebted to Miss Sophie Portal for the letters of Capt. Robert Portal, 4th Light Dragoons, and to Mr. Kenneth Moir for the letters of Cornet Fisher-Rowe, 4th Dragoon Guards.

I should like to record my obligation to Brigadier C. N. Barclay, C.B.E., D.S.O., who checked the manuscript from a military aspect, supervised the maps, and contributed much valuable advice, and to thank Mr. Michael Egan and many friends in Castlebar, Co. Mayo, for the trouble they took on my behalf and for local information of great interest. I am grateful to the authorities of the Royal United Service Institution for allowing me to use their library, and to Mr. T. Holland, the Librarian's Assistant, for his unfailing help. I have also to thank Mr. B. B. W. Goodden, who checked the legal points. By permission of Messrs. John Murray (publishers), Ltd., I have been allowed to quote from *Granville Leveson Gower (first Earl Granville), Private Correspondence, 1781–1821*, edited by Castalia Countess Granville, and by permission of Messrs. W. H. Allen & Co., Ltd., to use a letter from *A Queen at Home,* by Vera Watson.

C. W.-S.

Illustrations

Theirs not to reason why,
Theirs but to do and die:
Into the valley of Death
Rode the six hundred.

TENNYSON

CHAPTER

1

Military glory! It was a dream that century after century had seized on men's imaginations and set their blood on fire. Trumpets, plumes, chargers, the pomp of war, the excitement of combat, the exultation of victory—the mixture was intoxicating indeed. To command great armies, to perform deeds of valour, to ride victorious through flower-strewn streets, to be heroic, magnificent, famous—such were the visions that danced before men's eyes as they turned eagerly to war.

It was not a dream for the common man. War was an aristocratic trade, and military glory reserved for nobles and princes. Glittering squadrons of cavalry, long lines of infantry, wheeling obediently on the parade ground, ministered to the lust both for power and for display. Courage was esteemed the essential military quality and held to be a virtue exclusive to aristocrats. Were they not educated to courage, trained, as no common man was trained, by years of practice in dangerous sports? They glorified courage, called it valour and worshipped it, believed battles were won by valour, saw war in terms of valour as the supreme adventure.

It was a dream that died hard. Century followed century and glittering visions faded before the sombre realities of history. Great armies in their pride and splendour were defeated by starvation, pestilence, and filth; valour was sacrificed to stupidity, gallantry to corruption.

Yet the dream survived. In England, ten years after Waterloo, in spite of the harsh lessons of the previous fifty years, the humiliation and hunger of the Flanders campaign of 1794, the useless agony of Walcheren, the rags and fevers and retreats of the Peninsula, there were two men, still young, whose minds were obsessed by the desire for military glory. They were men of noble birth and wealth, who were also perhaps the two handsomest men in Europe, James Thomas Lord Brudenell, heir of the sixth Earl of Cardigan, and George Charles Lord Bingham, heir of the second Earl of Lucan.

The Brudenell family was ancient; Brudenell had succeeded Brudenell since the fourteenth century, wealthy, and strongly attached to the Crown. Indeed, it was from the Crown that they had derived their importance, rising in the world as courtiers and emerging from the respectable obscurity of county worthies through the ability to please a prince.

The first Brudenell to achieve consequence, Thomas Brudenell, was one of the original baronets created by James I upon the founding of the order in 1611. James's reasons for selecting him are not known, but when, in 1627, Thomas was raised to the rank and style of Baron Brudenell by Charles I, he first gave £5,000 in cash and a promissory note for £1,000 to the king's favourite, the Duke of Buckingham.

It was not a characteristic transaction. Bribery and backstairs dealings were foreign to Thomas Brudenell's nature: the mainspring of his conduct was loyalty.

When, in 1642, differences between King and Parliament ended in Civil War, Thomas Brudenell was a "zealous and faithful Royalist"; he raised a troop of horse for the King at his own expense, was captured, imprisoned in the Tower for two years, and fined £10,000. In 1648, when Charles became desperate, it was to Thomas Brudenell that he turned. Charles was a prisoner in Carisbrooke Castle, but believed he could escape if he had money. On September 5 he wrote in his own hand to Thomas Brudenell that if he would lend him £1,000, "I do hereby promise you, as soone as I have a great Seale in my owen Power, to confer on you the Tytle and Honnor of an Earle of this Kingdome; wherefor I hope you will take and trust to this my word."

Thomas Brudenell was himself in straits, his estate had been sequestrated; he had, he wrote, incurred losses of not less than £50,000 for the King's sake. Nevertheless the money was sent and the warrant made out on October 21, 1648. Within a few weeks Charles was taken to London, tried, and executed.

Thirteen years later, at the Restoration, Charles II fulfilled his father's promise and Thomas Brudenell was created Earl of Cardigan, on April 20, 1661, in the Banqueting Hall of Whitehall Palace.

The Brudenells were now great people, close to the King, moving in the innermost circle of the Court; powerful, and increasing their power by marrying their children into the first families in the kingdom. They were admirably fitted for their part. They were not scholars, philosophers, warriors, statesmen, nor patrons of the arts. They did not desire fame. They were content to be great people, with the only world they valued at their feet, firmly and arrogantly attached to the privileges of their class.

And above all they were good-looking. During the next two centuries the good looks of the Brudenells were to become proverbial.

Perhaps the most notorious, and the most sumptuous, of Restoration beauties was Anna Maria, Countess of Shrewsbury, the "woman made to punish men." Her reckless infatuation for the Duke of Buckingham forced her husband to challenge Buckingham to a duel. She is reputed to have disguised herself as a page, to have accompanied her lover to the duelling ground, to have

The Third Earl of Lucan at the Age of Twenty-two Wearing the Uniform of the Life Guards

The Seventh Earl of Cardigan at the Time of his Second Marriage

held the bridle of his horse while he ran her husband through the body, and to have spent the night with him while he wore the shirt soaked with her husband's blood. She was born Anna Marie Brudenell, daughter of the second Earl of Cardigan, and her portrait looks down from the wall at Deene, insolent, contemptuous, and superb.

For more than four hundred years Brudenells have lived at Deene Park, and the walls are lined with their portraits. Century after century, Brudenells look out from their frames, with hardly a plain face among them. Their hair clusters in silky curls, their skins glow, their eyes are large and brilliant, they are magnificently dressed, magnificently jewelled. Like splendid glossy animals they stare boldly at the world, with an arrogance springing not only from pride of birth, but from something deeper and haughtier; consciousness of physical beauty, pride of the flesh.

By the close of the eighteenth century the Brudenells had become of still greater consequence. Through a complicated series of events the immense estates of the Bruces, the Earls of Ailesbury, had come into the possession of a Brudenell. The third Earl of Cardigan married the only sister of the Earl of Ailesbury and had four sons. When the Earl of Ailesbury, in spite of three marriages, found himself without an heir, he adopted his sister's youngest son, Thomas Brudenell. It was impossible for the young man to succeed to his uncle's hereditary titles, but the additional title of Baron Bruce of Tottenham (the Ailesbury seat in Wiltshire) was conferred on the Earl of Ailesbury with a special remainder enabling the title to pass to his nephew; and in 1747, on his uncle's death, Thomas Brudenell became Lord Bruce. The Brudenells were still courtiers, and Thomas became Gentleman of the Bedchamber to George III, Chamberlain and Treasurer to Queen Charlotte, and was offered the post of Governor to the Prince of Wales. When George III wished to elevate him in the peerage, Thomas Brudenell asked that his uncle's title should be revived, and, to the confusion of future historians, he was created Earl of Ailesbury in his own right in 1776.

Thomas Brudenell, Earl of Ailesbury, became exceedingly important to the Brudenells. He had more ability than his brothers, and his possessions were immense—40,000 acres in Wiltshire, Hampshire and Berkshire; valuable estates in Yorkshire and the disposal of two seats in the House of Commons, Bedwyn and Marlborough. He became the great man of the family; his elder brothers treated him with deference and habitually asked and took his advice.

When, in November, 1793, Robert Brudenell, nephew and heir of the fifth Earl of Cardigan, wished to marry, he sought his powerful uncle's approval with some nervousness. He had reason to be nervous, for he had in fact, without asking anyone's permission, already engaged himself to a young lady who by no means came up to Brudenell standards. She had neither wealth nor title. She was a remarkably pretty Miss Cooke, Penelope Anne Cooke, the daughter of George Cooke, Esq., of Harefield, Middlesex.

Ailesbury was annoyed. Robert was only twenty-four, heir to the Earl of Cardigan and unusually handsome; absurd for him to throw himself away on a Miss Cooke. Robert must be made to see that the match was imprudent and ought to be given up. But, as Cardigan wrote to his brother on November 17, 1793, "There is no giving advice to a young man so much in love." Robert refused to be budged. What about the young lady herself? Ailesbury enquired. Had she been made fully aware of the imprudence of the match? At the end of November Cardigan wrote to report "a very long conversation with our nephew." Robert had "promised to communicate every particular to Miss Cooke," had "expressed himself as feeling very much obliged to us for the advice we gave him, and allowed there was much good sense in all I said." He "agreed he ought not to have made his proposals without consulting his uncles, cried very much and seemed very unhappy."

But, in spite of tears, he would not give up Miss Cooke, and on January 21, 1794, he wrote to Ailesbury "to announce my approaching marriage." He had called to see his uncle, but "finding you was dressing for the House of Lords, did not trouble you by coming in." He hoped "most sincerely" that the step he was going to take would meet with his uncle's approbation, "as nothing could make me so miserable as to forfeit your good opinion." Ailesbury's reply was brief. The match was imprudent, "therefore I never have nor can I now, express my approbation of the step you are going to take."

The marriage took place on March 8, 1794.

It was not a union which seemed likely to prosper, since its chief characteristics were imprudence, youth, and extreme good looks. But the married life of the young Brudenells unexpectedly turned out a rustic idyll. They chose to live quietly in the country at the Manor, Hambleden, Buckinghamshire, a Jacobean house set on gently rising ground and framed in chestnut trees. The rector of Hambleden at the time has left letters in which are glimpses of an amiable, charitable, and democratic pair. They preferred not to use their title and, even after Robert had succeeded his uncle as Earl of Cardigan, they were known in Hambleden as Mr. and Mrs. Brudenell. They were much given to good works, and Robert, "ever a good friend to Hambleden," bought two and a half acres of land and presented it to the village for cottagers' gardens; "these gardens are a great benefit and much prized." Penelope interested herself in the village women and the school. "She is a sweet woman, possessing .a temper both mild and engaging," wrote the rector.

And at the Manor on October 16, 1797, their second child and only male infant was born and christened James Thomas.

The circumstances surrounding his arrival were impressive. It was three generations since the succession of the Earls of Cardigan had gone direct from father to son. The much desired heir was of almost mystic importance, and, as he lay in his cradle, wealth, rank, power, and honours gathered round his head.

It was unfortunate that he was destined to grow up in a world that was almost entirely feminine. He already had an elder sister, and seven more girls followed his birth, of whom six survived. He remained the only son, the only boy among seven girls, unique, unchallenged, and the effect on his character was decisive. He was brought up at home among his sisters, and he grew up as such boys do, spoilt, domineering, and headstrong. No arm was stronger than his. No rude voice contradicted him, no rough shoulder pushed him. From his earliest consciousness he was the most important, the most interesting, the most influential person in the world.

He retained, however, from these early years, a liking for the society of women and a softness in his manner towards them which, having regard to his manner with men, struck his contemporaries with surprise. For a woman, a pretty woman, above all a pretty woman in distress, James Brudenell, later Lord Cardigan, had an almost mediæval deference, a chivalrous turn of phrase, a sometimes embarrassing readiness to protect and defend, which, though productive of astonishment and mirth, were nevertheless rooted in a genuine sympathy.

It was to be expected that his parents and sisters should be passionately attached to him, and natural affection and pride were immensely heightened by the circumstance of his extraordinary good looks. In him the Brudenell beauty had come to flower. He was tall, with wide shoulders tapering to a narrow waist, his hair was golden, his eyes flashing sapphire blue, his nose aristocratic, his bearing proud. If there was a fault it was that the lower part of his face was oddly long and narrow so that sometimes one was surprised to catch an obstinate, almost a foxy, look. But the boy had a dash and gallantry that were irresistible. He did not know what fear was. A superb and reckless horseman, he risked his neck on the most dangerous brutes. No tree was too tall for him to climb, no tower too high to scale.

He excelled in swordsmanship and promised to be a first-class shot. He had in addition to courage another characteristic which impressed itself on all who met him. He was, alas, unusually stupid; in fact, as Greville pronounced later, an ass. The melancholy truth was that his glorious golden head had nothing in it.

In 1811 his father succeeded as sixth Earl of Cardigan, and the family took possession of Deene Park. James was fourteen, and the young lord with his beauty and daring became a local legend. There is a tradition at Deene that through his reckless riding he had an accident which was responsible for the uncertainty and violence of his temper. The nearest town to Deene is Oundle, and it was his habit to scorn the road and gallop to Oundle across country. One day he was tearing along to Oundle on a young and intractable horse, forced the pace, was thrown at a gate, struck his head, and lay for weeks at death's door. When finally he recovered, his disposition had changed greatly for the worse. Where he had been imperious, now he was harsh and domineering; where he had been impatient, now he was uncontrollable and subject to fits of extraordinary and unreasonable rage.

In 1816 he went for two years to Christ Church, Oxford. Because he was a nobleman he was able to enter on a special and privileged footing. He wore a silk gown, brought his own horses and servants, provided his own food, and, had he taken a degree, would have been entitled to present himself after keeping fewer terms than a commoner. However, he left without undergoing any examination. A grand tour, more exciting than usual, followed, and when, in 1820, he was elected an original member of the Travellers' Club, he had visited Russia, Sweden, and Italy, and had acquired a taste for seeing the world which remained a pleasing characteristic. When he came of age, Lord Ailesbury gave him a seat in the House of Commons for Marlborough, one of the Ailesbury pocket boroughs.

The world was at his feet, and it was a world unimaginable today. It is almost impossible to picture the deference, the adulation, the extraordinary privileges accorded to the nobility in the first half of the nineteenth century. A peer was above the laws which applied to other men. He could run up debts, and no one could arrest him. When a famous set of roués and spendthrifts, including Beau Brummell, came to grief, one only, Lord Alvanley, survived, "invulnerable in his person from being a peer," wrote Greville. He could commit a criminal offence and no ordinary court had jurisdiction over him.

And the strange, the astonishing fact was that public opinion accorded these privileges not merely with willingness but with enthusiasm. Foreigners were struck by the extraordinary and eager deference paid by the English to their aristocracy. It was, as Richard Monckton Milnes wrote, "a lord loving country." Honest British merchants quivered with excitement in the presence of a peer, as if they were susceptible young men in the presence of a pretty girl. True, beneath the surface dark and gigantic forces were beginning to move, and in mines and mills, in rural hovels and cholera-infested city rookeries, half-starved, sub-human millions were beginning to stir in their sleep. But the wind of revolution that had blown from France seemed to have died away, and in England rank and privilege had never appeared more firmly entrenched. Flattered, adulated, deferred to, with incomes enormously increased by the Industrial Revolution, and as yet untaxed, all-powerful over a tenantry as yet unenfranchised, subject to no ordinary laws, holding the government of the country firmly in their hands and wielding through their closely knit connections an unchallengeable social power, the milords of England were the astonishment and admiration of Europe.

Of this aristocracy, James Brudenell, with his good looks and his physical prowess, was a superb specimen, and he had, even for his period, the prospect of enormous wealth. In spite of the imprudence of his father's marriage, the revenues of the sixth Earl of Cardigan were now estimated to be £40,000 a year.

What career should he adopt? Since the world lay at his feet, what use should he make of it? In an autobiographical document, preserved among the Brudenell papers, he writes that from boyhood he had only one desire, he wished to be a soldier; but he was prevented by his parents. He was an only son, the hopes of the family centred on him, and he was not to be allowed to endanger his life.

It was a bad moment to keep at home a boy who longed for soldiering. Throughout James Brudenell's childhood the Peninsular campaign was being fought, and the names of British victories, Vittoria, Badajoz, Salamanca, were on everyone's lips. He was eighteen at the date of Waterloo, lads younger than he took part in that great combat, and his mother's brother George Cooke commanded the first division and left an arm on the field.

But James, with his fearlessness, his physical energy, must stay at home; James the precious heir, the last of the Brudenells, must be kept safe. As a concession he was allowed, in 1819, to raise a troop of yeomanry from among the tenantry at Deene and to drill them in the Park.

There was perhaps a further reason. The violent estrangement between George III and his sons, those Royal Dukes whom Wellington described as, "the damnedest millstones that were ever hanged round the neck of any Government," had split Society into two camps. While the Royal Dukes and their friends were racing, drinking, piling up debts, and creating public scandals, surrounded by a cloud of mistresses, jockeys, and prize-fighters, the Court of George III and Queen Charlotte was sober, economical, and domestic. The Cardigans were loyal to the Court, and Lady Cardigan was Woman of the Bedchamber to Queen Charlotte as late as 1818, when George III was hopelessly insane and the Prince of Wales had become Regent.

But Lady Cardigan's family, the Cookes, had very different connections. Her brother, Colonel Sir Henry Frederick Cooke, a famous military dandy, was private aide-de-camp, secretary to, and intimate of the Duke of York, who had been Commander-in-Chief until in 1809 he was dismissed on the insistence of Parliament, following an enquiry into the sale of commissions by his ex-mistress, Mrs. Clarke. Though Greville said that the Duke of York was the only one of the Royal Dukes who had the feelings of a gentleman, he was also drunken, given to the society of disreputable women, perpetually in debt, and notorious for the coarseness of his language and humour. Colonel Cooke, known as Kangaroo Cooke from the immense length of his legs, wrote his letters and arranged his confidential business. In this direction he was employed not only by the Duke of York but by the hideous and vicious Duke of Cumberland, the most hated man in England. When the Duke of Cumberland was alleged to have made an indecent assault on Lady Lyndhurst, wife of the Lord Chancellor, Kangaroo Cooke was despatched to make things smooth. Famous for the daring elegance of his trousers and his cravats, moving in the best society, equally at home in London and Paris, and, thanks to his matchless knowledge of the lower side of high life, employed by the Government on important secret negotiations, Kangaroo Cooke was a man of immense backstairs influence.

By preventing James from entering the Army, his parents had wished to keep him morally as well as physically safe. They paid dearly for their decision. At this point something could have been made of him: he was young, he had courage, he had family affections. But since he could not be a soldier, he did nothing; and idle, frustrated, gloriously handsome, and immensely rich, he now formed a connection which was to prove fatal.

He had taken to spending a considerable amount of time in Paris. The pleasures which Paris offers, her elegance, the refinement of her luxury, had never been in sharper contrast to London than in 1823. Paris had invented the restaurant, and in place of the rough, bawling, steamy eating-houses of London were novel resorts with wood fires, thick carpets, snowy table-cloths. In place of the gargantuan excesses of the Regency, tables groaning under a mass of food, diners pouring bottle after bottle down their throats until they slid under the table, eating and drinking were raised to a delicate art. The city itself was still intricate, fantastic, and mediæval. Haussmann had not yet done his work, his boulevards did not exist, the Rue Richelieu was a fashionable street, the Palais Royal a fashionable promenade. The Second Empire, gaslight, the Rue de Rivoli, the Paris tripper had still to be born. Poor men did not come from London to Paris; it was a city of pleasure for the rich.

In Paris there was an English society, considerably more easy-going than society in London, and one of its leaders was Elizabeth, Countess of Aldborough, who had for many years reigned in Dublin as *maîtresse en titre* to the Lord-Lieutenant, Lord Westmorland. She declared that she had come to Paris for six weeks and stayed for six years, but the truth was that too many doors were closed against her in London. Though now approaching old age, she had still astonishing power to amuse, and almost every eminent person in Europe, including the Duke of Wellington, was her friend. She dressed and painted gorgeously, swore like a trooper, combined extraordinary effrontery with extraordinary good nature, and conversed with frankness of a past which had contained a remarkable number of lovers.

Her salon was one of the most entertaining in Paris, but it was hardly the circle the Cardigans would wish their only son to frequent. Moreover, in January, 1823, there was a special danger: Lady Aldborough was sheltering her beautiful granddaughter, Elizabeth Johnstone, who had just run away from her husband, Captain Johnstone, who happened to be an old friend of the Brudenell family.

Lord Brudenell and Mrs. Johnstone met and fell instantly and violently in love.

Elizabeth had been born a Tollemache, one of the family which owned the strange fairy-tale mansion of Ham House, a Sleeping Beauty's castle where almost nothing had been changed, or has yet been changed, since the seventeenth century. Her father, Admiral Tollemache, originally named Halliday, had assumed the name on inheriting property from an aunt. The

Hallidays had become rich as sugar-planters in Antigua, and some tropical heat and fury seemed to linger in their blood. Elizabeth's father was a violent man, who put one of his grown-up sisters-in-law across his knee in the drawing-room and gave her a beating for making fun of him, and the family history was full of sudden infatuations, elopements, and frantic jealousies. Violence, passion, and recklessness were in Elizabeth's blood, but her appearance was fragile. She was lovely, with a delicate pointed face, enormous dark eyes, a cloud of hair, a rosebud mouth, and a childlike wistful charm.

She had married Captain Johnstone against her parents' wishes. The match was not a good one; the Tollemaches were rich, while Captain Johnstone had only very moderate means. However, Elizabeth was wildly in love, and married they were. Within three months Captain Johnstone begged his wife's father to arrange a separation. Elizabeth could not endure being a poor man's wife, furiously resented being deprived of the luxuries she had at home, and made their life together intolerable. Admiral Tollemache attempted to reason with his daughter. Her temper equalled his, high words passed, and Elizabeth rushed from the house to her grandmother in Paris. There she found she was pregnant, and she was persuaded to return to her husband. A daughter was born and they set up house together again, living, according to Admiral Tollemache, "very unhappily" together. On January 7, 1823, Captain Johnstone went to stay at Crichel in Dorset to shoot with Mr. Henry Charles Sturt, who had recently married Lady Charlotte Brudenell, one of the seven Brudenell sisters. As soon as he had gone, Elizabeth left home, appeared at her father's house, quarrelled furiously with him once more, and once more fled to her grandmother in Paris.

This time she did not return, and during the summer her husband learned that she had eloped with Lord Brudenell and was living with him at Versailles.

In the autumn they came back to London and lived together as man and wife in an hotel in Bond Street; and the following

June Captain Johnstone brought an action for damages against Lord Brudenell, the first step in the long, costly, and cumbrous process, involving a special Act of Parliament, at that time the only method by which a marriage could be dissolved.

Captain Johnstone had known the Brudenell family all his life, and had been intimate with James Brudenell since boyhood. It was, however, repeatedly stated in the course of the action, and nowhere contradicted, that nothing had occurred between Mrs. Johnstone and Lord Brudenell until she was in Paris, "though as the wife of a friend she was known to him."

Lord Brudenell offered no defence and did not appear. He was represented by Counsel, who made a speech on his behalf submitting unreservedly to the discretion of the court. Lord Brudenell, said Counsel, "was a nobleman of the strictest honour, who had insisted that no slightest reflection was to be made, either upon the lady or the plaintiff in the case . . . his client would willingly submit to such damages as the jury might think it proper to award. . . . Whatever occurred between Mrs. Johnstone and Lord Brudenell did not occur until after the lady had quitted her husband. . . . Lord Brudenell could not be accused of having recourse to the arts of the seducer." References were made to the high station in life of both parties, to Mrs. Johnstone's "great personal charms and distinguished beauty," and to "Lord Brudenell's violent and irresistible attachment." The jury awarded Captain Johnstone £1,000.

After the trial Lord Brudenell sent a messenger to Captain Johnstone, offering to "give him satisfaction," to fight a duel with him for having run away with his wife. Captain Johnstone burst out laughing in the messenger's face. "Tell Lord Brudenell," he said, "that he has already given me satisfaction: the satisfaction of having removed the most damned bad-tempered and extravagant bitch in the kingdom."

Two years later, on June 26, 1826, a divorce having been obtained and a special Act of Parliament dissolving the marriage passed, James Brudenell and Elizabeth Tollemache were privately married in the Chapel at Ham House, among antique splendours of dark oak and crimson velvet, at the altar where a prayer book Charles II left behind still lies. Elizabeth was described as "being now single and unmarried."

The marriage was a disaster. They had been living as man and wife for more than three years, and he was aware that she was promiscuous, extravagant, and bad-tempered. Only a strict sense of honour, according to the second Lady Cardigan, compelled him to make her his wife. His contemporaries, even those who dislike him most, point to the union with Elizabeth Tollemache as the decisive misfortune of his life. There were no children of the marriage; he received no affection, no assistance, no control. It is too much to say that married to a different woman he might have been a different man, but perhaps married to a different woman his faults might not have been so public a nuisance.

Meanwhile, when it was too late, his parents had withdrawn their opposition to his entering the Army. Through the interest of the Duke of York a cornetcy was procured for him in the 8th Hussars, and he began his service in May, 1824. He was twenty-seven, a good deal older than was usual, but the Duke of York, he writes in his autobiographical sketch, "promised that if I paid attention to my military duties he would push me in the service." The Duke of York certainly kept his word. Six months after Lord Brudenell joined the regiment he was promoted lieutenant and, after two years' service, just before his marriage in 1826, he was promoted captain.

The next few years were comparatively serene. His mother, perhaps fortunately, died in 1826. He employed himself, he says, "attending with the greatest assiduity to his regimental duties," proving himself at once rigid, tireless, and meticulous, indefatigable regarding details of discipline and precedence and all matters relating to the arrangement of epaulettes and the colour and tightness of trousers. His own opinion of his military capacities was very high; he thirsted for command, nor did he hesitate to seize it when opportunity offered. On one occasion, the colonel being away on leave, and the senior major in bed with a cold, Lord Brudenell, happening to find himself senior officer present, instantly assumed command and ordered the regiment out for a field day, though it was winter.

He was not, however, merely ridiculous and a nuisance, he was dangerous, for it was a period when an assertive, quarrelsome man was exceedingly dangerous. His readiness to duel was notorious, he challenged on the slightest provocation, lying in wait, it seemed, during an argument for a chance to enforce his opinions with a pistol. Contradiction, correction, difference of opinion, even of the mildest kind, had a frightening effect on him; his face became suffused, the veins on his temples swelled, the good looks were wiped from his face.

Then in 1829 an event which seemed merely of family importance took place: his youngest sister Anne married George Charles Lord Bingham, eldest son of the second Earl of Lucan.

CHAPTER

2

The two young men disliked each other from the first. Indeed, it seemed as if nature had intended them to be rivals. Every characteristic, even their good looks, invited comparison. While James Brudenell was brilliantly fair, golden-haired, and blue-eyed, George Bingham was the very model of a Byronic hero, dark, passionate, romantic. Both were soldiers, fiercely ambitious in their profession; both were proud, narrow, overbearing, and peremptory. But George Bingham, three years the younger and far superior in intelligence, had achieved more than James. He had been a professional soldier since the age of sixteen, had seen active service, had been decorated, and now, at the age of twenty-six, was a lieutenant-colonel in command of the 17th Lancers, while James Brudenell at the age of twenty-nine had only reached the rank of captain.

The Brudenells and the Binghams sprang from very different roots, and the origin of the Binghams was stern and fierce. The family was founded by three brothers, Richard, George, and John Bingham, soldiers of fortune in the Irish wars of Queen Elizabeth. Richard Bingham rose to be military governor of the intractable province of Connaught, and his rule was so merciless that the ferocity of the Binghams became a legend, and to this day his name is execrated in the west of Ireland. Among many massacres, he ordered the execution of all Spaniards shipwrecked on the coast of Connaught after the Armada, and boasted that he had caused the throats of more than a thousand men to be cut.

The Binghams acquired a baronetcy, a stronghold at Castlebar, and vast acreages of wild land in Mayo, but they never became identified with Ireland. They remained, as such families did remain, foreigners, separated from the Irish population by religion and language, preserving through the centuries the outlook and behaviour of conquerors in an occupied country, regarding their Irish estates merely as the source which produced money to pay for English pleasures. As time passed, the wildness of the land abated and a market town grew up on Bingham property at Castlebar, but their great grey fortress, Castlebar House, was seldom occupied. Castlebar House stood frowning above the town, vast, empty, shuttered, and mouldering, while the Binghams lived in England. They were people of fashion and more than people of fashion; their fine town house in Charles Street, Mayfair, was a gathering place for men of intellect and wit, and Johnson, Gibbon, Reynolds, and Walpole were their friends.

An extraordinary and unexpected transformation had taken place, and the ferocious Binghams, the fierce cruel soldiers, had become devotees of culture and authorities on art.

Sir Charles Bingham, seventh Baronet, who succeeded in 1752, was a typical eighteenth-century dilettante. He spent a great deal of time in Florence and Rome, spoke Italian fluently, and collected ivories and intaglios. The most important achievement of his life was his marriage: in 1760 he became the husband of Margaret Smith, daughter and co-heiress of James Smith, a successful hosiery manufacturer. It was said that her origins were obscure and her pretensions laughable, but she had wealth, beauty, and "an extraordinary talent for being agreeable." She had also an extraordinary talent for painting. Horace Walpole, who at one time admired her extravagantly, declared she was a "miracle" and that she "transferred the vigour of Raphael to water-colours." Later, however, his admiration waned; Lady Bingham and her paintings ascended into very high circles indeed, and oddly enough he found her less and less likeable as she became more and more successful. In Paris her pictures became the rage, Louis XVI and Marie Antoinette declared themselves "amazed and charmed," and the Duke of Orleans had a studio fitted up for her in the Palais Royal. Under her capable direction ("she leads, he follows," wrote Horace Walpole), Charles rose in the world, and in 1776 he was created Baron Lucan of Castlebar. In 1781 their beautiful eldest daughter, Lavinia, made a match of dazzling brilliance by marrying the eldest son of Earl Spencer. Finally, in 1795, Charles was created Earl of Lucan. Walpole, who had now fallen out with Lady Lucan, wrote that the Lucans owed this last honour to the fact that Lady Lucan's favourite niece, Lady Camden, was at the moment "Vice-Queen."

Charles and his wife were "conscious of having done much to raise the consequence of the family." But in the midst of so much that was gratifying and successful the Binghams had one cause for anxiety—the character of their only son Richard. He seemed everything a parent could desire. He was very handsome, so handsome that it was feared his good looks would turn him into a coxcomb, and very gay, "the gayest of gay gallants," a contemporary calls him. Merriment bubbled from him. One sister describes him as being "always laughing and in high feather"; another longs for his arrival because "he always contrives to keep the house alive." His sisters adored him, "dear, dear, dear, dear, dearest Richard," they wrote, and signed themselves "your sister who loves you from the bottom of her heart." Nor was he wanting in intelligence. Schoolmasters, tutors, dons universally reported his parts to be excellent. His parents were exceedingly ambitious for him. Were they not the friends of Gibbon and Johnson, and was not his mother an international celebrity?

They expected him to be, as they constantly told him, a greater man than either Fox or Pitt.

Alas, nothing on earth, appeals, threats, bribery, or punishment, would make Richard work. He began his career by going to school at Westminster, but he did no good there; and at the age of sixteen he was taken away and sent to a tutor in Neufchâtel, to cram for the university. Gibbon was consulted on his historical studies, and advised memorising quantities of chronological tables to gain a sense of historical time. Richard was to write home weekly with a diary of his doings, to send his father his essays, and to be industrious, sober, economical, and punctual. He never wrote home, never forwarded his essays, if indeed he ever wrote any, devoted his time to dancing, fencing, and French poetry, bought fine clothes, and embarked on a love affair with a lady whom his favourite sister, Anne, described as "a Neufchâtel monster, a devilish b———h of a Madame, may the deuce take her." At Christ Church, Oxford, which he entered as a nobleman without an examination, he "frequented lazy and inglorious companions," spent his time "supping, hunting, lying in bed, and walking in the street with common whores," came constantly up to London without leave, stayed at a "blackguard hotel," and once more became involved in an undesirable love affair. "Almighty God teach you, my dear brother," wrote his sister Anne, "more wit and knowledge than to be taken in by a good for nothing destructive flirt and devil." Finally his health broke down, as a result of his dissipations, and his tutor recommended that he should be removed. After two years spent at the British Embassy in Vienna, he came of age; and his brother-in-law, now Earl Spencer, put him into Parliament as a Member for Northamptonshire. He became the gayest and most extravagant of young men about town, living with his aunt, Lady Dungannon, as he was on bad terms with his father.

In 1788, when Richard was twenty-three, he fell in love with Lady Elizabeth Belasyse, daughter of Earl Fauconberg. Neither his financial position nor his character was satisfactory. Lady

Elizabeth was a noted beauty, and in spite of their attachment the young couple were parted, and Lord Fauconberg forced his daughter to marry Mr. Bernard Howard, heir of the Duke of Norfolk. Lady Elizabeth was married in tears, and declared that she would rather go to Newgate than to her marriage bed. Richard left London, fell into a decline, and remained away for more than a year. In 1791 they met by chance, passion flared up, there were clandestine meetings, jealousy, scenes; and on July 24, 1793, Lady Elizabeth left home in her coach, ostensibly for "Mr. Gray's shop," in fact never to return.

She was already far advanced in pregnancy, and the lovers buried themselves in a remote country manor, Washingley, near Stilton, where a daughter was born. Here, where they rarely saw another human being, they lived for each other, Richard, to the surprise of his friends, settling down to family life, and "I swear to you," writes one of his friends, "taking as much notice of the baby and being as stupid about it as its mother." In 1794, after an action for damages in which Mr. Howard asked for £10,000 and was awarded £1,000, Lady Elizabeth's marriage was dissolved by Act of Parliament, and they were married. Richard's family were bitterly disappointed, and the favourite among his sisters, Lady Anne, refused ever to receive Elizabeth or her children.

The subsequent history of the marriage was curious. Year after year they lived on at Washingley, in what seemed perfect happiness. Richard succeeded as Earl of Lucan in 1799, a family of children was born, and still the idyll continued.

After ten years they suddenly returned to the world, were seen at Brighton, "observed to bicker," and in 1804 they separated ". . . more from disagreement of temper and extreme absurdity on both sides than for any other cause," wrote Lady Bessborough, sister of Earl Spencer.

He had the gout, she took to racketing and neglected him; he grew low spirited and scolded her. Incessant wranglings ensued, mix'd up with accusations of flirtation on the one side and stinginess on the other. This continued for near two years, when, after a violent quarrel, he return'd one night half inclin'd to make it up, but unfortunately mention'd having talk'd on the subject to his Sister (who never would consent to see Lady L or her children). Lady L put herself into a great passion; said it was dishonourable to consult her greatest enemy, and that, far from accepting his proffer'd forgiveness, she never would forgive him or remain another night in the house, and accordingly she set off and went to one of her Sisters in Yorkshire.

Upon this Richard immediately took out articles of separation, removed his children from their mother, and, with what seems a refinement of cruelty, set up house with his sister Anne. "How extraordinary," comments Lady Bessborough, "after giving up the world for each other and living happily near ten years."

The eldest son of this marriage, born in 1800, was George Charles Bingham, later third Earl of Lucan.

He was an exceptionally attractive little boy. With his younger brother he was sent away early to school, and the principal feminine influence in his life was his beautiful aunt Lavinia, Countess Spencer. Lady Spencer used to have the two little boys out from school on Sundays, and one of her daughters wrote enthusiastically, "They are very fine fellows indeed, and the elder, in particular, has the frankest, most open and affectionate manners that I ever saw."

No description could be less like the character George Bingham became. Some unrecorded experience, some unknown frustration, transformed the frank, open, affectionate little boy into the stern, harsh, suspicious man. He grew up a Bingham in the old style, a throw-back, with the military tastes, the courage, the ruthlessness which had earned his ancestors the epithet ferocious.

At the age of eleven he went to Westminster, and when he was sixteen a commission was bought for him in the 6th Regiment of Foot. Then began the series of exchanges, of quick switches to half-pay, of large payments to buy steps in rank which were accepted operations under the purchase system; and which enabled George Bingham, within ten years, at the age of twenty-six, to attain the rank of lieutenant-colonel in command of the 17th Lancers, one of the most famous regiments in the British Army. The same system enabled his brother-in-law, James Brudenell, to become lieutenant-colonel in command of the 15th Hussars within eight years, at rather more expense.

The purchase system, under which a man first bought his commission and then paid for each subsequent step in rank, and which enabled a rich man to buy the command of a regiment over the heads of more efficient officers, appears at first sight so childishly unjust, so evidently certain to lead to disaster, that it is almost impossible to believe that sensible people ever tolerated, much less supported it. Yet the purchase system expressed a principle which is one of the foundations of the British Constitution; famous victories were won by the British Army while it was officered by purchase, and it was upheld by so great a master of military administration as the Duke of Wellington.

No sentiment is more firmly rooted in the English national character than a hatred of militarism and military dictatorship. "An armed disciplined force is in its essence dangerous to liberty," wrote Burke, and Parliament in its dealings with the Army has always been concerned, above all else, to ensure that no British Army shall be in a position to endanger the liberties of the British people.

The vital period in the formation of Britain's policy towards her Army was the period of government by Cromwell's major-generals. The people of England were then subjected to a military dictatorship, they were ruled by Army officers who were professional soldiers, and who, though admittedly the finest soldiers in the world, usually had no stake in the country, and often were military adventurers. Their government was harsh and arbitrary, and the nation came to detest the very name of the Army.

After the Restoration, nation and Parliament were equally

determined that never again should the Army be in the hands of men likely to bring about a military revolution and impose a military dictatorship. With this object, purchase was introduced when a standing Army was formed in 1683. Men were to become officers only if they could pay down a substantial sum for their commission; that is, if they were men of property with a stake in the country, not military adventurers. As a secondary consideration the purchase price acted as a guarantee of good behaviour; a man dismissed from the service forfeited what he had paid. From that date it was the settled policy both of Parliament and of the Crown to draw the officers of the British Army from the class which had everything to lose and nothing to gain from a military revolution. The formation of an Army on the lines of Continental models, officered by professional soldiers, dependent on their pay and looking to the service to make their fortunes, was deliberately avoided. "Parliament has never sought to attract to the command of the army men dependent on their pay, either to hold their place in Society as gentlemen, or to maintain the higher social status assumed by Military officers over the civil community," wrote Clode, the nineteenth-century authority on military administration. Men of no fortune were not wanted; if they chose to come in it was at their own risk. It was laid down that "the pay of an officer is an honorarium, not a merces," and as late as 1869—purchase was substantially abolished in 1870—the pay of officers remained almost precisely what it had been in the reign of William III, though the pay of private soldiers and non-commissioned officers had been repeatedly increased.

As the eighteenth century passed into the nineteenth, the people of England had reason to congratulate themselves. Gazing across the Channel they observed country after country groaning under military despotism. They observed the fate of France, bled white for Napoleon's wars, passing from revolution to revolution; Spain starving under military oppression; Austria, ruled by an army, where even to speak of liberty was a crime. They alone were free. Thanks to their military system, the country which had the finest troops in Europe, which had broken Napoleon's power in the Peninsula and crushed him at Waterloo, had not, and had never shown any signs of having, a revolutionary army.

During the first half of the nineteenth century any attempt to attack the purchase system was howled down as an attempt to provoke revolution. In 1856 Lord Palmerston told the Commission on Purchase that he

thought it was very desirable to connect the higher classes of Society with the Army; and he did not know any more effective method of connecting them than by allowing members of high families who held commissions to get on with more rapidity than they would by seniority. . . . If the connection between the Army and the higher class of society were dissolved, then the Army would present a dangerous and unconstitutional appearance. It was only when the Army was unconnected with those whose property gave them an interest in the country, and was commanded by unprincipled military adventurers, that it ever became formidable to the liberties of the nation.

The purchase system became hallowed, as the public-school system was hallowed. It was allowed to have grave faults, to lend itself to abuse, even, to foreign eyes, to appear ridiculous, but it suited Englishmen. And it worked. Had not the British Army defeated the most formidable army in the world, were not the British masters of three continents?

It was useless, of course, to deny that the hardships inflicted by the purchase system were very great. Gronow, himself a Peninsular veteran, wrote of the men who fought at Waterloo, "Under the cold shade of the aristocracy, men, who in France would have been promoted to the highest grades of the army, lived and died, twenty or thirty years after the battle, with the rank of lieutenant or captain." "Society," wrote *The Times*, "abounds with military men who attribute their low position in the Army, or their retirement from it in disgust, to nothing but the purchase system—they had no money, so how could they get on." For men who could not find the sums necessary to buy promotion the outlook was hopeless. Sir John Adye, in his *Recollections*, mentions a captain who had been twenty-three years in that rank, and cites a regiment in which, in 1845, there were three officers who had fought at Waterloo thirty years before, of whom only one had attained the rank of major. When the Commission on Purchase was set up in 1856, Jacob Omnium, the radical journalist, described it as "ordered to enquire whether promoting officers because they were rich, and preventing those who were poor from rising in the Army, was, or was not, of advantage to the service."

With an avowed bias in favour of aristocracy and wealth, the Government allowed men of wealth and birth to manipulate the system to suit their own convenience. Half-pay, for instance, had been devised as a retaining fee. Officers whose services were temporarily not required went on half-pay, but could be called up at any time. All half-pay officers were recalled and given marching orders at the time of the Jacobite rising in 1715. But in the nineteenth century half-pay was used as a means of avoiding distasteful service and hastening promotion. Although each step was bought, the ladder of promotion had to be climbed rung by rung, and no man could be promoted until he had attained the immediately preceding rank. A young man would buy a vacant captaincy in a regiment in which he had no intention of serving, and next day he would go on half-pay; though no service was done with the regiment, he had become a captain, which qualified him to buy his next step as major in a more desirable regiment. Transfer to half-pay was made by Royal Sign Manual, countersigned by the Secretary for War. It was granted at discretion, and the service of a single day gave a claim to it as complete as the service of twenty years.

By going on half-pay, or by exchanging, at a price, into another regiment, wealthy officers avoided uncomfortable service abroad. When a fashionable regiment had to do a turn of duty in India, it was notorious that a different set of officers went out from those who had been on duty at St. James's Palace or the

Brighton Pavilion. When the regiment returned, the Indian duty officers dropped out and a smarter set took their place.

These, however, were minor grievances; the major, the over-whelming evil of the purchase system, was the enormous size of the sums expended to buy promotions, especially command. Legally the sum to be paid was fixed. In 1821 the War Office issued an official tariff laying down the amounts to be paid for a commission and for subsequent steps in rank in the different types of regiment in the service. Any payment in excess was declared illegal, and was to be punished by prosecution in the King's Bench, a fine or imprisonment, and cancellation of the transaction. In fact, such prosecutions never took place, and additional payments were almost invariable. Indeed, officers who did not wish to retire would be bribed to do so by the offer of a sum of money, and officers who did intend to retire would refuse to send in their papers until they had secured an amount far in excess of the regulation figure.

It was by this method that George Bingham obtained the command of the 17th Lancers. He joined the regiment as a major on December 1, 1825. He was then twenty-five years of age, had been in the Army nine years, had twice bought a step and next day gone on half-pay, and had appeared on the roster of five different regiments. His cavalry experience, however, was limited to a single appointment with the Life Guards.

It happened that the senior major of the 17th Lancers, Anthony Bacon, was an outstanding officer with a long and brilliant service to his credit. He had served in the Peninsula and taken part in the great assault on San Sebastián, the passage of the Bidassoa, the battle of the Nivelle, and the crossing of the Nive and the Adour. He had fought at Waterloo, and Lord Uxbridge, who commanded the cavalry, had said of him, "Anthony Bacon is without doubt the best cavalry officer I have ever seen." His personal history was romantic. He had married Lady Charlotte Harley, daughter of the celebrated Lady Oxford, with whom both the Prince Regent and Byron were in love. Lady

Oxford's children, from the suspected variety of their fathers, were known as the "Harleian Miscellany." When Lady Charlotte was a lovely child of eleven, Byron dedicated the first canto of *Childe Harold* to her. The match was reckless, neither Anthony Bacon nor Lady Charlotte had any money, but their devotion became a legend, they were never apart, and Lady Charlotte, a superb horsewoman, rode with her husband in his campaigns.

But Anthony Bacon did not, as he confidently expected, succeed to the command of the 17th, even though he was senior major and a brilliant officer with a lifetime in the service. In November, 1826, eleven months after joining the regiment, George Bingham bought the command for £25,000, paying £20,000 above the regulation price. Anthony Bacon, in despair, sold out and entered the service of the King of Portugal as a mercenary, and one of the finest cavalry officers in Europe was lost to the British Army.

George Bingham now had his chance to show what he was made of, and, as the 17th soon discovered, he was made of very stiff material indeed. True, he poured money into the regiment, the men had their uniforms made by a fashionable tailor, they rode blood-horses and were nicknamed "Bingham's Dandies," but in return he demanded perfection.

Officers and men began to groan. Drills, parades, inspections came upon them in an unending procession, followed by reprimands, punishments, floggings. George Bingham was a martinet. He worked incessantly, rose before dawn, and expected his officers to do the same, ate and drank little, and unquestionably possessed abilities of a high order. But there was a fatal flaw— with all his talents he had no common sense. He was totally unable to distinguish between what was important and what was not. He was perpetually entangled in trifles, forever struggling in a web of trivialities. His temper was irritable, and his severity grew. With a literal mind and a furious conviction of being always in the right, he enforced every law to the letter and exacted each pound of flesh with ruthless accuracy.

Presently his harshness began to be talked about. The regiment was said to be "always in hot water," at mess tables the 17th was "an object of pity"; George Bingham himself was described as quarrelsome, troublesome, and difficult. When he had been in command of the regiment for ten months, in October, 1827, his aunt Lavinia, Lady Spencer, thought it her duty to write him a letter of remonstrance, "however painful it may be for you to read and for me to write." She had been staying, she wrote, at Cassiobury, where she had heard "universal criticisms of your conduct as Colonel of the 17th . . . your martinet zeal, reputation of great severity and harshness, lack of self control and unpopularity with your officers." She implored him

to moderate your desire of producing perfection, temper your eagerness to produce faultless performance . . . and soften your manners towards those who are subordinate to you. . . . You are entitled by your station in society, by your professional ambition, and by the natural advantages which belong to you, to look forward to every distinction which can attend military life. . . . Every professional feather will float on to your helmet, *if* you conduct yourself so as to acquire the good will and the estimation of the well judging public. . . . A few years hence, when Time shall have silvered o'er that black pate of yours, you will have found that Man is governed by a thread, if it is imperceptible, when a cable will not turn him if it is imprudently displayed. . . . I have run the risk of displeasing you by conveying this to you . . . but believe me nothing but the tenderest concern for your welfare impelled me.

It was the voice of good sense, but alas that voice he was incapable of hearing. Time had done its work, and only the eye of affection could now discern the frank affectionate open little boy in the complicated suspicious violent young man. Yet the letter had its effect; he who could not endure the mildest criticism kept it among his private papers all his life, and he wisely left the regiment for a time. The Russians were engaged in the Balkans in a campaign against the Turks, and early in 1828 he managed to obtain an appointment on the staff of Prince Woronzow, who was commanding a brigade outside Varna.

As a fighting man he was successful. He ignored discomfort, was indifferent to hardship, and possessed great physical courage. As one of his officers was to say twenty-six years later in the Crimea, "He's brave, damn him!" Very encouraging reports came home to Lady Spencer. "Lord Bingham never let slip an opportunity to be in the fighting, even more than I could wish," wrote Prince Woronzow on September 23, 1828, and Lord Heytesbury, the British Ambassador to Russia, forwarding the letter, added,

His conduct has been such as to draw the attention and merit the approbation of the Emperor. The Empress was pleased to inform me a few days since that the Emperor had mentioned him upon more than one occasion in his private letters to her, doing full justice to his zeal and gallantry and adding that he was "Un fort bon garçon."

At the close of the campaign he received the order of St. Anne, second class, and reached England early in 1829. In June he married Lady Anne Brudenell, youngest of the seven Brudenell sisters, tall, extremely handsome, but, according to Queen Adelaide, who had observed her behaviour at Court, "worldly and not over-wise." After a prolonged honeymoon abroad, the young couple went to Ireland, where George Bingham reassumed the command of the 17th Lancers.

A curious incident now occurred. In 1826, after a violently contested election, George Bingham had been returned to Parliament as member for Mayo. A number of votes in the constituency were controlled by a Major Fitzgerald, who caused them to be cast for Lord Bingham, alleging that he was induced to do so by the promise of "a comfortable appointment, either civil or military, in a good climate," in spite of other tempting offers, notably from Lord Sligo. However, the Government went out of office, George Bingham went to the Balkans, no comfortable appointment was forthcoming, and financial disaster overtook Major Fitzgerald, who "with a numerous family was compelled to flee the country and reside at Ostend." Letters, first of complaint and then of threat, pursued George Bingham through the Balkans, on his honeymoon, and then to Ireland. Finally, in 1830, Major Fitzgerald played what he evidently considered to be a trump card: he issued a challenge. Someone had misinformed Major Fitzgerald as to George Bingham's character, and the major was under the delusion that he would rather pay then be shot at. Immediately on receipt of the letter George Bingham obtained leave from the Commander-in-Chief and hurried with a second to Ostend, where he knocked the major up in the middle of the night and offered to fight him then and there. The major's consternation was not to be described; he attempted to temporise, there had been some misunderstanding, no challenge had been intended, and as a matter of fact he had mislaid his pistols. George Bingham would allow no delay, the major must fight or apologise—and he would lend him pistols. A meeting was fixed for dawn, but unfortunately the major took the wrong road. George and his second waited. The major appeared, but now his second had taken the wrong road. The major disappeared once more, and still George Bingham and his second waited. The sun was high in the sky when the major's second at last appeared without the major, but with an apology. George Bingham set out at once for England with the apology in his pocket.

Within a few months a whispering of scandal began. It was said that no duel had taken place because Lord Bingham had refused to fight, that he had first ruined Major Fitzgerald and then denied him satisfaction. By January, 1831, statements were being made in the press, and an article in the *Telegraph and Connaught Ranger* asserted that as a result of his behavior in the duel with Major Fitzgerald, Lord Bingham was to be removed from the command of the 17th, which was to be given to—Lord Brudenell. A copy of the issue containing this article was sent, by some unknown person, to the mess of every regiment in the service. In Dublin, the district where the 17th was stationed, a paragraph appeared in the *Freeman's Journal* stating as a fact that Lord Bingham was to be removed from the command of the 17th and that Lord Brudenell was to be appointed, and the estate agent wrote from Castlebar urging that there should be a public contradiction, as Ireland was humming with gossip. A captain in the 61st Foot, a complete stranger, wrote to Lord Bingham, "Your courage is more than doubted. From the same source it is rumoured that you are retiring from the 17th in favour of my Lord Brudenell. . . . For God's sake, my lord, vindicate your character."

George Bingham refused to descend to explanation. He published the correspondence with Major Fitzgerald in the *Court Journal,* he submitted a long private memorandum, describing the affair to the Commander-in-Chief, Lord Hill; beyond that he would do nothing. Nevertheless, his brother-in-law, James Brudenell, did not get the command of the 17th, the 17th remained "Bingham's Dandies." In the following year, however, Lord Brudenell did achieve a command: he bought the lieutenant-colonelcy of the 15th Hussars, at a cost, it was stated in *The Times,* of between £35,000 and £40,000.

The 15th King's Hussars reckoned themselves to be a happy and fortunate regiment. Their commanding officer, Colonel Thackwell, later Lt.-Gen. Sir Joseph Thackwell, G.C.B., K.H., was an altogether exceptional officer. He had been with the regiment for thirty-two years and had fought with it through the Peninsular campaign and at Waterloo, where he had two horses shot under him and lost his left arm; he had made a study of military science both in England and in Germany, and was esteemed one of the finest cavalry commanders in Europe. Though he exacted a very high standard of smartness and efficiency—"Thackwell's eagle eye" was proverbial—he was humane, the defaulters' list was short, and floggings and courts-martial were rare. "The regiment," ran a report, "was in beautiful order, and the duties of officer and trooper throughout the corps were discharged with ease, efficiency and cheerfulness."

On handing over the regiment Colonel Thackwell congratulated Lord Brudenell "most sincerely on succeeding to the command of one of the best regiments in His Majesty's service."

Such was the happy family into which Lieutenant-Colonel Lord Brudenell new entered. The task before him was not easy. He was to assume command of men who had been majors before he got his cornet's commission, who had met and beaten the most formidable of foes in the greatest battle of modern history, who were bound to the regiment by a lifetime of service. His sole qualification was a peace-time service of eight years, of which only three had been spent in regimental duty.

Lord Brudenell, however, did not embark on his new duties with misgiving, or even with diffidence, but with thoroughgoing contempt. It was a class contempt—of the lord for the commoner, of the rich man for the man of moderate means, of the man who has been born within the charmed circle of privilege and influence for the man who has not. Such arrogance and such contempt were native to Lord Brudenell, but it happened that in 1832 his feelings had been violently inflamed by contemporary events.

That year of 1832 was the year of the Reform Bill. At this distance of time it seems a moderate and sensible measure, framed to correct the grosser injustices of Parliamentary representation by a redistribution of seats. But it was the cause of extraordinary contemporary violence. The Tory aristocracy, seeing the reins of government slipping from their hands, frantically opposed Reform with coercion, with severe penal laws, with military force; while the great blind mass of the people, sensing that power for the first time was within their grasp, fought as frantically back.

Shrieking mobs patrolled the streets of every large town, riots took place, the centre of Bristol was burned and Nottingham Castle destroyed, troops were called out and fired on the mob, and many persons were killed. In the country people shivered in their beds as night after night the sky was reddened by burning ricks, and country houses were attacked and wrecked by masked bands. In London Queen Adelaide was stoned, the Duke of Wellington had to be rescued by troopers from the hands of the mob, whole streets had their windows broken, and the gaieties of the London season were cancelled as the shadow of the guillotine seemed to fall across London squares.

Revolution was averted by the passage of the Bill in June,

and in the winter of 1832 the first general election of the Reformed Parliament took place. The Tories gathered themselves together to fight for the control of the country. Among the fiercest opponents of reform were the Cardigans and Ailesburys; and James, Lord Brudenell, the most rabid and reactionary of Tories, stood for the Northern Division of Northamptonshire.

To James Brudenell, Tory principles were of infinitely more importance than a political creed—they provided the justification for his existence. His enormous faith in himself was based on the principle of hereditary aristocracy. By virtue of that principle he could brush aside the facts that he was perhaps more stupid than other men, that there were ideas he could not grasp, conclusions which eluded him, results he failed to anticipate. The question was one of divine right; his rank gave him a divine right to command and to be obeyed. It was a conviction which would have aroused no surprise in the seventeenth or even the eighteenth century, but in a world in which railways and steamships had been invented, and in which gaslight was dispelling the gloom of centuries, the divine right of Lord Brudenell appeared startling indeed.

The elections of the winter of 1832 and the spring of 1833 were fought with frightful bitterness, and Tory landlords openly resorted to coercion. Mr. Brown, a tenant of the Earl of Ailesbury, received notice to quit because he had "circulated bills to weaken Lord Ailesbury's influence over the election of members of Parliament," though he protested that he had been obliged to deliver the bills in the performance of his duty as postmaster. Mr. Shrimpton, a farmer, was warned his tenancy would be terminated unless he compelled his two sons to vote for Lord Ailesbury's candidate. Mr. Jordon, a blacksmith, not only lost Lord Ailesbury's custom but was informed that no tenant of his lordship's would be permitted in future to employ him, because he had attended a meeting of the Reform candidate. In Northamptonshire the Brudenells went further. Mr. Smith had his farm sold up because "notwithstanding his being Lord Cardigan's tenant, he had voted against Lord Brudenell . . . he being the landlord's son." Enormous sums of money, said to amount to £30,000, were spent to ensure Lord Brudenell's return, and were spent successfully: Lord Brudenell got in, but only after scenes had occurred which made the Northamptonshire election notorious. The reactionary violence of Lord Brudenell's speeches and the haughtiness of his bearing provoked outbreaks of fury; and *The Times* repeatedly deplored the inflammatory nature of his language and conduct. It was his practice to ride to the hustings with a party of friends as splendidly mounted and splendidly dressed as himself, to face the crowd with scorn, and when an uproar started, to gallop off, scattering the mob with a thunder of hoofs, and pursued by yells, shrieks of hatred, groans, hisses, and a shower of missiles.

At Wellingborough, after he had made a violent speech against the Corn Laws, a serious riot took place. Troops had to be summoned from Weedon to rescue Lord Brudenell and his friends, but not before Lord Brudenell had suffered "considerable personal injury." It was with nerves inflamed, and obstinacy and arrogance thoroughly aroused, that he crossed to Ireland and assumed command of the 15th.

For more than half his life, since he was a boy drilling the yeomanry in Deene Park, he had waited for the moment when he should have command of a regiment. He had visions of a regiment that was nothing less than perfection, of movements executed by men like automatons, more exactly, and above all more swiftly, than ever before. He was in love with speed, the thunder of a charge made him restless with pleasure, and it was observed that the excitement of the horses communicated itself to him, his eye too rolled, his nostrils too dilated. He had plans for new movements, galloping movements, charges from new angles not in the drill book. Mounted on splendid glossy chargers, with brilliant uniforms and dazzling accoutrements, his regiment was to form, reform, wheel, charge, halt, with the precision of a swooping hawk—at break-neck speed.

Though the 15th was a notably efficient regiment, the new commanding officer viewed it with disgust. He demanded more glitter, more dash, and he set to work to drill, polish, pipeclay, reprimand, and discipline the 15th to within an inch of their lives.

All the old comfortable habits of the regiment were swept away. Horses were clipped and groomed as for Hyde Park, field days took place as often as twice a week, movements were performed, not very successfully, at a gallop, drills on horse and on foot seemed never ending. The appearance of the regiment was severely criticised, and the new lieutenant-colonel held frequent inspections, after which, without consulting the officers concerned, he ordered such new items of uniform and equipment as he considered necessary to render the appearance of the regiment impeccable. Even the food eaten by the officers of the 15th earned the new lieutenant-colonel's scorn, and he ordered that, in the mess, French dishes should replace plain roast or boiled.

He was genuinely surprised to encounter opposition. His nature had a curious simplicity, so that, but for his violence, he would have been childlike and naïve. He was completely absorbed in one object, himself. It was not, as one realised when one became familiar with him, that he deliberately disregarded other men's opinions and feelings—they simply did not exist for him. Like a child playing in a corner of a nursery with his toys, he was wholly absorbed in himself, the rest of the world was an irrelevance. Nor did he ever attempt to conceal his absorption; his nature was wholly without guile, so that, as Kinglake said, he was as innocent as a horse.

Like a child, however, he found opposition intolerable, and surprise was swiftly succeeded by furious indignation. The very horses of this miserable regiment seemed determined to thwart him. He took it from Newbridge to Carlow, as a smart regiment should be taken, at a good round pace, and afterwards he was told that 70 per cent of the horses had sore backs. The excuse was that they had become so thin through extra work that the saddles rubbed them, but he knew better. The officers had been inefficient and had not seen that the horses were properly looked to. He had set his heart on the regiment riding into Dublin in style, but it could not ride: the horses were not fit. He broke out to the adjutant that he was being thwarted, and of set purpose. Had he not issued orders, not merely by dozens but by sheaves and bales, altering, and of course improving, every step of procedure in stables? Had he not positively ordered that the horses were not to get sore backs? Were the officers of the 15th unaware that he was commanding officer with an absolute right to have his orders obeyed—and still the horses had sore backs. The truth rushed in on him—there was a conspiracy against him. The inefficient officers of the 15th were banding together to prevent him from bringing the regiment to perfection. There were exceptions: one or two officers had privately assured him that they supported his endeavours, and they should certainly be recommended for promotion. But the rest were obstinate, insubordinate, and inefficient. And for his purpose they were perfectly useless. Never could these middle-aged, serious family men become the smart, dashing officers he needed for the regiment of his dreams. Economy—they talked of nothing but economy. How could a regiment be brought to perfection by economy? Of how a gentleman should live, how he should be mounted, of the elegance of his dress, the luxury of his table, the officers of the 15th had no conception.

And as the months went by, it began to be noticed that his disapproval and dislike of the officers of the 15th were becoming concentrated on one man, Captain Augustus Wathen.

Augustus Wathen was perhaps the most popular and certainly the most intelligent officer in the regiment. He had more than twenty years' service behind him, he had fought through the full three days at Waterloo, and he had devised a method of teaching cavalry tactics by means of models which had been sympathetically received by the War Office. He was an unusually quiet man, with a gentle kindly manner, highly esteemed in the service. But he was not the wealthy and dashing officer Lord Brudenell desired. Though he was well connected (his wife is mentioned as Lady Wathen), his means were only moderate, and his home in London was one of the smaller of the newly built houses in Cadogan Place, Sloane Street. Moreover, his gentle manner concealed something more than a fair share of obstinacy; he was given to raising objections, and had on one or two occasions written to the Commander-in-Chief to draw his Lordship's attention to points with which he found himself unable to agree. He had, for instance, boldly criticised the cavalry movements laid down by the Board of Cavalry Commanding Officers, and been smartly snubbed. Certainly Captain Wathen was not the man to give way to the new lieutenant-colonel, or to humour him.

Presently it was noticed that the mere presence of Captain Wathen was sufficient to drive the lieutenant-colonel into a rage. He summoned him with a shout, screamed orders at him, "in a very irritating and domineering manner," and refused to grant him leave. Captain Wathen was not to be drawn, nor would he give way. He continued to perform his duty quietly, making no reply to Lord Brudenell's outbursts, but not concealing the fact that he found Lord Brudenell's sheaves of orders unnecessary and unreasonable, nor that he disapproved of the expense in which Lord Brudenell's mania for smartness was involving the regiment.

As the summer of 1833 wore on, the conduct of the lieutenant-colonel became so outrageous as to be embarrassing. It seemed that he was a man possessed. Captain Wathen had become a mania, he thought of nothing but Captain Wathen, saw his hand in everything and everywhere. Captain Wathen was inciting the regiment against him, Captain Wathen was slandering him, Captain Wathen had gone to a lawyer. The lieutenant-colonel muttered of evils that must be suppressed, strong measures that must be resorted to, and sent for the adjutant. Notes were to be taken of the conversation of officers, both in the orderly room and outside the regimental office. The notes must be taken secretly, without the knowledge of the officers concerned, and brought to him. The adjutant was surprised, but the lieutenant-colonel said shortly, "It is an order." Two sergeants from Captain Wathen's troop were then summoned, and the lieutenant-colonel suggested that they should listen to the conversation of the men in Captain Wathen's troop and report to him.

In September, 1833, an explosion occurred. In his high-handed manner the lieutenant-colonel ordered new stable jackets for Captain Wathen's troop, without consulting Captain Wathen. At this date responsibility for clothing the soldier rested entirely with the colonel of his regiment. The colonel received a fixed sum, called "off-reckonings," for every man in the regiment, out of which he was bound to provide clothing according to patterns fixed by a clothing board, chosen annually by the Board of General Officers. To ensure the proper use of clothing, each troop or company kept a book in which new articles of clothing issued were debited, and the extent of this debit was not expected to exceed a reasonable sum. Any balance remaining from off-reckonings was retained by the colonel as part of his emolument.

The obvious fault of the system was the opportunity for making illicit profits; and what the Army called "clothing colonels," by depriving their men of clothing to which they were entitled, and receiving payments for men who did not exist, succeeded in pocketing large sums.

Almost equally detestable to regimental officers, however, were colonels who lavished money out of their own pockets on regimental clothing. True, the colonel who required his men to be magnificent paid for much of their splendour himself, but he required his officers to be equally splendid, and he did not pay for them. Nor did captains care to see their books heavily debited for gorgeous new clothing while there was still wear in the old.

On September 5 Captain Wathen requested an interview, protested that the new stable jackets ordered by the lieutenant-colonel were unnecessary, that the men did not want them, and brought one of the old jackets to prove it. Face to face with Captain Wathen, Lord Brudenell was unable to control himself; in a paroxysm of rage, he snatched the jacket away, flung it across the room, and put Captain Wathen under arrest. He remained under arrest until October 20, and was then released by order of the Commander-in-Chief, Lord Hill. Lord Brudenell demanded a court martial, but it was refused and he received a reprimand himself; and Captain Wathen resumed his duties with the regiment.

The lieutenant-colonel was barely able to contain his fury: it was observed that he ground his teeth and shook with the vehemence of his anger; and at the end of October he had an opportunity to vent his rage. In the course of an inspection Captain Wathen trotted by with his troop in a position which, though it had been in use for many years, had just been altered by a new order. Lord Brudenell had Captain Wathen out on the parade ground in front of the regiment, and he shouted a reprimand at him in the most offensive terms, describing him as ignorant, inefficient, and insubordinate, and threatening to put a junior officer over his head to command his troop since he was evidently incompetent to handle it.

When a brother officer was asked how Captain Wathen behaved on this occasion, he said, "Captain Wathen seemed very hurt."

On November 8 Maj.-Gen. Sir Thomas Arbuthnot inspected the regiment, and the result was a triumph for the lieutenant-colonel, for Sir Thomas warmly congratulated him on the appearance and smart performance of the 15th. Later Sir Thomas inspected the regimental accounts, and the lieutenant-colonel was able to draw his attention to the amount of debt incurred by Captain Wathen's troop; Sir Thomas commented unfavorably. The lieutenant-colonel hastened to communicate both these pieces of news to Captain Wathen, adding that Sir Thomas was writing a message of congratulation on the appearance and order of the regiment—it was to be read aloud to his troop by every captain.

In due course Sir Thomas separately inspected each troop book, and when it came to Captain Wathen's turn Captain

Wathen requested leave to speak. The amount of the debt in his troop book, he said, was due to the issue of new stable jackets, which in his opinion were unnecessary and had been ordered without his consent; the men had grumbled at getting them and, further, though every troop in the regiment had been issued with new jackets, his troop alone had been debited.

Sir Thomas was flustered: it seemed "very strange to him that such things should be said of a commanding officer." Had Captain Wathen told Lord Brudenell the jackets were not necessary and that the men did not want them? He had. Sir Thomas then requested the presence of Lord Brudenell.

The interview was unsatisfactory. Lord Brudenell denied everything, could not keep his temper, contradicted Sir Thomas, called Captain Wathen a liar, had repeatedly to be told not to interrupt, and was finally sent out of the room.

A brief and informal enquiry followed. Officers of the regiment spoke of the lieutenant-colonel's irritating and domineering manner to Captain Wathen, and were furiously contradicted by the lieutenant-colonel. Captain Wathen stuck firmly to his point: the lieutenant-colonel had made a complaint on the extent of his troop debt when he was well aware that the debt of other troops would not merely have equalled but exceeded his if the stable jackets had been charged to them. Sir Thomas, evidently feeling he had stepped into a hornet's nest, collected what facts he could, remarked once more that the whole affair was very strange, and departed.

Four days later Captain Wathen was once more under arrest. On November 12 Lord Brudenell had sent for him and furiously harangued him for more than an hour. At the end of that time he suddenly accused him of disobeying orders—he had not read Sir Thomas's message of congratulation aloud to his troop. Captain Wathen, "making himself heard with difficulty owing to constant interruptions," stated that the message had been delivered verbally. The lieutenant-colonel ordered him to repeat what he had said; Captain Wathen said that the lieutenant-colonel's interjections made repetition impossible, and was ordered to write down his words. He did this, and the lieutenant-colonel then ordered him to sign his statement. Captain Wathen refused, saying his mind was in too great a state of confusion; he was put under arrest.

Once more Lord Brudenell applied for a court martial, and this time it was not refused. On December 23, 1833, Captain Wathen was court-martialled at Cork, the prosecutor being his commanding officer, Lieutenant-Colonel Lord Brudenell, on the following six charges:

1. On November 8, 1833, at Cork he said in an invidious and improper manner to Major-General Sir Thomas Arbuthnot that new stable jackets had been issued to the men of his troop without his knowledge.
2. That the men did not want them.
3. That he had told Lord Brudenell that the men did not want them.
4. That he had not told his men that Lord Brudenell commended their appearance.
5. That when he did address his men he told them their appearance had been approved by some strangers or civilians, and said that he had no doubt that if they had gone abroad they could have done their duty in spite of unpleasantness which might have occurred in the troop and did not tell them Lord Brudenell had censured them for want of attention to their horses.
6. That he refused to obey an order given him by Lieutenant-Colonel Lord Brudenell to repeat verbally what he had said to his men, and when he had been allowed to write down what he said refused to leave the statement in the regimental office.

The court martial took nearly a month and aroused great excitement. Though the press was not admitted, *The Times* printed lengthy eye-witness accounts and commented in three leading articles. Public feeling was becoming suspicious of the administration of the Army. It was a stronghold of the Tory aristocracy—had it also become a weapon of reaction? Tory lords had been heard to declare that it signified nothing what the people thought or what they expressed as long as the Army could be depended on. What was going on within the Army, what manner of men were its officers? If the answer was men like Lord Brudenell, then the situation was startling indeed.

In the cool and factual atmosphere of the court Lord Brudenell's behaviour took on an extraordinary improbability. His orders to take down officers' conversations secretly, his cross-examinations of sergeants and men unknown to their officers, the "insolence and unrelenting hostility of his manner," his habit of shouting, of "taunting" officers less rich and well born than himself—these, related in cold blood, appeared astonishing. Captain Wathen had been the principal but by no means the only object of the lieutenant-colonel's detestation. There had been other victims, other arrests, other public taunts and shouted reprimands.

From the first day of the trial Lord Brudenell was reported to be "in a state of high excitement and extreme emotion"; he fidgeted, grimaced, seemed unable to sit still, and when the evidence was against him his fury was barely to be restrained.

In examination he cut a poor figure. It was one thing to shout on the parade ground that Captain Wathen's troop was the worst in the regiment, the worst in the service, but another to particularise. In what respects was Captain Wathen's troop unsatisfactory? asked the Court. His Lordship hesitated, he meant . . . he meant . . . well he meant that the men were idle. In what way were they idle? After some dozens of questions it was discovered his lordship meant that they did not cut the coats of their horses sufficiently short. The Court passed to another subject—the allegations his lordship had made regarding secret underground workings against him, strong measures that had been forced on him to suppress evils: what precisely did his lordship mean by these statements? His lordship grew confused and sulky, the

Court pressed him, and finally he brought out that he had been "consistently thwarted and opposed by Captain Wathen." He was pressed again; would his lordship kindly particularise? He answered in an angry rush, "Upon my speaking to a man of his troop in strong terms, relative to the man's misconduct and that of other men of the troop, Captain Wathen in an insubordinate and menacing manner told me that if I brought such charges against the troop I should substantiate them. This comes under the heading of thwarting and opposing a commanding officer, in my opinion."

The Court digested this in silence. Then the adjutant, who had been present, was called. Had Captain Wathen's manner been menacing? No, his manner was not menacing, but he often seemed very much wounded.

On January 18 Captain Wathen rose to make the statement for his defence; it had been drawn up with the assistance of his wife, and was described by *The Times* as masterly. Defence, however, was almost unnecessary; after the weeks of testimony from officers, from men, from sergeants and veterinary officers, from Maj.-Gen. Sir Thomas Arbuthnot and representatives of the Horse Guards, the charges had ceased to exist. The matter of the stable jackets stood revealed as a childish little plot; the charges relating to Sir Thomas Arbuthnot's message had been hardly worth examining—it even transpired that in fact the message had been read; the charges relating to the men were trifles based on hearsay. There could be no doubt of the outcome of the trial, and the fury and excitement of the lieutenant-colonel, "who had continued in a very distressing state of mind since the commencement of the proceedings," became "such as to be the cause of much anxiety to his friends."

On the 20th Captain Wathen closed his defence; emotion in the court was running very high, and when he referred to the fact that he had been under arrest in all for nine weeks, and "alluded modestly to his twenty years' service and to his having fought the full three days at Waterloo," many of the veterans in the court were observed to shed tears, and there were loud and irrepressible cheers. He then laid upon the table many original letters from commanding officers and others high in the service testifying that his character as an officer and a gentleman was irreproachable, and withdrew, followed by loud and prolonged applause.

The decision of the court martial was not announced for a fortnight, but meanwhile *The Times*, "taking for granted that Captain Wathen has had a most honourable acquittal and that Lord Brudenell has been reprimanded," enquired, in two leading articles, how the situation had ever arisen at all.

How came Lord Brudenell—an officer of no pretensions or experience comparable to those of a hundred other gentlemen who had seen and beaten a foreign enemy—how came such an unripe gallant as this to be put over the heads of so many worthier candidates, to be forced into a command for which, we may now say, he has proved himself utterly incompetent. . . . This officer was a man of no experience. We are told he never did regimental duty for more than three years of his life. He was not less incapacitated for command by temper, than by ignorance of his duty as a commanding officer, both professional and moral. Such a man ought never to have been placed at the head of a regiment.

On February 1, 1834, the findings of the court martial were published in a general order.

The Court, having taken into serious consideration the evidence produced in support of the charges against the prisoner, Captain Augustus Wathen, of the 15th, or King's, Hussars . . . is of opinion that he is not guilty of any of the charges preferred against him. The Court therefore honourably acquits him of each and of all the charges.

The Court then proceeded further.

Bearing in mind the whole process and tendency of this trial, the Court cannot refrain from animadverting on the peculiar and extraordinary measures which have been resorted to by the Prosecutor. It appears, in the recorded minutes of these Proceedings, that a junior officer was listened to, and non-commissioned officers and soldiers examined, with a view to finding out from them, how, in particular instances, the officers had executed their respective duties. . . .

Another practice has been introduced into the 15th Hussars, which calls imperatively for the notice and animadversion of the Court—the system of having the conversation of officers taken down in the orderly room without their knowledge—a practice which cannot be considered otherwise than as revolting to every proper and honourable feeling of a gentleman, and as being certain to create disunion and to be most injurious to His Majesty's service. . . . Upon a full consideration of all the circumstances of the case, His Majesty has been pleased to order that Lieutenant-Colonel Lord Brudenell shall be removed from the command of the 15th Hussars.

The decision of the Court was to be entered in the general-order book and read aloud at the head of every regiment in the service.

It might now, not unreasonably, have been supposed that Lord Brudenell's military career was at an end. No such idea ever crossed Lord Brudenell's mind; his conviction that he was now, and always, in the right never wavered. He rushed to the Horse Guards and protested to Lord Hill; he called on Lord Melbourne and Lord John Russell; he demanded a reconsideration of the court martial; he demanded to be court-martialled himself; his sense of being wronged was so overwhelming that if anyone disagreed with him he did not notice it. In his autobiographical note he writes, "All thought it a case of grave injustice." Finally, he obtained an interview with the Duke of Wellington.

Though the Duke had resigned the command of the Army to Lord Hill on becoming Prime Minister in 1828, his influence in Army matters was omnipotent. His enormous prestige, his vast experience, the power of his astonishing mind, the reverence, amounting to worship, accorded to him as the Saviour of Europe, combined to place him in a position that has been occupied by no other human being before or since. The Commander-in-Chief, the Cabinet, the King, went to the Duke on military matters as to a sacred oracle.

It was Lord Brudenell's firm impression that he received encouragement from the Duke. His position as heir of the Earl of Cardigan, "who and what you are," as the Duke phrased it, was, he thought, appreciated; certainly he was told to keep quiet for a year at least, but he understood the Duke to say that he saw no reason why, at the end of that time he should not be placed again at the head of a regiment.

Accordingly in September, 1835, after being "quiet" for eighteen months, he wrote confidently to the Duke. He had the prospect of a lieutenant-colonelcy in a regiment at present in India. He had been at the Horse Guards in March, and an arrangement had been made which he "considered as equivalent to the promise of the appointment"; would the Duke "induce" Lord Hill to obtain the sanction of the Government? Lord Melbourne and Lord John Russell were on his side, and other members of the Cabinet were, he knew, in his favour. "I therefore cannot believe that any opposition to my appointment would be persisted in."

The Duke was taken aback: it was his first experience of the limited vision of Lord Brudenell; and by return he wrote a very sharp letter.

I must . . . tell you that you entirely misunderstood me if you supposed that I ever fixed, in my own mind, much less stated to another a period after which you should be recalled. . . . I cannot but think you are mistaken respecting the feelings and sentiments of the Ministers in your case. . . . Lord Hill knows well that if he should consult my opinion on any matter it will be communicated to him frankly and that I shall have no object in the communication excepting to promote the honour and convenience of His Majesty's service. I must add that I never ever interfere with an opinion, excepting when requested.

Still Lord Brudenell was not to be deterred. True, he had been removed from his command, but he had not been dismissed from the Army, he had only been put on half-pay; whatever the

Duke might say, he was still a soldier with a perfect right to negotiate for a new appointment. There was also an all-important circumstance in his favour. At this moment the influence of the Brudenells at Court was very great; indeed, they were in a position to bring almost irresistible pressure to bear on the Throne itself.

Harriet, the only clever woman, and James Brudenell's favourite among his seven beautiful sisters, had married Richard Penn Curzon, Earl Howe, rich, handsome, amiable, and a most reactionary Tory. On the accession of William IV in 1830, Lord Howe was appointed Chamberlain to Queen Adelaide, and very soon the world was astounded by the spectacle of an inexplicable passion between the Queen, who resembled a German governess of the stricter type, "with her spare form, her sour countenance and her straight stiff German back, squeezing out gracious smiles," and the handsome, agreeable Lord Howe.

Howe is devoted to the Queen [wrote Greville in December, 1832] and never away from her . . . he is never out of the Pavilion, dines there almost every day, or goes there every evening, rides with her, never quitting her side, and never takes his eyes off her . . . he is like a boy in love with this frightful spotted Majesty, while his delightful wife is laid up (with a sprained ankle and dislocated joint) on her couch.

It was not in accordance with Queen Adelaide's strict German principles to separate husband and wife, and Lady Howe was required to appear invariably at Court with her husband. Lady Howe was not easy to refuse when she asked a favour from the Queen.

The verdict in the Wathen court martial had been a frightful shock to the Brudenells. "The blow struck at the heir," wrote the *Morning Chronicle*, "vibrated through every branch of the noble house," and the grief of the old widowed Earl was "terrible to witness."

The Queen assented to join with Lady Howe to induce the King to agree to the reinstatement of Lord Brudenell in a command.

At first the King refused to listen, and Lady Howe and the Queen implored, and even wept, in vain. He "would not interfere in what he most emphatically called Lord Hill's righteous judgment." As a last resort the King was persuaded to see the Earl of Cardigan, bowed by infirmities and sorrow but still magnificent in old age. The grief of the old man at the disgrace of his only son moved William IV "after female tears and pleas had failed," and the King, himself the affectionate over-indulgent father of ten troublesome illegitimate children, "reluctantly declared that if Lord Hill would consult him, he would give consideration to their entreaties." It was enough. The Queen then and there sent for Lord Hill, and he came at once to the Palace.

Though Lord Hill was an efficient and successful commander, the Duke of Wellington had written, "I am not sure he does not shrink from responsibility." At the top of his official letter-book Lord Hill wrote in his own hand, "A soft answer turneth away wrath," and the troops, by whom he was greatly loved, called him "Daddy" Hill. To a kind heart he united extreme Toryism: he had refused to vote for the Reform Bill, even at the personal request of the King, and was a staunch upholder of the aristocracy.

The combination of the Queen, the Earl of Cardigan, and Lady Howe was too much for Lord Hill. "Overcome by the distress of a noble family," he gave way. If Lord Brudenell obtained a command, the appointment would be approved. He then, it was reported, "closed the interview with these memorable words, 'I have consented to this step because I am unable to endure the distress of this noble family, and because I hope that the author of this distress is now sensible that he cannot be permitted to follow the dictates of his ungovernable temper. I trust this lesson has not been thrown away.'"

In March, 1836, two years after he had been removed from the command of the 15th Hussars, Lord Brudenell was gazetted to the lieutenant-colonelcy of the 11th Light Dragoons, then at Cawnpore but due to return home in 1838, in succession to Lieutenant-Colonel Childers. The purchase price was said to exceed £40,000.

A storm of indignation followed. The press, led by *The Times*, demanded to be told who had appointed Lord Brudenell to the command of the 11th Light Dragoons, who had been able to reverse the decision of the court martial? If a man was pronounced unfit to command one regiment, how could he be fit to command another? Had the Cabinet no control over military appointments, was the nation, who paid for the Army, helpless in the hands of a military and aristocratic oligarchy? The storm did not blow itself out in the press: Sir William Molesworth, member for East Cornwall, gave notice of a motion in the House of Commons—"That a select committee be appointed to enquire into the conduct of the Commander-in-Chief of the Forces in appointing Lieutenant-Colonel Lord Brudenell to the Lieutenant-Colonelcy of the 11th Light Dragoons."

On May 3, 1836, the motion was brought forward. In the course of a long speech Sir William Molesworth read the verdict of the Wathen court martial and listed the long and distinguished services of the 11th Light Dragoons in Egypt, in the Peninsula, at Waterloo, and, for the last seventeen years, in India. The two majors had served with the regiment for thirty and twenty-five years respectively, since 1806 and 1811.

With what feelings [asked Sir William] will they view the advancement over their heads of this young officer, who has never heard the sound of a musket, except in the mimic combats of a review; who entered the Army in 1824, with unexampled rapidity obtained an unattached Lieutenant-Colonelcy in 1830, in 1832 the command of a regiment, in 1834 was removed from that command for alleged misconduct, and now in 1836 is deemed the fittest and most proper person to command their regiment? They will murmur . . . they will say that which is said in every part of this town when the question is discussed—

they will say that courtly influence, courtly favour and courtly intrigue have biased the otherwise sound judgment of the Commander-in-Chief and compelled that distinguished and otherwise irreproachable officer to make this seemingly most reprehensible appointment—an appointment which cannot fail to produce the painful belief in the minds of all connected with the British Army, that, provided an officer possesses wealth and influence, it matters not what his past conduct may have been—it matters not that the solemn decision of a court-martial may have been against him; neither that conduct, nor that decision will be a bar to his future promotion, nor an impediment to his advancement, over the heads of veterans, to the command of those whose conduct has been irreproachable.

Sir William sat down. There was no applause; indeed, he had been frequently interrupted by cries of "Oh! oh!" "Question, question," and "Divide, divide." The incredible had happened, and the House of Commons was taking Lord Brudenell's side.

For this result William Molesworth himself was responsible, for he was a fatal champion. Personally he was unpopular, politically he was regarded as a most dangerous man. It was only four years since the Reform riots, the Chartist movement was now reaching its height, and an active fear of revolution was common to Whig and Tory. William Molesworth was an extreme radical detested by both parties. True, the measures he advocated, the abolition of flogging in the Army and Navy, the secret ballot in elections, colonial self-government, and the abolition of transportation for convicts, have been adopted and today seem commonplaces of good sense, but to his contemporaries he was a revolutionary and a traitor to his class. The friend of Bentham, John Stuart Mill, and Grote, he had violently shocked public opinion by denying the divinity of Christ; twice he had wished to marry, and on each occasion the young lady had been forbidden to receive the addresses of an infidel and a radical.

The effect of Sir William Molesworth on the Army authorities was electric. Always jealous of their powers, a public attack made in the House of Commons, by a radical, on their administration was unendurable to them. High military officials drew together to do battle, and the merits of the *casus belli*, Lord Brudenell's reinstatement, were forgotten.

Most important of all, behind the attitude of the House of Commons might be discerned the all-powerful influence of the Duke. It was one of the Duke's cardinal principles that the Army must be kept free from the faintest suspicion of political control. The British Constitution rested on the fact that the British Army was not a political instrument; the House of Commons must never therefore be allowed to interfere in matters relating to the discipline of the Army. "To create such a precedent," wrote the Duke, "was fraught with possibilities of the most dangerous description." The principle of freedom from political control was to be upheld, and with it, incidentally, Lord Brudenell.

Lord Brudenell meanwhile was whole-heartedly triumphing. None of the irritation and high excitement displayed during the Wathen court martial was to be observed. The events now occurring appeared perfectly simple to him. He had always known he was in the right, and here he was, being vindicated. Hard words, and from a radical, he treated with contempt.

He made, rather to the surprise of the House, a straightforward and unassertive speech in his own defence. A series of panegyrics followed as honourable Member after honourable Member rose to testify to the character and military accomplishments of Lord Brudenell. Officers of the highest rank, Sir Hussey Vivian, Master-General of the Ordnance, Maj.-Gen. Sir Henry Bouverie, Lieutenant-General Lord Stafford, Maj.-Gen. Sir Frederick Ponsonby, sent glowing testimonials though it was observed that these were all of very recent date. Major-General Sir Edward Blakeney even wrote that "Lord Brudenell was one of the most intelligent officers who ever served under my command." At this, however, there were cries from all sides of "Oh! oh!"

Lord Brudenell then laid the testimonials on the table, bowed, and withdrew in order that the debate might continue without his presence, followed by "loud and continuous cheers."

When Joseph Hume, the celebrated radical, rose to support Sir William Molesworth, the outcome of the debate was a foregone conclusion, and Hume, who had earned the particular detestation of the Army authorities by his efforts to abolish flogging, made himself heard with difficulty. Through shouts of "Divide, divide," cries of "Oh! oh! oh!" and intervals of confusion, he was heard to assert that everyone in the House knew there had been an intrigue—a poor man without friends or high connections would have no chance of standing where the noble Lord stood today. The Commander-in-Chief, for whose personal character he had the highest respect, had been forced to act in deference to high influences, the decision of a court martial had been set aside by means of intrigue. Every officer who spoke on the subject of flogging in the Army said that it was necessary for the maintenance of discipline. Let the House draw the comparison between the punishment of soldiers and their officers. What were privates to think of the justice of the punishment inflicted on them when they saw placed at the head of a regiment a man whom the Commander-in-Chief had censured in the strongest terms?

Major-General Sir Henry Hardinge closed the debate. He was an officer of great experience in administration, had been Secretary for War, and was the intimate friend of the Duke of Wellington. With almost angry vehemence he approved both Lord Brudenell and his reinstatement. If it had been intended that the noble Lord should be considered a person unfit ever again to serve His Majesty, then the noble Lord would not have been placed on half-pay. The verdict of the Wathen court martial was curtly dismissed, the court had "travelled out of its proper course to censure Lord Brudenell." Sir Henry then had some difficulty in dealing with Lord Brudenell's fitness to command, and was forced to concede that it might possibly be said that the testimonials Lord Brudenell had produced were all of very recent

date and had been given for a particular purpose to bolster up a
weak case; however, many of the testimonials had come from
general officers who were not of the noble Lord's political party.
Then, abruptly dropping fact for feeling, he remarked that "he
hoped the question would be decided by that impartial spirit of
justice that ought to characterise and always had characterised
English gentlemen," and sat down to the sound of loud cries of
"Hear! hear!" and cheers.

The feeling in favour of Lord Brudenell was now so evident
that Sir William Molesworth offered not to take up the time of
the House by dividing. Lord Brudenell's friends, however, called
loudly for a division, and a division was taken. The result was
Ayes, 42; Noes, 322. The reinstatement of Lord Brudenell was
therefore approved by a majority of 280.

Lord Bingham, however, was not impressed. For Lord Bingham was heard to observe that in his opinion his noble brother-
in-law was not fit to have charge of an escort.

CHAPTER

4

The new lieutenant-colonel was in no hurry to join his regiment in the dust and heat of Cawnpore. He lingered in London for the greater part of the season, leaving in June to visit the Duke of Orleans at Compiègne, where the Duke held a review of 2,300 troops in his honour. Then, accompanied by his wife, he travelled by easy stages through Italy, Malta, and Egypt to Suez, where a vessel was hired to convey the pair to Bombay "in a more comfortable and agreeable manner than the ordinary steamer." Leaving Bombay in January, 1837, they made a leisurely progress in a series of hired vessels round the coast of India, breaking their journey at frequent intervals to see the country and be entertained at balls, dinners, and picnics by a series of high officials, including the Governor-General. It was not until October that they floated up the Ganges to Cawnpore, where Lord Brudenell took over the command of the 11th on October 24.

He was delighted to find that he had two other regiments, in addition to the 11th, under his command—it was almost as if he had obtained promotion. "I had attained my object," he writes, "and had the command of a brigade in the field; the 11th and two other regiments."

Cawnpore, however, soon palled on him. The new lieutenant-colonel was frequently absent, and in January, 1838, when the regiment began to make preparations to return to Europe, Lord Brudenell left Cawnpore for good. He stayed with the Commander-in-Chief, visited hill stations, shot tiger. While in camp near Meerut he received the news that his father had died in August, 1837; he was now seventh Earl of Cardigan, with an income of £40,000 a year.

Meanwhile the regiment had been brought down from Cawnpore and embarked in the *Repulse* for the long voyage home round the Cape. Their new lieutenant-colonel did not go with them. Hiring another vessel, the Earl and Countess of Cardigan sailed once more round the coast of India and up the Red Sea, stayed in Cairo, in Rome, in Paris, and reached England in June, 1838. Lord Cardigan had been away from England for two years, but he had spent only about four weeks with the 11th Light Dragoons.

To the 11th, wrote Capt. Harvey Tuckett of the regiment, those weeks seemed like years. It was obvious that deprivation of military authority had increased Lord Cardigan's appetite for command, and he fell on the 11th voraciously. When he received the regiment it was free from crime, but no sooner was he in command than the regimental prison cells were filled; "not one was left unoccupied, and most had two tenants. In less than a month his Lordship had eight courts martial and more than a hundred men on the defaulters list." History repeated itself—nothing pleased the new lieutenant-colonel: his angry eye saw laxity, slackness, and bad discipline everywhere.

The courts-martial under his lordship's command were unsatisfactory to him. There was a moderation in the exercise of justice of which he did not approve. A private had been imprisoned for some offence and a court-martial was ordered to assemble. On the morning of the court-martial Lord Cardigan called his officers round him. He intimated to them that he did not consider his authority had received the support it ought to have done; and if the sentence of the court-martial about to be held was not satisfactory, he warned them that he should report them to Sir Henry Fane, the Commander-in-Chief in India, and to

Lord Hill, the Commander-in-Chief in England. Under this intimidation the sentence was satisfactory, and that evening a soldier of twenty years service was flogged. Directly the punishment was over, the Adjutant was ordered to drill the regiment for an hour, on foot.

During the long voyage home, when the lieutenant-colonel was absent, only one court martial was held, and fewer than twenty men were on the defaulters list.

It was with grave forebodings, then, that the officers and men of the 11th Light Dragoons, now stationed at Canterbury, prepared to receive their commanding officer on his return to England.

It happened that the 11th contained an unusually intelligent young officer, Lt. William Charles Forrest, who rose to be General Forrest, C.B., and colonel of the 11th. He had a strong sense of humour and a high degree of self-control, and, however provocative Lord Cardigan became, he usually contrived to keep his temper. Many of his letters have been preserved, a startling record of the extreme difficulty of being commanded by the seventh Earl of Cardigan.

Before the new lieutenant-colonel had been in England with the regiment a week, the officers of the 11th made a painful discovery—he had an obsession. He could not endure "Indian" officers, that is, British officers who had served in India, and the 11th had been in India for seventeen years. Admittedly the type of officer Lord Cardigan desired for the 11th, the wealthy, fashionable man-about-town, was not, except on the rarest occasions, to be found serving in India. Since it was not in the lieutenant-colonel's nature to conceal his feelings, the situation of the "Indian" officers of the 11th quickly became intolerable. He sneered at them on the parade ground and in stables, growled at them in the mess. He supposed, he said loudly, that the officers of the 11th had no conception of the proper performance of their regimental duties. Where, indeed, could they have learned them—in India? How could they have any comprehension of the way a smart regiment should be disciplined and turned out—he did not imagine they had gained much experience in Cawnpore. Nothing about the regiment satisfied his lordship, from the colour of the sheepskins which covered the saddles, which were not white enough, to the state of the uniforms, which were not new enough, and the regiment's performance on the parade ground, which was not fast enough. He announced his determination to have a galloping field day within six months of his arrival. Discipline was tightened, parades and inspections were doubled, and his displeasure fell constantly and heavily on officer and man. In the first six months of his command he held fifty-four courts martial, desertions were numerous, and Canterbury gaol became so filled with soldiers of the 11th that it was said to have become their regimental barracks.

The authorities began to be uneasy. It seemed as if the lesson impressed on the lieutenant-colonel two years ago by Lord Hill had failed in its effect. Was it possible that from his experiences with the 15th Hussars Lord Cardigan had learnt nothing? Sir Charles Dalbiac, the Inspector-General of Cavalry, sent the lieutenant-colonel a letter of reproof. After careful study of the minutes and evidence of the courts martial, it was Sir Charles Dalbiac's opinion that the manner in which Lord Cardigan carried on the discipline of the regiment was unnecessarily severe. Lord Cardigan paid no attention and continued to scold and discipline the 11th as furiously as before; and several "Indian" officers, seeing no future under his command, left the regiment. They were replaced by rich young men ready to spend lavishly on their mounts and themselves; and the 11th began to get a reputation for glitter and dash.

Among the "Indian" officers was Capt. Harvey Tuckett; this officer had considerable wit and a ready pen, had contributed to newspapers, and had written a number of regimental skits.

Meanwhile on August 5 six young officers of the 11th, amusing themselves with a cross-country gallop, rode across crops belonging to Mr. Brent, a prosperous miller and alderman of the city of Canterbury. Mr. Brent intercepted them and attempted to remonstrate. The officers rode their horses at him, forcing him against a wall, but Mr. Brent, with considerable courage, seized one of the horses by the bridle and demanded the young men's names. With a loud guffaw someone shouted "Snooks!" and the party galloped away. Mr. Brent pursued them to the barracks, and had the gate slammed in his face. Thoroughly enraged, he wrote first to Lord Cardigan, who did not answer; next to Lord Hill, who replied after several weeks that Mr. Brent's recollection of the affair differed from that of the other parties concerned; and finally to the editor of the *Morning Chronicle*.

With gleeful alacrity the *Morning Chronicle* published Mr. Brent's account of the affair and disclosed that "the Earl of Cardigan is none other than Lord Brudenell, whose reappointment after being dismissed so much surprised every right-thinking person"; he "seems to have very little idea of what is due from one gentleman to another." Lord Cardigan flew to his pistols and challenged Mr. Brent (a generous offer, he asserted, "since Mr. Brent, though a magistrate, was no gentleman"); he challenged the editor of the *Morning Chronicle,* and he threatened to call and horse-whip the newspaper's leader-writer. With even greater glee the *Morning Chronicle* published his letters and assured the noble Earl that if he attempted to force his way into the office he would be handed over to a police officer. Angry letters came in from readers protesting against the conduct of the Earl of Cardigan, the scandal of the 15th Hussars was revived, and the authorities found that they had another attack on aristocratic favouritism in the Army on their hands. It was a warning of what lay ahead as a consequence of having reinstated the Earl of Cardigan. But ill-advised as his conduct in 1839 might seem, it was the merest shadow of what was to follow in 1840.

That year opened in triumph. Incessant drilling, constant field days, lavish expenditure on uniform and equipment had had their effect, and the 11th was a very fine regiment indeed. In October, 1839, the Duke of Wellington, as the guest of Lord

Cardigan, had seen the 11th exercise in the field, and he wrote that he had never seen a regiment in higher order or one the appearance of which did the commanding officer and the officers more credit. Lord Cardigan unquestionably possessed certain qualities of efficiency; indeed, his contemporaries agreed he would have made an excellent sergeant-major.

In February, 1840, the 11th was the regiment chosen to meet Prince Albert at Dover and escort him to London for his marriage to Queen Victoria. The Prince became Colonel-in-Chief, the name of the regiment was changed from the 11th Light Dragoons to the 11th, Prince Albert's Own, Hussars, and new uniforms were designed. Hussars are the most brilliant of cavalry, and the 11th Hussars were superb. They wore overalls (trousers) of cherry colour, jackets of royal blue edged with gold, furred pelisses, short coats, worn as capes, glittering with bullion braid and gold lace, high fur hats adorned with brilliant plumes. "The brevity of their jackets, the irrationality of their headgear, the incredible tightness of their cherry coloured pants, altogether defy description; they must be seen to be appreciated," wrote *The Times*. This gorgeousness was largely achieved at Lord Cardigan's personal expense, and he also added £10 out of his own pocket to the price allowed by the Government for each horse in the regiment. It was estimated he spent £10,000 a year on the 11th out of his private income.

He was now in his glory. When he went to London, it was his practice to give a number of his smartest men a day's leave and five shillings, and each posted himself at some point which he intended to pass. People ran to stare as Lord Cardigan sauntered down St. James's Street, saluted at every few yards by his Hussars, brilliant as parakeets.

But if only he could have got rid of the "Indian" officers—it was incredible to him, he used to remark to his friends, that any of them could be so thick-skinned as to stay. No "Indian" officer ever received an invitation to his own house, and when cards of invitation for dinners and balls were sent to the mess by gentlemen living in the neighbourhood, he had made it a rule that they were not to be given to those officers whom, he said, he had "found sticking to the regiment in the East Indies." Yet "Indian" officers obstinately remained, a perpetual hindrance to his work of bringing the regiment to perfection.

Take their drinking habits. In India it had been the custom for officers to drink porter—it was healthier and cheaper. To this the lieutenant-colonel furiously objected. Porter was the drink of factory hands and labourers, and he wished to make the 11th famous for its splendid hospitality, for he loved the pomp and ceremony of "great" dinners. He forbade bottled porter to appear on the mess table.

On May 18, 1840, Major-General Sleigh, the Inspector-General of Cavalry, and his staff were to dine in the mess of the 11th after an inspection. Arrangements were made on a magnificent scale, and the lieutenant-colonel gave orders that nothing but champagne was to be served at dinner. The result of the inspection was most gratifying: Lord Cardigan was highly complimented on the brilliant appearance, the magnificent mounts, and the fine performance of the 11th, and as he entered the mess with General Sleigh he was seen to be in high good humour.

At dinner one of General Sleigh's aides was sitting next to a certain Capt. John Reynolds, an "Indian" officer and the son of a distinguished "Indian" officer. General Sleigh's aide asked if he might have Moselle instead of champagne, and John Reynolds gave the order to a mess waiter, who, anxious to supply the wine at once, did not stop to decant it, but placed it on the table in its bottle. At this moment Lord Cardigan looked down the table, and there, among the silver, the glass, the piles of hot-house fruit, he saw a black bottle—it must be porter! He was transported with rage. John Reynolds, an "Indian" officer, was drinking porter under his very nose, desecrating the splendour of his dinner table. When it was explained to him that the black bottle contained Moselle, he refused to be appeased; gentlemen, he said, decanted their wine. Next day he sent a message to John Reynolds through the president of the mess committee, a Captain Jones, who was one of his favourites. Captain Jones found him with two other officers, one of whom did not belong to the regiment. "The colonel has desired me to tell you," said Captain Jones, "that you were wrong in having a black bottle placed on the table at a great dinner like last night. The mess should be conducted like a gentleman's table and not like a pot-house." John Reynolds was "utterly astonished," especially as the message was delivered before an audience, but, controlling himself, he told the other "in a quiet manner, that he had no right to bring him an offensive message, and as a brother captain it would have been better taste if he had declined to deliver it." Almost at once he was summoned to the orderly room, where, before Captain Jones and the adjutant, Lord Cardigan attacked him in furious rage. "If you cannot behave quietly, sir, why don't you leave the regiment? That is just the way with you Indian officers; you think you know everything, but I tell you, sir, you neither know your duty nor discipline. . . . Oh yes! I believe you do know your duty, but you have no idea whatever of discipline. I put you under arrest."

John Reynolds remained silent. Captain Jones then offered his hand, but Reynolds refused to shake it. "I have no quarrel with you," he said, "and nothing has passed that makes shaking hands necessary."

Lord Cardigan burst out in a loud voice, "You have insulted Captain Jones." John Reynolds quietly repeated, "I have not, my lord." Lord Cardigan shouted, "I say you have. You are under arrest, and I shall report the matter to the Horse Guards." John Reynolds replied, "I am sorry for it," and retired.

He was then placed under close arrest, but brought up from time to time, to be examined by Lord Cardigan, who railed at him, taunted him with being an "Indian" officer, and ordered him to explain himself. These interviews lasted as long as two hours, and John Reynolds stated, "I never can describe the mental torture I underwent during the probing and cross-examination of my feelings, lest I should say something that might afterwards be used against me, especially as Lieutenant-Colonel the Earl of Cardigan condescended to assure me that he waived the consideration of being my commanding officer, and afterwards resumed it, so that I had great difficulty in knowing when I was addressing his Lordship as a private gentleman and when in his capacity as Lieutenant-Colonel."

After three days he received a memorandum from Lord Hill, the Commander-in-Chief, recommending him to admit the impropriety of his conduct towards his commanding officer and to resume friendly relations with Captain Jones. He obeyed the first instruction, but refused to drink wine with Captain Jones or to shake hands with him, and remained under arrest. On June 9 Major-General Sleigh came once more to Canterbury, summoned the officers of the 11th to appear before him, and, without holding an investigation, read aloud a letter from headquarters, condemning John Reynolds in the strongest possible language and approving and supporting Lord Cardigan. Reynolds's behaviour was described as "pernicious and vindictive," and an enquiry was "absolutely refused" on the ground that "many things would come to light which are not for the good of the service." John Reynolds then asked that he might be court-martialled for the offences he was alleged to have committed, and at this General Sleigh flew into a rage. There was to be no court martial, no enquiry, no further discussion of the affair; the Commander-in-Chief had made up his mind once and for all that the matter was to be considered as settled. And, turning angrily on John Reynolds, General Sleigh told him that he had "forfeited the sympathy of every officer of rank in the service."

General Sleigh and Lord Cardigan then left the room together, and Capt. John Reynolds resumed his regimental duties with the 11th. The following week the regiment left Canterbury for duty at Brighton Pavilion.

The Army authorities had found themselves in a dilemma; since Lord Cardigan had been reinstated, for better or worse he must be supported. It was too late to draw back, and the best policy seemed to be firmness: the officers of the 11th must be shown that it was useless to oppose Lord Cardigan.

Unfortunately the "black bottle" affair became a nine days' wonder, the phrase caught the public fancy, and "black bottle" became a catchword. Jokes about the 11th appeared in newspapers, and mock reports were circulated of "The Battle of the Moselle, in which His Royal Highness Prince Albert's Regiment has severely suffered, being so completely broken in pieces as to require *'reforming.'* " A private of the 11th was arrested for assaulting a guardsman in the street; when reprimanded by Lieutenant-Colonel Lord Cardigan, the man stammered out, "But, my Lord, he called me a black bottle." Meanwhile Capt. John Reynolds's guardian (his father had died in India) pestered Lord Hill for an explanation of General Sleigh's reprimand, for production of the correspondence, and for a court martial. When he got no satisfaction, he sent an account of the affair and copies of his letters to Lord Hill to every leading newspaper in London, and in almost every instance they were printed in full.

To Lord Cardigan, however, "black bottle" brought unmixed satisfaction. Once more he had been supported, once more he had been proved right. He assumed an air of importance even greater than before, his temper became even less controlled, his bearing haughtier.

Brighton was a station after the lieutenant-colonel's own heart. As the 11th paraded through the streets they attracted crowds by the brilliance of their uniforms and the rich dresses and splendid mounts of their officers. He took a house in Brunswick Square and entertained lavishly, bringing his fashionable friends down from London for dinners, balls, gambling, and racing.

Yet the ointment contained a fly—there were still "Indian" officers in the regiment. John Reynolds had been put in his place, but there was another "Indian" officer named Reynolds, no relation, they said, but equally obnoxious. Lieutenant-Colonel Lord

Cardigan was beginning to find Richard Reynolds, senior captain of the regiment, impossible to tolerate.

Richard Reynolds had been in the service for fourteen years, of which thirteen had been spent with the 11th in India, a service which, he said, "Lord Cardigan was in the habit of treating with contempt and reproach." The treatment to which he was now subjected followed a familiar pattern. He was called out in front of the regiment and publicly reprimanded; at the mess table he was told to hold his tongue; when he asked for leave he was invariably refused. During his service in India both his father and mother had died, leaving him in charge of ten younger brothers and sisters, but Lord Cardigan had given "positive orders that Capt. Richard Reynolds was not to be granted even a day's leave of absence on any pretext whatsoever."

On August 26, 1840, Lord Cardigan gave a large evening party at his house in Brunswick Square to which the military and social world of Brighton was invited, but not John or Richard Reynolds. During the evening a young lady asked Lord Cardigan why the two Captain Reynoldses were absent, and in the presence of a number of people, and "with strong excitement," Lord Cardigan replied, "As long as I live they shall never enter my house." The words were repeated, and next day Richard Reynolds wrote Lord Cardigan a letter of protest, ending, "I cannot but consider this report highly objectionable, as it is calculated to convey an impression prejudicial to my character, and I therefore must insist that your Lordship will be good enough to authorise me to contradict it."

On August 28, on parade, Lord Cardigan called Richard Reynolds out before the regiment and furiously reprimanded him, shouting at him, describing his letter as "disrespectful, insubordinate, and insulting," and finishing with the taunt that he supposed such conduct was only to be expected from "Indian" officers.

On September 1 *The Times* printed an angry letter demanding that all officers who had seen Indian service should convene a public meeting and insist that the Commander-in-Chief India exact an apology from the Earl of Cardigan. A stream of indignant protests followed: the head of the Indian service officers of the British Army was the Duke of Wellington himself, and the tactics which defeated the generals of Napoleon in the Peninsula had been learned on the plains of India. The Earl of Cardigan should be compelled to apologise to the Duke.

Meanwhile Richard Reynolds had lost his temper, and on the evening of September 1 he wrote Lord Cardigan a fatal letter. Number 60 in the Articles of War laid down that "Any . . . officer who shall give, send, convey, or promote a challenge to any other officer to fight a Duel—or shall upbraid another for refusing a challenge . . . shall on conviction of any of the aforesaid offences be liable to be cashiered." In his letter Richard Reynolds accused Lord Cardigan of taking advantage of article number 60 to avoid a duel. "Your Lordship's reputation as a professed duellist . . . does not admit of your privately offering insult to me, and then screening yourself under the cloak of commanding officer."

The accusation was unjust. Lord Cardigan's physical courage was beyond question. True, the article in question had often been ignored, and Lord Cardigan would not ignore it, but the explanation was not cowardice, but his meticulous respect for the letter of the law. An immense effort was needed before the lieutenant-colonel could take in an idea, but, once admitted, it was swallowed whole; it could never be modified or relinquished.

His reply to the letter was to put Richard Reynolds under arrest and to apply for and be granted a court martial.

On September 4 a letter appeared in the *Morning Chronicle* attacking Lord Cardigan with intimate knowledge and extraordinary virulence. Headed, "To the Officers of the British Army," the letter said that Lord Cardigan on many occasions had grossly and wantonly insulted officers at the mess table, and when called to account had pleaded his privilege as commanding officer to avoid a duel. Repeated applications for an enquiry into Lord

Cardigan's conduct had been made to the Horse Guards, to the Prime Minister, and to Prince Albert—all in vain.

Lord Cardigan has now insulted the senior captain of the regiment, has again pleaded his privilege as commanding officer and placed Captain X under arrest. Many a gallant officer has waived the privilege which nothing but wealth and an earldom obtained for Lord Cardigan. ... I therefore sincerely trust, gentlemen, that you will aid me in calling for an enquiry, and it may no longer be imagined that a commanding officer may outrage every gentlemanly feeling of those under his command with impunity.

The authorship of the letter was an open secret: it had been written by Capt. Harvey Tuckett, the "Indian" officer celebrated for regimental skits, who had recently left the regiment. Lord Cardigan sent a friend, Captain Douglas, down to the Poultry, where Captain Tuckett carried on business as an East India agent, to demand an apology. But Captain Tuckett refused: every statement he had published was, he maintained, correct in every particular. As he had left the regiment, Lord Cardigan was not committing a breach of the Articles of War by fighting a duel with him, and a rendezvous was fixed at the Windmill, Wimbledon Common, at five in the afternoon of Saturday, September 12.

The Windmill was a well-known rendezvous. But the miller was a constable, and as soon as he saw two post-chaises approach, he and his wife ran up to the platform of the mill and saw five gentlemen with cases, which evidently contained pistols, alight. The miller ran down to fetch his staff of office. Meanwhile Lord Cardigan and Capt. Harvey Tuckett had been placed at twelve paces distance from each other. Shots were exchanged without effect, each was given another pistol, shots were exchanged again, and then Captain Tuckett fell to the ground, wounded in the back part of the lower ribs.

Upon this the miller went up to Lord Cardigan, who still held the smoking pistol in his hand, arrested him for a breach of the peace, and confiscated the pistols. The party then went into the mill, and since Captain Tuckett was unconscious and bleeding profusely, a well-known surgeon, Sir James Anderson, who accompanied the party, was allowed to take him to his own house, while the miller took Lord Cardigan and Captain Douglas to the Wandsworth police station. There, so notorious had the affairs of Lord Cardigan become that the inspector recognised him and said he hoped he had not been fighting a duel with Capt. Richard Reynolds. Cardigan "stood up erect and with the utmost disdain said, 'Oh no; do you suppose I would condescend to fight with one of my own officers?' " Bail was granted over the week-end, and on Monday, September 14, Lord Cardigan and Captain Douglas appeared before the magistrates and were released upon entering into a recognisance to appear when called for.

Lord Cardigan then returned to Brighton in a state of extreme excitement.

It was now Lt. William Forrest's turn to fall foul of the lieutenant-colonel. William Forrest was posted for duty at the Pavilion for the short period of a week, and as there was almost no accommodation at the Pavilion beyond the guardroom, he did not give up his room in barracks, but merely turned the key. A certain Lieutenant Jenkinson, a young man of family and wealth, who succeeded later as Sir Charles Jenkinson of Hawksbury, one of Lord Cardigan's favourites, wished to use the room, found it locked, and reported William Forrest to the lieutenant-colonel. On September 18, at half-past five in the afternoon, Lord Cardigan driving his phaeton along the Steyne, saw William Forrest, instantly reined up, leapt out, and attacked the lieutenant at the top of his voice in violent language, to the surprise of bystanders. It was evident, wrote Forrest, that the lieutenant-colonel was much wrought up at the time. "Do you suppose, sir, that you can hold two rooms?" he shouted. "I have sent an order for the key to be given up, and given up it shall be. How dare you, sir, oppose your commanding officer?" William Forrest respectfully pointed out that he had nowhere else to keep his property and that the accommodation at the Pavilion was such that he had nowhere to dress; had he been asked for the loan of his room he would willingly have lent it, but for the short period of a week it was not reasonable to require him to relinquish his room, nor was it customary. He also ventured to say that he was not aware that he was infringing any standing order by retaining the key of his room. The lieutenant-colonel interrupted him in a paroxysm of rage. "You try to come the letter of the law over me, do you, sir? I could understand your feeling inconvenience if you had been accustomed to two or three suites of apartments at St. James's—but, really, for you! Why, if I choose I can keep you here for a month, and you have no right to go into the barrack at all except for your breakfast and dinner. I order you to give up the key of your room to Lieutenant Jenkinson before night." Lieutenant Forrest saluted and withdrew.

At a quarter past six Lord Cardigan came to the Pavilion stables and enquired if the key had yet been handed over, and when William Forrest said that he had not yet had time to do so, he was placed under arrest. The next day the lieutenant-colonel forwarded a complaint of Lieutenant Forrest's conduct to the Commander-in-Chief. In a written explanation Lieutenant Forrest pointed out that it was the lieutenant-colonel's "offensive and irritating manner and language which were in a great degree the cause of the fault I committed in neglecting immediate compliance with the order; had I received the slightest courtesy I should not now find myself in the painful position of being reported to the Genl. Commanding-in-Chief."

Lieutenant Forrest being known to be exceptionally good-humoured and an outstanding officer, Lord Hill became uneasy. On September 29 he wrote—it was the first of many similar letters—asking Lord Cardigan for a "clear statement as to his reasons for putting Lieutenant Jenkinson in Lieutenant Forrest's room for one week during Lieutenant Forrest's turn of duty at the Brighton Pavilion." The lieutenant-colonel did not answer, and after an interval Lord Hill wrote Lieutenant Forrest a mild reprimand.

Meanwhile the court-martial on Richard Reynolds had begun

at Brighton on September 24. Public interest was intense: the Tuckett duel, and the arrest of Lieutenant Forrest, following swiftly on "Black Bottle" had earned Cardigan fresh notoriety. In a leading article *The Times* adjured him to "abrogate a little of that aristocratic hauteur which characterizes his demeanour"; other newspapers described the 11th as "lying helpless at the mercy of spies and tale-bearers . . . none but sycophants were said to be able to escape the wrath of the Lieutenant-Colonel." A current joke concerned the uniform of the 11th: "In the new uniform of Lord Cardigan's regiment are there many frogs?" "I don't know, but there are plenty of toads (toadies) under the coats."

Lord Cardigan himself became an object of public execration. Tall, handsome, opulently dressed, carrying himself with a mixture of arrogance and self-importance said to make one lose one's temper just to look at him, he was greeted, as he whirled through Brighton in his phaeton, with hisses and groans.

Though the court martial on Richard Reynolds lasted a fortnight, the verdict was a foregone conclusion, and he himself admitted that the letter he had sent his lieutenant-colonel was a breach of the military code, which must prove fatal. The authorities were determined not to risk another Wathen court martial, there was to be no wave of sympathy for Richard Reynolds. He was not allowed to call evidence to prove the habitual insolence with which Lord Cardigan treated his officers, and when the lieutenant-colonel gave a version of the scene at the evening party, which differed materially from the earlier account, there were no questions from the Court. Lord Cardigan was much agitated and gave his evidence in a loud and rapid voice, but he did not grimace or become incoherent. No insecurity disturbed him; he knew victory was his.

Reynolds conducted his defence with dignity; he established the fact that he had evidence he was not allowed to call, and described with restraint the treatment to which he had been subjected by the lieutenant-colonel, the "long course of violence, insolence and vindictiveness," the shouts, the taunts, the sneers, the unreasonable refusal of leave, the public reprimands on parade "where the Lieutenant-Colonel was well aware it was impossible to answer."

On October 19 the verdict of the Court was announced: Capt. Richard Reynolds was cashiered. An eye-witness reported that when the verdict was read Lieutenant-Colonel Lord Cardigan, "made no attempt to disguise his overwhelming satisfaction and delight beyond measure." By being cashiered, Reynolds lost the value of his commission, but fortunately he possessed some private means.

The Army authorities were by no means easy in their minds, however, and the papers in the Reynolds court martial and the disputes in the 11th had been sent to the Duke of Wellington for his advice. And the Duke was horrified. He tried (he wrote to Lord Hill on October 15) "to recollect any similar instance of which my experience in the Service, and in command may have given me knowledge," and "could bring to mind only one." It was not the position of the officers of the 11th under the command of Lord Cardigan which horrified the Duke—he was concerned only with the threat to the discipline of the Army. To take a sentimental view of the state of the 11th, to be concerned with the feelings of the men involved, was foreign to the Duke; a commander must necessarily train himself to be indifferent to the fate of individuals. Here officers had "acted in a spirit of party against their commanding officer," there had been "want of subordination and respect," and finally one of the Articles of War had been violated. Should such conduct be repeated, the discipline, efficiency, and well-being of the British Army would be endangered. The fate of Richard Reynolds, the propriety or impropriety of Lord Cardigan's behaviour were matters of indifference to Wellington: the supreme, the over-riding necessity was to maintain discipline. In a memorandum to Lord Hill dated October 14 he wrote:

. . . there is no alternative left for the court martial excepting to pass the sentence upon an officer who provokes another to send a challenge; that he shall be cashiered. I commanded armies for many years of my life; and was entrusted by my superiors with the power of ordering General Courts Martial to assemble for the trial of officers and soldiers for breaches of discipline; I don't recollect an instance of an officer sending a challenge, or provoking another to send a challenge, who upon conviction was not cashiered. The perusal of Captain Richard Reynolds letter of the 28th August can leave no doubt that it was intended as a provocation to Lord Cardigan to take steps which would have terminated in a duel.

Lord Cardigan should be advised "to interfere as little as possible in personal matters, to conduct them through the official channels of the Regimental staff. . . . He will thus have time to consider every Act and every Expression. He will have Witnesses for the whole of his conduct and it will not be so easy for Parties to act against him."

In a covering letter the Duke wrote to Lord Hill with feeling. The disputes were "lamentable."

At a moment at which the Queen's Service may require the greatest professional effort on the part of every organised military body, it may be found that this fine corps, in the highest order and discipline, the conduct of its non-commissioned officers and men excellent, is unfit to perform the service required from it on account of these party disputes between the officers and the Commanding Officer upon petty trifles. . . . I think that when the sentence of the General Court Martial is confirmed it would be desirable that you should send down a general officer to the 11th Hussars to communicate to the officers your feelings and opinions on the state of the Regiment in consequence of their disputes.

On the 20th Lord Hill wrote to the Duke, "Nothing can be more important than the papers you have written. . . . I shall implicitly follow all your instructions."

On Thursday, October 22, the officers of the 11th were ordered to be present in the mess. When they had assembled, a roll call was taken, the doors were locked, and Sir John Macdonald, the Adjutant-General, who had come down from London, read an "admonition" from Lord Hill, the Commander-in-Chief; and in spite of the precautions, the admonition was fully reported in *The Times* two days later. "It was perfectly useless," said the Adjutant-General, "for them to make any further complaints against the Earl of Cardigan, for that Lord Hill had determined to listen to nothing about that which had heretofore occurred—that on this point Lord Hill was peremptory; but that any future conduct of the Lieutenant-Colonel of the regiment should be promptly enquired into and redressed." Sir John then urged the development of friendly feeling, remarking that no regiment can acquit itself properly on active service where there is not co-operation between the commanding officer and his officers. Then, turning to the Earl of Cardigan, Sir John said, "with great distinctness" that Lord Hill "trusted that in the command of the regiment the noble Earl would in future exercise moderation and forbearance. It was Lord Hill's opinion that the numerous complaints which had been made to him as Commander-in-Chief would never have occurred if the Lieutenant-Colonel of the 11th Hussars had evinced the proper degree of temper and discretion in the exercise of his command."

The reprimand was totally unexpected, and the effect on the lieutenant-colonel remarkable. His features became distorted, and he seemed to writhe. "When he found himself reproved and reprimanded before those officers whom he had so frequently treated with arrogance, oppression and insult, his countenance changed, and the agony of his soul was perceptible to all."

The sentence on Richard Reynolds was received by the public with furious indignation. Meetings were held in London and the country to petition the Queen to remove Lord Cardigan from the command of the 11th, a subscription was started to compensate Reynolds for the loss of his commission, and *The Times* inquired why Lord Cardigan should for "the second time in his life be whitewashed from his offences, offences which would have cashiered any officer not protected and sheltered by overwhelming influence." Richard Reynolds behaved admirably. In a letter to that newspaper on November 3 he asked that demonstrations should cease. There was, he could not deny, an unanswerable case against him; the letter he had written to Lord Cardigan was, by the military code, unforgivable. "I cannot lay my hand on my heart and say that I have not offended grievously against the laws of the Army."

Meanwhile Lord Cardigan, seen at the Brighton station taking the train for London, was "assailed with loud boos" and had to be hurried into a carriage and protected by the railway staff. On October 30 he appeared in a box at the Brighton Theatre, to be greeted with a storm of hisses which continued for half an hour; it was impossible to begin the performance, and at the request of the management he left the box, "upon which three cheers for Capt. Richard Reynolds were called, amid loud acclamation and enthusiasm." A few days later, on November 2, a benefit performance at the theatre was announced, "under the patronage of the Right Honourable the Lieutenant-Colonel the Earl of Cardigan and the officers of the 11th Hussars." No sooner did the audience catch sight of Lord Cardigan than pandemonium broke loose. Hisses, yells, groans were succeeded by the chanting in unison of the names of Richard Reynolds and Black Bottle, and fists were shaken towards the lieutenant-colonel's box. *The Times* condemned Cardigan for appearing at all. "Such effrontery, such a defiance of public opinion was not looked for even from the commander of the 11th Hussars."

The unpopularity and notoriety of Lord Cardigan were soon more than merely local—he became a figure of national detestation.

On December 22, for example, he attended a performance at Drury Lane Theatre. "The first audible indication of his presence was a cry of 'The Black Bottle,' followed by a general hiss. A crowd gathered under his box, shaking their fists and shouting, 'Turn him out!' 'Shame!' " Lord Cardigan sat in his box, ignoring the demonstration, until the uproar became so great that it was obvious no performance could take place. "His Lordship then, advancing very deliberately to the front of the box, put on his great coat, and making a bow, retired amid one universal shout of disapprobation."

A week later he was recognised at a Promenade Concert.

At the end of the first piece a few gentlemen began hissing. In about ten minutes there was a complete uproar; every eye in that vast circle fixed upon one spot; necks craning, bodies twisting round pillars; all to gaze on, or cast insult on, one small party. From nine o'clock until eleven there was one continued uproar, not a note of music could be heard.

Lord Cardigan sat it out with great coolness, determined not to be bullied, sitting in his box with his arms folded and a haughty expression on his face, but was finally forced to withdraw.

Demonstrations, unpopularity, had not the slightest effect on Lord Cardigan. His view was simple. Once again he had been proved right, once again there had been a conflict and he had won, and in his autobiographical sketch he wrote simply, "I placed an officer under arrest, he was court-martialled and cashiered." As for Lord Hill's admonition, he paid no more attention to it than to Lord Hill's warning on his reinstatement in 1836. Indeed, from the date of the admonition he began to disregard Lord Hill; when Lord Hill wrote to him, he did not answer, and there was, it appeared, nothing Lord Hill could do.

As month followed month, the affairs of the officers of the 11th continued to occupy the attention of the press, and almost daily some revelation appeared. Officers had been forced to sell out and leave the Army because it was impossible to serve in the 11th under Lord Cardigan, and he would not sanction an exchange to another regiment; officers who at courts martial had given evidence not in favour of Lord Cardigan were relentlessly pursued by the lieutenant-colonel's vengeance. These letters and articles were cut out by Lord Cardigan and posted to Lord Hill with a demand that they should be contradicted instantly and officially. Lord Hill did not reply. On his side the Commander-in-Chief sent cautions and requests for explanations on various points to Lord Cardigan, and Lord Cardigan did not reply.

On Sunday, December 8, as the regiment was leaving church, Mr. Sandham, the junior surgeon, had difficulty with the fastening of his cap. He stayed behind to adjust it and caught up with the regiment by using a side door, instead of the main door, of the church. As soon as the regiment had reached barracks, Lord Cardigan sent for Mr. Sandham and, before he could say a word, "personally assailed him with violence, shouted at him, cancelled his leave, and ordered him to leave the room, refusing to allow him to make any explanation." Mr. Sandham lost his temper, told the lieutenant-colonel he was unjust and was placed under arrest. Mr. Sandham then formally complained to Lord Hill. On December 17 Lord Hill wrote to Lord Cardigan with considerable sharpness.

The Commander-in-Chief "could not but express his regret that if your lordship thought it your duty to notice this apparent irregularity, a fault of an unimportant character of which Mr. Sandham was wholly unconscious, you did not at the same time take the necessary steps to enquire into the circumstances which gave rise to it . . . had this obvious course of action been adopted . . . the valuable time of Lord Hill would not again be occupied by regimental controversies of this painful nature between your lordship and an officer of the 11th Hussars."

Lord Hill went on to direct that Lord Cardigan should place this letter in Mr. Sandham's hands, and that Mr. Sandham should read it in his lordship's presence.

Lord Cardigan took no notice of Lord Hill's letter, and on December 27 Lord Hill wrote asking for an acknowledgment. Lord Cardigan did not reply. On January 3 Lord Hill wrote a third time desiring to be informed if his instructions had been carried out, but still Lord Cardigan did not reply; and the Commander-in-Chief, apparently helpless, did not write again.

Another matter intervened. At the end of December Lord Hill

was once again asking Lord Cardigan for an explanation about Capt. John Reynolds, "Black Bottle," who had applied for leave to sell out. Reynolds stated that it was being made impossible for him to remain in the regiment, so he had applied for leave to become a student in the Senior Department of the Royal Military College, the forerunner of the Staff College, but that Lord Cardigan had refused to grant leave, and he therefore had no choice but to sell out and leave the Army. His application was received with something verging on consternation at the Horse Guards, and Lord Hill wrote very sharply indeed. His Lordship the Lieutenant-Colonel was to report forthwith his reasons for refusing Capt. John Reynolds leave to become a student in the Senior Department; unless those reasons were borne out by the General Regulations and Orders of the Army, they could not be supported or approved. "In reporting your reasons for refusing, it is to be clearly understood that they are to have no reference to any differences which may have taken place between your Lordship and Captain Reynolds." Early in January John Reynolds was summoned to a private interview with Lord Fitz-Roy Somerset, Military Secretary to the Horse Guards, who later, as Lord Raglan, became Commander-in-Chief in the Crimea. Lord FitzRoy Somerset was noted for tact and charm, and he exerted all his persuasiveness to persuade the captain not to sell out. In his account of the interview John Reynolds says he refused on the ground that he did not feel safe with the Earl of Cardigan—he knew the value of his commission was not secure for a day whilst he was under the Earl's command; the Earl's conduct to him was overbearing, his language abusive. Lord FitzRoy Somerset, a personal friend of the Earl of Cardigan, continued to press Reynolds: if he would withdraw his resignation, he should have what terms he liked. Finally he appealed, as one soldier to another: for the good of the service, John Reynolds ought to withdraw his resignation. Reynolds then consented on terms, "the first being that he should never again be required, even for a single day, to serve under the Earl of Cardigan"; he was also to receive a recantation of the censure passed on him by General Sleigh in the "Black Bottle" affair, six months' leave to make up for the leave consistently refused him by the Earl of Cardigan, and permission to study for two years at the Senior Department.

The appointment was announced on January 18, 1841, and received by the newspapers with pæans of praise, *The Times* suggesting that Lord Hill might well be forced to resign, "it now being realised that he has personally interfered much on behalf of his friend Lord Cardigan"; and an early reconsideration of Captain Richard Reynolds's case was predicted.

A lull now followed in the affairs of the officers of the 11th. On October 20, the day after the verdict of the court martial on Richard Reynolds was announced, the Earl of Cardigan and his second, Captain Douglas, had appeared at the Old Bailey, where a grand jury found a true bill against them on three counts: intent to murder, maim, and cause grievous bodily harm to Capt. Harvey Garnett Phipps Tuckett. By virtue of his rank the Earl of Cardigan was not to be tried in an ordinary criminal court, but by his peers, and he was summoned to appear before the House of Peers in full Parliament on February 16, 1841, there to be tried for felony; the maximum penalty was transportation for life. For the moment, therefore, Lieutenant-Colonel the Earl of Cardigan was occupied, and not much with his regiment.

5

The law of England upon duelling is uncompromising and severe. To kill a man in a duel is to murder him, to fight a duel with him is to attempt to murder him. From time to time more severe penalties have been imposed. In 1828 Lord Lansdowne's Act made it a capital offence to shoot at another man with intent to kill, disfigure, maim, or do him grievous bodily harm; thus to fight a duel, whatever the result, became a crime punishable by hanging. In 1837 the law was modified, and to fight a duel remained a capital offence only if a wound were inflicted; if shots were exchanged harmlessly and no blood was shed, the penalty was three years' hard labour with the treadmill, or transportation, either for life or for fifteen years.

In practice the penalties were almost never imposed. The Duke of Wellington was not hanged for fighting Lord Winchelsea; Lord Castlereagh was not transported when he wounded Mr. Canning; the fifth Lord Byron was not executed for killing Mr. Chaworth; nor did the Duke of York go to the treadmill for fighting Colonel Lennox. In 172 duels known to have been fought between 1760 and 1820, though 91 persons were killed, the death penalty was imposed only twice, and in one instance there was almost a certainty of foul play.

Duelling was an aristocratic practice—workmen and clerks

did not run each other through the body for insults in a beer-house on Saturday night—and it was accepted as part of the code of that separate priviliged world, the world of high life which existed outside the world of ordinary citizens. Moreover, though the thought of a duel provoked a shudder, dueling had a flavour of wild poetic justice. Judges and juries found themselves unable to view a deadly combat in which each contestant took his life in his hand in the same light as a murder, or to put a Wellington or a Castlereagh on the same level as a Charles Peace or a William Palmer.

By 1841, however, public opinion had changed. To the age of railways, steamers, and gaslight, of popular education and popular science, duelling appeared criminal and absurd. The intelligent artisan, the powerful and rising middle class were learning to resent aristocratic privilege, and nowhere was it more clearly manifested than in the practice of duelling. Members of the aristocracy had licence to commit a criminal offence and escape the penalty—and only, it seemed, members of the aristocracy.

Two years before, in 1838, on the very ground, the Windmill Wimbledon Common, where Lord Cardigan fought Captain Tuckett, a duel had taken place between a Mr. Elliot and a Mr. Mirfin, in which Mr. Mirfin was killed. The duel was decidedly not in high life. Mr. Elliot had pretensions to gentility as the son of an officer, but Mr. Mirfin was the son of a prosperous linen draper, and lived at an unfashionable address in Lambeth. The duel arose not out of a point of honour, but on account of a collision between the one's gig and the other's phaeton on the Epsom Road on Derby Day.

After Mr. Mirfin's death, Mr. Elliot, the two seconds, and a friend who had been present were taken into custody and charged at Wandsworth police station with murder. Mr. Elliot and his second broke their bail and fled, but the dead man's second and his friend were tried at the Old Bailey for aiding and abetting the murder of Mirfin and sentenced to death. The sentence was subsequently reduced to a year's penal servitude with hard labour, and the two men were at that time serving their sentence in the Guildford House of Correction, on the treadmill.

On September 29 *The Times* demanded the same treatment for the Earl of Cardigan.

Let his head be cropped, let him be put on an oatmeal diet, let him labour on the treadmill. Let not occasion be given for anyone to say that the same which was visited as a felony on the associates of the linen-draper Mirfin is excused as an act worthy of a man of honour in the Earl of Cardigan.

Meanwhile, slowly and cumbrously the antique, costly machinery for the trial of a peer on a criminal charge was being set in motion. In January, 1841, the case was transferred from Mr. Justice Bosanquet at the Old Bailey to the Lord High Chancellor in the House of Lords, and since no similar trial had taken place since 1776 a committee was set up to determine procedure. On February 2, Lord Cardigan appeared at the bar of the House in the custody of Black Rod, was admitted to bail with two sureties for £20,000, and the trial was fixed for Tuesday, February 16.

Very elaborate preparations were made. The Houses of Parliament had been burned down in October, 1834, and the Peers were sitting in the Painted Chamber; more than £2,000 was spent on reconstructing the interior for the trial. Seating for 640 persons was provided, new galleries were put up, and "extensive timber work" undertaken. Lord Cardigan was to sit on a stool within the bar of the House; the Strangers' Gallery was reserved exclusively for peeresses, crimson carpets and matting were laid, and crimson cushions provided for the seating. Seamstresses and upholsterers were reported to be working night and day to complete the work in time.

The prospect of heavier penalties than a prison sentence lay before Lord Cardigan. Should he be convicted—and the facts of the case seemed beyond dispute—he would be a felon, and his lands and goods would automatically become forfeit to the Crown. Early in February he executed a deed of gift making over his property to Viscount Curzon, eldest son of his favourite sister, Lady Howe. The stamp duty on the transaction was said by *The Times* to amount to £10,000, sufficient to cover the cost of the trial.

There were, however, indications that once again the Earl of Cardigan was to escape. According to the law of 1837, duelling was an offence punishable by death if a wound were inflicted, and Capt. Harvey Tuckett had indisputably been severely wounded. But in the three counts of the indictment against Lord Cardigan the Crown ignored the wounding and dealt only with intent—shooting with a leaden bullet with intent to kill and murder, shooting with intent to maim and disable, and shooting with intent to do grievous bodily harm; the omission of wounding meant that he would evade the maximum penalty of the law. Then on the day before the trial it was learned that Capt. Harvey Tuckett was not to be called to give evidence. In an angry leading article *The Times* predicted that there was a plot to leave a loop-hole for Lord Cardigan's acquittal.

On the morning of the trial, February 16, 1841, by a strange coincidence both the Lord Chancellor and the Solicitor-General found themselves suffering from severe indispositions which prevented them from appearing. The office of Lord High Steward, the judge at the trial, was filled by the Lord Chief Justice, Lord Denman, whom Greville described as "an honourable high-minded gentleman but no lawyer and one of the feeblest Chief Justices who ever presided over the court of Queen's Bench."

Lord Denman entered the House in his robes at eleven in the morning, preceded by the Serjeant with the Mace, Black Rod carrying the Lord High Steward's Staff, and Garter with his Sceptre. The roll of peers was called, the indictment read, and the Earl of Cardigan brought to the bar. On approaching it he made three reverences and knelt until directed to rise. The indictment was read, and the Deputy Clerk to the Crown asked him, "How say you, my Lord, are you guilty of the felony with which you stand charged, or not guilty?" Lord Cardigan replied, "Not guilty, my lords." "How will your lordship be tried?" "By my peers." The Deputy Clerk to the Crown then responded, "God send your lordship a good deliverance," and the trial began.

The Attorney-General led for the Crown, and after explaining the law on duelling and recounting the facts of the case, he turned aside to deal with a curious scandal. It was being asserted in the press that Lord Cardigan had not behaved fairly in the duel, that while Captain Tuckett had used duelling pistols Lord Cardigan had used non-duelling pistols, with rifled barrels, which aimed more accurately, and hair triggers, which released the bullet faster. Lord Cardigan flatly denied, to the police and to *The Times*, that his pistols had either rifled barrels or hair triggers, but the police sent the pistols to three gunsmiths for independent examination, and after reading Lord Cardigan's denial, the gunsmiths asked *The Times* to publish their report. They testified unanimously and with a wealth of technical detail that "Captain Tuckett's were the common kind of duelling pistols but that Lord Cardigan's were of superior manufacture, with hair triggers and French rifled." However, on October 15 Captain Tuckett had written to *The Times* stating he was "sure the Earl of Cardigan had not the most distant idea of taking advantage of him in the duel."

The Attorney-General now opened his prosecution by handsomely clearing Lord Cardigan, but he gave Captain Tuckett no credit for his generosity. The Earl of Cardigan was

at once acquitted of anything unfair in the conduct of this duel. Something had been said about rifled barrels. However that may have been he, the Attorney-General, had the most firm conviction that nothing but what was fair and honourable was intended. . . . Nor did he suppose that there was in the mind of Lord Cardigan any grudge against Captain Tuckett—any personal animosity or rancour. . . . Under these circumstances if death had ensued it could have been regarded rather as a great calamity than a great crime.

The Attorney-General then appeared to recollect that he was, after all, prosecuting Lord Cardigan, and finished rather hastily by saying that, "although moralists of high character have excused or even defended the practice of duelling, their Lordships must consider what it is by the law of England."

Evidence for the prosecution was then called. The facts of the case were indisputable, but it was very soon evident that the defence was not interested in facts, only in the identity and nomenclature of Captain Tuckett. The miller had seen a man fighting a duel who described himself as Capt. Harvey Tuckett, and had gone to a certain address, asked for Capt. Harvey Tuckett, and seen the same man, but it was pointed out that he had no previous knowledge of Capt. Harvey Tuckett, and therefore had no means of telling if the man so describing himself were in reality he. The miller said that he had been handed a card by the wounded man; the defence protested that the card was not admissible as evidence. Lord Denman directed that the decision on the card should be postponed, and it was temporarily withdrawn.

When Sir James Eglinton Anderson, M.D., the surgeon who had been present at the duel and taken Captain Tuckett home, was called, Lord Denman informed him that he was not bound to answer any question that might tend to incriminate himself, and he therefore refused to give any information whatsoever. After evidence from the police, a Mr. Walthew, a chemist at 29 The Poultry, where Captain Tuckett occupied rooms as offices, was called. Mr. Walthew, closely examined on his knowledge of Captain Tuckett's names, said he knew only that Captain Tuckett rented accommodation from him and gave his address as 13 Hamilton Place. Had he ever been at 13 Hamilton Place? No. What were his tenant's Christian names? Mr. Walthew knew him only as Harvey Tuckett.

Mr. Edward Septimus Codd, an Army agent, followed. He stated that he paid Captain Tuckett his half-pay, that he saw him only at his place of business, that he had never been to 13

Hamilton Place, and that he knew him by the Christian names of Harvey Garnett Phipps Tuckett.

Sir William Follett, who led for Lord Cardigan's defence, now announced that he had no objection to the card being put in as evidence. On the card was engraved CAPTAIN HARVEY TUCKETT, 13 HAMILTON PLACE.

Upon this Sir William Follett declared that no case had been made out which called for an answer from the prisoner at the bar.

The prosecutor is bound to prove the Christian and surnames of the person against whom the offence is alleged; if he fails in either, he fails in the proof of his case. Every count in the indictment contains the name of Harvey Garnett Phipps Tuckett. There is no evidence to show that the person at whom the noble lord shot upon the 12th September was Harvey Garnett Phipps Tuckett. Mr. Codd received the half-pay of Captain Harvey Garnett Phipps Tuckett, who had been in the 11th Hussars, but there is nothing to connect this Mr. Tuckett with the person who is said to have been on Wimbledon Common on the 12th September. Mr. Codd does not know where that Mr. Tuckett lives, he never saw him but at his own office. . . . A witness is called who comes from The Poultry and who states that a certain Captain Tuckett occupies rooms in his house, where he carries on the business of an Indian and Colonial Agent, and he states that his name is Harvey Tuckett, but he does not know his other names and he does not know where he lives. There is, therefore, no evidence to connect the Captain Tuckett spoken of by Mr. Codd as bearing those Christian names with the Captain Tuckett spoken of by the other witnesses. . . . My Lord, this point has been expressly decided . . . it is laid down in all the books on this point, that it is essentially necessary to prove the Christian and the surnames of the party against whom the offence is alleged to have been committed and in this case there is no proof . . . to show the Christian names of the gentleman who was there [upon Wimbledon Common] upon that day.

A few minutes later, strangers having withdrawn and the Earl of Cardigan having been removed in the custody of the Yeoman Usher, Lord Denman gave it as his opinion that there was "an absolute want of circumstance to connect the individual at whom the pistol was fired, and who afterwards was seen wounded in Hamilton Place, with the half-pay officer known to Mr. Codd as bearing the names set forth in the indictment" . . . and he "ventured to declare . . . that the Earl of Cardigan is entitled to be declared not guilty."

Strangers were again admitted, proclamation was made for silence, and Lord Denman, standing up, called every peer by his name, beginning with the junior baron, and asked him: "John, Lord Keane, how says your lordship; is James Thomas Earl of Cardigan guilty of the felony of which he stands indicted, or not guilty?"

Whereupon John, Lord Keane, standing up in his place, uncovered, and laying his right hand upon his breast, answered, "not guilty, upon my honour."

All the peers present answered in the same manner with the exception of the Duke of Cleveland, who answered, "Not guilty legally, upon my honour."

Lord Denman, the Lord High Steward, then made the same declaration, and the Earl of Cardigan was brought to the bar and informed that he had been pronounced not guilty by a unanimous sentence. His Lordship, after bowing, retired, and "the white rod being delivered to Lord Denman, the Lord High Steward, by the Gentleman Usher of the Black Rod, his Grace stood up uncovered, and holding the staff in both hands broke it in two and declared the commission to be dissolved."

On the night of his acquittal Lord Cardigan appeared in a box at Drury Lane, and a riot took place. Yells, hisses, shrieks, groans made it impossible for the performance to begin; it being feared that the Earl would be attacked in his box, he was taken out of the theatre by a side door. The next day *The Times* thundered out a furious leader attacking the integrity of the judicature, and casting doubts on the sincerity with which the officers of the Crown had performed their duties. Particular exception was taken to the "tender consideration" with which the Earl had been treated by the Attorney-General and Lord Denman. Had the noble Earl been a linen draper, perhaps Lord Denman would not have so kindly reminded a material witness before his examination began that he need not answer a single question unless he liked.

On March 5, in the House of Commons, Joseph Hume took advantage of a debate on Army estimates to raise the question of the conduct of the Earl of Cardigan once again. He referred to the "extreme irritation of the public mind" and the "extraordinary conduct of the Commander-in-Chief, Lord Hill, in consistently refusing to take notice of the behaviour of the Lieutenant-Colonel of the 11th Hussars." What had been the history of the 11th since the noble Earl was reinstated in its command? He would like to see a return of officers who belonged to the regiment when Lord Cardigan joined it, what complaints were made, what remonstrances had taken place, how many had quitted the regiment. He ventured to say that no man henceforward could join the regiment under its present commander without having "slave" branded on his forehead, and he called on the Secretary for War for an explanation in the case of Capt. Richard Reynolds of the 11th Hussars, an officer of fourteen years' standing, who, after receiving the praise of every individual officer under whom he had served, had been dismissed from the service for a single offence, with many extenuating circumstances.

The Secretary for War was Thomas Babington Macaulay, the celebrated historian and essayist, who had, says his biographer, "to put the best face he could on these ugly stories." He "admitted that the topic of Lord Cardigan was one of violent irritation and great general excitement, and that the Government had acted in the face of the whole Press and the general cry of the country. Could Lord Cardigan go to a theatre that he was not insulted? Could he take his place in a train without having a hiss raised against him? Was there ever a case in which a man was more violently and intemperately assailed?" But, he inquired, what was the Government supposed to gain by shielding Lord Cardigan, who was not a supporter of the Government? The Government was a Whig Government, and Lord Cardigan was notoriously a violent Tory. The truth, said Macaulay, was very different. The Commander-in-Chief, Lord Hill, supported "by the authority of one other name, which stands even higher than Lord Hill's in general estimation and professional eminence"—the Duke of Wellington—had decided that there was no ground for instituting proceedings by court martial against the Earl of Cardigan, that it was impossible to resort to half-pay as a punishment, and that it would be unjust to dismiss him from the service without a court martial, and thus to establish a precedent for the dismissal of an officer for faults of manner and temper of such a nature that it was impossible to make them capable of proof before a court martial. "Having deliberately come to that opinion," finished Macaulay, "the clamour which has been raised has only determined the Government to adhere to it more firmly. I say nothing of Lord Cardigan, I don't pretend to say he is faultless, but I insist that the principles on which the Government acted are sound ones."

The House, however, was not satisfied. Lord Howick, who as Secretary for War had supported Lord Cardigan's reinstatement in 1836, demanded that Richard Reynolds should be restored to his rank; it was the very greatest error, he said, that an enquiry into the conduct of the Earl of Cardigan had not been ordered; and when Colonel Sir George de Lacy Evans wound up the debate by putting it to the vote that the matter should not be allowed to rest, the vote was carried with loud applause.

The debate took place on Friday night, but by Monday an extraordinary change had taken place. The astonishing influence of the Duke of Wellington had made itself felt during the week-end, and his inflexible resolution had prevailed. The Army was not to be dictated to by the House of Commons, the great principle designed to save the country from military domination was to be preserved, even if with it was preserved Lord Cardigan. Lord Howick and Colonel Sir George de Lacy Evans were silent, and only the small and unpopular band of radicals continued to press for an enquiry. Daniel O'Connell, the Irish liberator, supporting Joseph Hume, opened his speech by stating that he had hoped someone of more influence in the House than himself would have taken the matter up, but no one had come forward. His plea for an enquiry fell flat, and when Sir Richard Hussey Vivian, Master-General of the Ordnance, said that in his opinion it was always very objectionable to bring questions relating to the discipline of the Army into the House of Commons, the House concurred. The debate dwindled to a close, no division was taken, and the House adjourned.

Within a month Lord Cardigan was again in the public eye. Once more the papers were filled with violent outcries against him, once more the populace was infuriated—so infuriated that he had to drive about London in a closed carriage with the blinds down. With extraordinary lack of good sense and good feeling, he had had a soldier flogged on Easter Sunday in the building which had just been used for public worship, and in such a way that the punishment appeared to be a continuation of divine service.

The 11th Hussars were stationed at Hounslow, and while at Hounslow the chaplain held church services in the riding-school. On Easter Sunday, April 11, 1841, the regiment attended morning service, and as soon as it was over they were marched to their quarters; there a short inspection took place, and then they were marched back at once to the riding-school, where they witnessed the flogging of one of their comrades.

The press flung itself on the news. In a violent leader on

April 21, headed "The Atrocity Committed by Lord Cardigan,"
The Times demanded his removal in the name of common
humanity and common decency. On April 20 Joseph Hume asked
a question in the Commons, supported by an indignant House.
Amid loud "hear, hears" from all sides, Mr. Macaulay admitted
that

the immediate infliction of punishment on a Sunday after divine service
was clearly contrary to the religious feelings and habits of the people
of this country and could not be reconciled either with good taste or
good feeling. [Loud applause.] In fact, however, a disposition to inflict
corporal punishment, whatever imputations might be cast on Lord
Cardigan, was not one which could justly be thrown on him. This was
the first instance of corporal punishment in the regiment for two years.
Such notice, however, had been taken of the proceeding, and such further
notice would be taken, as to render it impossible that a recurrence should
take place.

He sat down amid loud "hear, hears."

On April 22 Lord Hill issued an order of the day, which was
circulated to every regiment in the service, censuring Lord
Cardigan.

It is well known that it is not the practice of this country to carry
the penal sentences of the law into execution on the Lord's Day; neither
is it the practice of the army, whether abroad or at home. The General
Commanding-in-Chief is therefore surprised that an officer in the situation of Lieutenant-Colonel commanding a regiment should have carried
such a sentence into execution on Sunday.

Lord Hill's rebuke was not enough. Public feeling in the
country against Lord Cardigan was dangerously strong, and the
Government saw the very situation arising which they had
striven at such cost to avoid: a great outburst of popular indignation would be expressed through the Commons which the military authorities would not be able to resist. A special meeting of
the Cabinet was summoned. It was decided that Lord Cardigan
must go, and the Prime Minister, Lord Melbourne, saw Lord Hill

and told him he must advise the Queen to remove Lord Cardigan from his command. On April 22 Lord Melbourne wrote to the Queen preparing her for Lord Hill's visit.

We have had under our consideration at the Cabinet the unfortunate conduct of Lord Cardigan. The public opinion on it is very strong, and it is almost certain that a motion will be made in the House of Commons for an address to your Majesty to remove him from the command of his regiment. Such a motion, if made, there is very little chance of resisting with success, and nothing is to be more apprehended and deprecated than such an interference of the House of Commons with the interior discipline and government of the Army. It was also felt that the general Order issued by the Horse Guards was insufficient to meet the case: and in these circumstances it was thought proper that Lord Melbourne should see Lord Hill and should express to him the opinion of the Cabinet, that it was necessary that he should advise your Majesty to take such measures as should have the effect of removing Lord Cardigan from the command of the 11th Hussars. The repeated acts of imprudence of which Lord Cardigan has been guilty, and the repeated censures which he has drawn upon himself, form a ground sufficient for such a proceeding, and indeed seem imperiously to demand it. Lord Melbourne has seen Lord Hill and made to him the communication, and has left it for his consideration. Lord Hill is deeply chagrined and annoyed, but will consider the matter and confer with Lord Melbourne upon it tomorrow.

Very great pressure was being put on Lord Hill, reported *The Times*. Mr. Macaulay was said to have pointed out to him that further resistance by the military authorities was absolutely dangerous.

The very principle which was at stake, that of preserving the Army from political control, would be sacrificed, because a change in the management of the affairs of the Army would be called for in a tone so imperative as to make further resistance to public opinion impossible. It had therefore been reluctantly decided that the Earl must take the earliest possible opportunity to sell out, thus being afforded the grace of having originated his own retirement.

Even as *The Times* leader-writer was penning his lines the

situation changed; once again the Duke of Wellington interposed. Immediately after seeing Lord Melbourne, Lord Hill had hastened to consult the Duke, and the strength of mind, the indifference to popular opinion, and the inflexible principles of the Duke's extraordinary character had their invariable effect. The Duke was not to be moved: he was not going to allow the Army to submit to political control, the Army must manage its own discipline according to its own code. Lord Hill went from the Duke to Lord Melbourne, and next day Lord Melbourne wrote to the Queen in a very different tone.

. . . this question may materially affect the discipline of the Army by subjecting the interior management of regiments to be brought continually under the control and inspection of the House of Commons, upon complaints of officers against their superiors, or even of private men against officers.

The danger of the whole of Lord Cardigan's proceedings has been lest a precedent of this nature should arise out of them. . . . Lord Melbourne has desired the Cabinet Ministers to assemble here at four o'clock, in order to consider the subject. Lord Melbourne has seen Lord Hill again this morning, and Lord Hill has seen and consulted the Duke of Wellington, who has stated his opinion very fully.

The opinion of the Duke is that the punishment on Sunday was a great impropriety and indiscretion on the part of Lord Cardigan, but not a military offence, nor a breach of the Mutiny Act or of the Articles of War; that it called for the Censure of the Commander-in-Chief, which Censure was pronounced by the General Order, upon which the Duke was consulted before it was issued, and that according to the usage of the Service, no further step can be taken by the Military authorities. This opinion Lord Melbourne will today submit to the Cabinet Ministers.

Sympathy for Lord Cardigan came also from a powerful and unexpected quarter—the Queen. With Queen Victoria Lord Cardigan was, and remained, on terms of surprising amiability. He had met Prince Albert when he arrived in England, the Prince had become Colonel of the 11th, the regiment bore the title of Prince Albert's Own, and both the Queen and the Prince admired the brilliance and smartness of the 11th under Lord Cardigan's command.

Lord Cardigan was not removed from the command of the 11th Hussars, and when it became known he had been retained on the Duke of Wellington's advice the clamour died away. On Cardigan himself the effect of this latest disturbance was extremely slight. In his autobiographical sketch he writes merely that there was one detail, the Sunday flogging, in which his conduct was not approved by his military superiors.

However, in the summer and autumn of 1841 his attention was not exclusively taken up by military matters: he was working, desperately hard, to get himself appointed Lord Lieutenant for the County of Northamptonshire. As an Earl, a Brudenell of Deene, one of the largest landed proprietors in the county, and a staunch Tory, he considered the Lord Lieutenancy of Northamptonshire to be his due; and, after the attacks on his reputation, the appointment was extremely desirable. The present Lord Lieutenant, Lord Westmorland, was known to be in failing health, and Lord Cardigan had already written to Sir Robert Peel in May, 1839, asking, indeed demanding, that Sir Robert should give a promise to appoint him should a vacancy occur and the Tory Government be in power.

Sir Robert Peel severely refused, but Lord Cardigan would not be put down. He wrote again, at length, to Peel and to the Duke, repeating his claims of rank, property, and political service, tactfully adding in a covering note that no answer was expected. In September, 1841, a disturbing idea struck him— could it be that he had received no promise of the Lord Lieutenancy on account of his trial in the House of Lords? He had been acquitted, and unanimously acquitted—surely the trial could not be held against him, and he wrote off to Sir Robert Peel on September 18 asking once more for a firm promise of the Lord Lieutenancy. "I hope you will not consider the trial to which I was subjected in the House of Lords last spring as any disqualification for the appointment." On December 15 Lord

Westmorland died. Some days passed, but Lord Cardigan received no intimation of his appointment, and on December 23 he wrote to Sir Robert Peel with irritation. Were his services to the Tory Party to be ignored? He reminded Sir Robert that he had had to give up his seat at Marlborough in 1829 in consequence of supporting Sir Robert and the Duke on Catholic emancipation, and had been "forced to make a considerable pecuniary sacrifice" to obtain another seat; he had fought a severely contested election after the Reform Bill in Northamptonshire, and had secured the seat for the Tories. Was he to receive no reward, no recognition, even in his own county?

The fact was that Peel and the Duke had already settled the appointment, and Cardigan's name had not been mentioned. On January 6, 1842, the appointment of Lord Exeter to the Lord Lieutenancy of Northamptonshire was announced.

"Cardigan is very angry he has not got it," wrote Greville. He was more than angry—he was deeply wounded. He insisted on seeing Sir James Graham, Secretary of State, and demanded an explanation. Sir James told him bluntly that his conduct with regard to the 11th Hussars made it impossible to appoint him. Lord Cardigan was astounded, and on January 9 he wrote to Sir Robert Peel a hurt and angry letter—the conduct to which Sir James Graham referred had *on each separate occasion, as it occurred, in detail* (with one exception) been approved by my military superiors." Because of the outcry in the press, he had been deprived of an honour "to which I may safely say it is generally thought I have the highest pretensions" and which he "could not but feel confident would have been conferred on me by a Government the Leader of which I had so long and faithfully supported." A "marked slight" and a "stigma" had been inflicted on him in his own county, on account of "a single act of indiscretion."

He did not stop at reproaching Sir Robert Peel, he reproached the Duke also. His disappointment at not being Lord Lieutenant, he wrote to the Duke on January 14, 1842, was "extreme." Sir

Robert Peel had told him, when he "personally applied for the situation," that the Duke would be consulted, and for twenty-two years he had undeviatingly supported the Duke's Governments under all circumstances at great personal sacrifices—"much greater sacrifices than any other person who aspired to lay claim to the situation can possibly claim to have made." He could not, "having regard to these great material services refrain from expressing his great disappointment that he should not have been thought worthy to receive this honour." At the same time he begged the Duke to exonerate him "from any other wish or intention than of addressing your Grace with the most profound respect. I am incapable of any other course, for I may safely assert that of all your Grace's adherents and admirers, the Humble Individual who addresses you has ever been one of the most firm and most ardent." The Duke replied through his secretary that he was sorry for Lord Cardigan's disappointment.

Yet, though Lord Cardigan was enraged, resentful, and wounded, no single doubt crossed his mind; his self-confidence, his faith in himself, remained unshaken. In March, 1842, a vacancy occurred in the Order of the Garter, the highest honour the British Crown has to bestow, and Lord Cardigan at once applied to be elected. It was, he wrote on March 3, due to him, to make up for not having been elected Lord Lieutenant of Northamptonshire. Sir Robert Peel received the request with surprise. Only once before in all his experience, he wrote to the Queen on March 20, had a direct application been made for a Garter. The Queen, however, supported Lord Cardigan—evidently he had discussed his disappointments with her. It happened that in April Prince Albert was officially advised by Sir Robert Peel that it was desirable for him to retire from the Colonelcy of the 11th Hussars and become Colonel of the Guards. On April 20, 1842, the Queen wrote,

The Queen encloses the Prince's letter to Sir Robert Peel, containing his acceptance of the Guards. At the same time the Queen and the Prince feel much regret at the Prince's leaving the 11th. . . . The Queen fears, indeed knows, that Lord Cardigan will be deeply mortified at the Prince's leaving the regiment, and that it will have the effect of appearing like another slight to him; therefore the Queen much wishes that at some fit opportunity, a mark of favour should be bestowed on him. . . . The Queen hopes Sir Robert will think of this.

In spite of the Queen's wish, Sir Robert did not recommend Lord Cardigan for the Garter. In September another vacancy occurred, and Lord Cardigan at once applied again, complaining vigorously that no slightest mark of the Queen's favour had been bestowed on him. Again he was refused. In July, 1843, there was a third vacancy; once more Lord Cardigan pressed his claim, and once more he was refused.

However, Lord Cardigan was not only occupied in seeking public honours—much of his attention was engrossed by his personal affairs. His marriage had long since failed. Within a year of his marrying Elizabeth Tollemache only fear of public scandal kept them together. With his violent temperament, remarkable good looks, and great wealth, entanglements were inevitable. Lord Cardigan's love affairs became legendary, and whole villages in Northamptonshire were said to have been populated by him with the children denied him in marriage.

In 1842 the papers were filled with Lord Cardigan's name, as a result of his relations with Lady Frances Paget, wife of Lord William Paget, second son of the Marquis of Anglesey. The affair has a decided flavour of knight errantry. Lady Frances was very lovely and had been married very young, Lord William was said to be brutal, to neglect her for months at a time, and to be unfaithful. One day Lady Frances, who was being watched by her husband's orders, rushed up from the country and summoned Lord Cardigan to her house off Berkeley Square. A man named Winter was hastily concealed under her drawing-room sofa, while Lord William posted himself in a cab in Berkeley Square. Lord Cardigan appeared, Lady Frances took him into the back drawing-room and shut the folding doors; and so, though Winter remained under the sofa for more than two hours, he "could not be certain what happened." After two hours Lord Cardigan drove away, Lord William emerged from his cab, very high words were heard to pass between husband and wife, and Lady Frances was later observed to have a black eye. She, however, steadfastly denied that anything had passed "beyond friendship," and on September 11, 1841, Lord William took the extraordinary step of writing a letter to *The Times* declaring his determination of proving Lord Cardigan's innocence or guilt by a trial at law.

The affair dragged on for two years, receiving an enormous amount of publicity. Lord William offered to fight a duel, but was informed that "Lord Cardigan could never again fight a duel in England." Finally, on December 22, 1843, an action appeared in the list at the Guildhall, brought by Lord William Paget against the Earl of Cardigan for "crim con"—criminal conversation, adultery—with Lady Frances Paget. Public excitement was intense. The court was packed, and a special jury had assembled when, "like a thunderclap," it was announced that the case had been withdrawn. Winter, Lord William Paget's principal witness, was not to be found.

In a letter which he sent to every newspaper in London, Lord William Paget asserted that Lord Cardigan was guilty of "the wicked and infamous crime of having bought and sent out of the way the principal witness against him." Lord Cardigan published an angry denial, and the affair petered out in an enraged correspondence, printed by *The Times,* in which furious assertions by Lord William were countered by equally furious denials by Lord Cardigan. It was admitted that Winter, a disreputable character with a police record for blackmail, had approached Lord Cardigan's solicitors, but denied that any offer had been made him.

But when the lieutenant-colonel did find time to turn his attention to his regiment, the 11th found him as rigorous, as exacting, and as much a law unto himself as ever. Even with Lord Cardigan at a distance, disturbances continued, and in February, 1842, the adjutant left the regiment, in consequence of being required to supply secret reports on the behaviour of his brother officers.

In August, 1842, however, a change of immense importance took place in the administration of the Army. Lord Hill's health failed, he retired, and was succeeded by the Duke of Wellington, who became Commander-in-Chief for life on August 15. Just previous to assuming the command, the Duke had had a unique experience: he had been overruled in a military matter which concerned the Earl of Cardigan. The Government continuing to be uneasy about the case of Capt. Richard Reynolds, pressure was put on Lord Hill by the Cabinet, and against the Duke's strongly expressed advice, the verdict of the court martial was rescinded and Richard Reynolds was gazetted to a captaincy in the 9th Lancers on April 18. No sooner had the Duke taken up his appointment as Commander-in-Chief than he found himself involved in a fresh series of unpleasantnesses arising from the conduct of the Earl of Cardigan.

It was one of Lord Cardigan's characteristics that his wounds remained always fresh: time exercised no soothing influence on his mind, and those who had offended him years before were pursued with a vindictiveness as active as if offence had been given yesterday. Captain John "Black Bottle" Reynolds had escaped the lieutenant-colonel's vengeance by going to the Senior Department of the Royal Military College, but he had taken a batman from the 11th with him, and the batman drank. There were no means of disciplining or controlling the man at the Military College, and Lord Cardigan refused to allow another batman to be sent from the regiment. The batman's drunken habits became a nuisance, John Reynolds protested, angry letters were exchanged. Then Lord Cardigan sent the papers to the Duke, and the Duke was extremely annoyed. Drafting a letter to Lord Cardigan, he ordered him to "let the *de facto* authorities of the regiment decide this case and drop it. . . . I suggest this for my sake, as I really have not leisure time to consider all the nice details of these trifles." On the side of his draft the Duke scribbled, "I must add that it will be quite a pleasing occupation to command the army if I am to have many such commanding officers as Lord Cardigan."

The ink was hardly dry on the Duke's letter when he received a complaint about Lord Cardigan's treatment of William, now Captain, Forrest. Cardigan had not forgiven Captain Forrest; the matter of the key of his room at Brighton still rankled in his mind, and he refused to allow Forrest any leave, though he had been seriously ill and was still convalescent. Captain Forrest, however, had a brother-in-law, Maj. Carmichael Smyth of the 93rd (Argyll and Sutherland) Highlanders, who was known to the Duke. The Carmichael Smyths were a remarkable family; one brother, Sir James of the Engineers, had drawn the plans for Waterloo for the Duke and another had become Thackeray's step-father and was the model for Colonel Newcome.

And in October Maj. Carmichael Smyth wrote to the Duke respectfully imploring him to investigate the Earl of Cardigan's conduct not only towards Captain Forrest, but towards other officers.

The Duke made enquiries, and wrote severely to Lord Cardigan. It was his "earnest suggestion that you carry out the provisions of the General Regulations and orders of the Army in a spirit of Conciliation and Indulgence, and, above all, exercise your command in such a manner as shall prevent your being involved in fresh dispute on trivial regimental matters."

But it was not easy to make an impression on Lord Cardigan. In April, 1843, the 11th Hussars were sent to Dublin. The lieutenant-colonel went with them, and as soon as he was living with his regiment fresh disturbances broke out. By September the newspapers were busy with the 11th Hussars again.

Lord Cardigan's "system of harshness and oppression towards his officers," wrote *The Times*, was in no way mitigated. He had placed his senior lieutenant under arrest for being ten minutes late for stables; he had arrested three officers who had mistakenly supposed a field day to be terminated and were separated from their horses when he suddenly gave an order to remount. In each case an appeal had been made to the general commanding, who ordered their release. Senior officers had written to the general in command to complain of Lord Cardigan's language on parade, and a round robin had been addressed to the Duke of Wellington, the Commander-in-Chief, complaining of Lord Cardigan's habit of scolding officers before the assembled regiment.

On receipt of the round robin, the Duke sent down a message to the officers of the 11th, and it was copied down by Captain Forrest.

The constant disagreement between Lord Cardigan and the officers serving under him having been brought to the notice of the Commander-in-Chief the Duke of Wellington, he proposes, should these dissensions continue, to put a stop to them by dispersing all the officers through various regiments in the service.

The Duke did not spare Lord Cardigan.

In future should any officer of the Regiment address any complaint or remonstrance to Lord Cardigan, such letter, together with a copy of the proposed reply from the Lieutenant-Colonel is to be submitted to the General Officer who should be so unfortunate as to have the Regiment under his command.

"This," wrote Captain Forrest, "hit us all very hard." The effect on Lord Cardigan, however, was negligible. Arrests, reprimands, complaints continued; disputes incessantly took place about accommodation, about hunting, about leave. All these, with copies, with explanations, with amplifications were forwarded to the general in command, and finally to the Commander-in-Chief, the Duke of Wellington.

In the winter of 1843, Captain Forrest, after a great deal of difficulty obtained leave to take his wife, who was expecting a baby, to her relatives in England for her confinement. When they arrived, Mrs. Forrest became suddenly ill, the baby was born, and on the advice of the doctor, Captain Forrest applied for an extension of leave. Lord Cardigan refused an extension; all the same Captain Forrest stayed with his wife. A violent quarrel followed and the papers were sent to the Duke.

The Duke addressed a withering memorandum to Lord Cardigan.

Upon reading the letters before him, the Duke considered that nothing could be more fair and proper than that Captain Forrest should apply for leave to escort his wife to her friends under the circumstances of her approaching confinement, nor could anything be more natural than that he should make such application to the Commanding Officer. It became necessary for Captain Forrest to apply for an extension, and the Duke considers that Captain Forrest had a perfect right to do so until after his wife's confinement and until after such time as her medical advisers and her friends should cease to wish for his presence. . . . The Duke must observe that in the whole of his experience he had never known the time of the staff of the Army to be taken up in so useless a manner as in the present instance, that if any other Regiment in Her Majesty's Service gave such trouble and could not be commanded without such voluminous correspondence and such futile details an additional Staff would be necessary for conducting the affairs of that Regiment. The details of the foolish quarrels of the officers of the 11th among themselves had gone to such an extent that if they continued the Duke might think it necessary to submit to Her Majesty some plan to relieve the Department from an intolerable annoyance.

Whether the Duke then summoned the Earl of Cardigan to Apsley House to one of the terrible interviews from which men emerged shivering and strangely shrunken is not recorded, but after the incident of Captain Forrest's wife's baby, no more was heard of disturbances in the 11th. Lord Cardigan bore the Duke no grudge, and in 1844 wrote him a number of letters with the object of securing an appointment as aide-de-camp to the Queen. In this, however, he was disappointed.

In 1846 the regiment returned to England, and Lord Cardigan separated from his wife on account of her liaison with Lord Colville, "a mere blockhead," wrote Greville. There was no second divorce, and Lord Cardigan became a celebrated grass-widower.

At Deene Park he entertained magnificently, and kept up the house on a great scale: sixteen men were employed to keep the fires going and the fabric in order, twenty worked in the winter to collect ice for summer use. He also occupied the family mansion in Portman Square. Hunting was his passion, and a famous hunting character, "Gumley" Wilson, describes him during these years, the hardest of hard riders, with head well up, going as straight as a bird, not to be stopped by any fence, but jealous to a degree, and ready to fight anyone and everyone on the slightest provocation. It was generally thought that his unfortunate marriage had soured him.

On three occasions the 11th Hussars were inspected by Prince Albert and the Duke, and "the appearance of the regiment and the precision and celerity with which the field movements were executed elicited tokens of the utmost approval."

At last it seemed that he had found his niche. Captain Wathen, "Black Bottle," Richard Reynolds, the Sunday flogging were forgotten. Now he had achieved his ambition; the British Army had no smarter regiment than the 11th Hussars—their precision, their operatic splendour were famous. Certainly he had had disappointments, but he had consolations, too: his riches, his rank, his pleasures, his brilliant Hussars saluting him as he walked down St. James's Street. He was becoming elderly, and now that he was over fifty much of his time was occupied in treatment for an irritating bladder complaint, and he was also subject to chronic bronchitis. It seemed reasonable to suppose that his troubles must now be in the past.

CHAPTER

6

Meanwhile George Charles Lord Bingham, the brother-in-law whom Lord Cardigan so cordially disliked, had achieved considerable success. He was intelligent; indeed his intellectual capacities were said to be "of a very high order." The Duke of Wellington, an old family friend, "thought well of him" and predicted that he would have a distinguished military career; while Sir Robert Peel thought well of his performance as Member for Mayo in the House of Commons. Admittedly his character was difficult, but looks and wits went far to cloak irritable obstinacy, and pride seemed pardonable in one who had been endowed by Nature with so much to be proud of; the general verdict agreed with the opinion expressed by Peel to Wellington—"a fine high-spirited young fellow."

After his marriage to Lady Anne Brudenell, the young couple spent much of their time at Court in London and at Windsor. At a review of the 17th Lancers in Windsor Park Lord Bingham was in command, much admired, and "flying about on a charger"; Lady Anne was in brilliant looks, but it was observed that she had the Brudenell lack of discretion and allowed her beauty to be too much admired, "especially by Lord Falkland." However, for the moment the domestic life of the Binghams was serene; their marriage in 1829 had been followed by the birth of an heir in 1830, and he was succeeded by other handsome, healthy children.

Yet by 1836 Lord Bingham was restless: he found the life of a soldier in peace-time frivolous and dull. True he had brought his regiment, "Bingham's Dandies," to a remarkable pitch of perfection, and was an exception to his contemporaries in going "to very great pains to study his profession," learning tactics and making himself acquainted with military history—but to what end? Battles, danger, hardship he would have welcomed, but his fierce, tearing energy found no outlet in the reviews and banquets, the guest nights and parades, of peace-time soldiering. He despised any man who could conceive that such a life was the pursuit of military glory and his special scorn was directed at his gorgeous brother-in-law, the Earl of Cardigan—he called him "the feather-bed soldier."

He was, moreover, seriously concerned about the family estates in Ireland. The Binghams had never enjoyed such wealth as the Brudenells, and though their estates round Castlebar in Mayo were vast, they were unremunerative. No industries had been founded, few roads had been built, few buildings erected, the immense acreages of wild land had never been transformed into a smiling countryside of prosperous farms. Mayo remained poverty-stricken, backward, inhospitable, and the Binghams, absentee landlords, turned their backs on Mayo and Castlebar. When Castlebar House was burned down in the troubles of 1798, it was not rebuilt and in 1803 Richard Bingham, second Earl of Lucan, bought land at Laleham, near Chertsey, on the banks of the Thames. Here, in the civilised and domesticated prettiness of Middlesex, he built himself an immense exquisite stylised villa in the classical taste, with plaques by Thorwaldsen, in the hall a Greek frieze after the Parthenon, marble floors, and magnificent porphyry pillars. This masterpiece of sophistication, set in park land with conservatories, walled gardens, and meadows sloping to the Thames, became the Binghams' home.

George Bingham never visited Castlebar until, at the age of

twenty-six, he stood as Member for Mayo; his father, after the purchase of Laleham, was never seen at Castlebar at all. The estates were left to an agent, whose business was to squeeze out the utmost possible amount of cash to satisfy the requirements of the second Earl, since, as that gayest of gay gallants flitted between Paris, Florence, Rome, and Laleham, applications for money came constantly to Castlebar.

It had never been easy to extract large sums from the wild lands of Castlebar, but since 1826 the years had been disastrous. Money was slow in coming, then did not come at all; the estate accounts fell into arrears, first for months and then for years. Disquieting reports trickled across the Irish Channel—the agent was taking extraordinary liberties, had even moved with his family into the family mansion. Someone must go over and take control at Castlebar.

George Bingham had lately become interested in improving the family property. Farm management suited his active, autocratic temperament; he had become converted to the profitable possibilities of new farming methods, and the improvement of cultivation had become an object second only to his desire for an active military career. He made up his mind to go to Ireland to tackle the immense acreages of Bingham property in Mayo. His father declined to leave England, the worries and discomforts of Castlebar would, he declared, be the death of him.

In May, 1837, George Bingham relinquished the command of the 17th Lancers and went on half-pay. The regiment parted from him with every expression of goodwill and regret. He was presented with a piece of "emblematic plate," gave a cup to the mess in return, and entertained the non-commissioned officers and men, at his own expense, to a dinner in the riding-school, which was decorated for the occasion, a large set piece of laurel leaves and gilt with the words "Bingham and Prosperity" being greatly admired.

In the autumn he crossed to Ireland and drove to Castlebar by coach, traversing the country from the classic elegance of

Dublin and the English-looking fields of Kildare to the bogs, the treeless heaths, the rocks, the mud huts of Mayo.

Castlebar had preserved the appearance of a feudal town. Though the castle had vanished, on its site fortifications still frowned above steep and narrow streets, the houses were beautiful and ancient, built, with enormous solidity, of grey cut stone, adorned with cornices, stone-wreathed windows, and carved doorways. In the late eighteenth century a Mall had been added to the town, with formal walks under rows of trees, but the streets tailed off abruptly into mud cabins, curlews wheeled and cried in the centre of the town, and the walkers in the Mall had bare feet. After 1798 what remained of the castle and Castlebar House had been turned into a barracks for the English garrison, and an unpretentious square villa in the demesne called sometimes the Lawn, and sometimes the Summer House, became the Irish residence of the Earls of Lucan, and was officially described as Castlebar House.

For more than thirty-five years the agency at Castlebar had been held by an O'Malley, first father and then son. Their reign had been absolute; confidence in them had been complete, and the younger St. Clair O'Malley had been treated by the second Earl "almost as a son." As a result, he had assumed considerable pretensions—he shot over the Castlebar estates, he hunted, he sat on the Bench, by virtue of his position as agent for the Earl of Lucan. In the absence of the family, he lorded it in Castlebar, moving into Castlebar House, because, he said, the house without an occupant was getting damp. His character exhibited a mixture of pretension, evasiveness, inefficiency, and subservience which would have been intolerable even to a less stiff-necked man than George Bingham; the two quarrelled violently, and when in 1839 George's father died and he succeeded as third Earl, he discharged St. Clair O'Malley.

He proved to be amply justified. The estate was heavily in debt. The accounts which had been extracted from the O'Malleys only after the second Earl's death were "of the most irregular and unsatisfactory description," and the new Earl's solicitors in London wrote that "it was the most extraordinary thing that affairs had been allowed to go on in this way for so long." To get rid of the O'Malleys, however, was not easy. When St. Clair O'Malley refused to accept dismissal, a series of scenes took place, and in 1840 Lord Lucan advertised throughout the Irish press that he had discharged the O'Malleys, father and son, from the agency of the Castlebar estates.

The affair proved an unfortunate introduction to Irish life. The new Earl was already unpopular; his proud and irritable manners were resented, and it was said that he was trying to rule his estates with military despotism. He had also quarrelled with the English garrison, and had forced the commanding officer to have the windows of the barracks, which overlooked the demesne of Castlebar House, blocked up because, he said, the officers stared at his beautiful wife as she took her walks.

The O'Malleys were related to half Castlebar, and had served the Binghams for a lifetime. It was felt that though they might have made mistakes, the Earl was hard. A party against Lord Lucan formed in Castlebar, and St. Clair O'Malley embarked on a war of defiance, continuing to shoot over Lord Lucan's land, and even leasing part of a house from one of Lord Lucan's tenants in order that he might shoot with more convenience. He offered to fight Lord Lucan, and was contemptuously refused; then he armed himself with a thick stick and swaggered about Castlebar announcing his intention of thrashing Lord Lucan should Lord Lucan dare to cross his path.

In 1842, after repeated warnings, Lord Lucan summoned St. Clair O'Malley for poaching. The case was heard at the Petty Sessions Court at Castlebar in October, and was remarkable in that both plaintiff and defendant sat on the Bench of Magistrates. Newspaper reporters from all over Ireland thronged the court, and every possible provocation was offered by the O'Malleys; they invited officers from the garrison to attend, all available seats were occupied by their partisans, and St. Clair O'Malley himself attended, flourishing his big stick.

Under these trying circumstances Lord Lucan's temper failed him, and a violent quarrel took place in court. O'Malley demanded that Lord Lucan should leave the Bench while the case was heard, upon which Lord Lucan declared that he had a right to sit there and no individual could or should compel him to leave his seat. O'Malley then assured Lord Lucan that he held him in the greatest contempt, and everything that came from him he treated with utter contempt. Lord Lucan called on the Bench to "protect him from that Miscreant"; in return O'Malley described Lord Lucan as a cowardly blackguard, and threatened to break every bone in his body. The court broke up "in a state of the utmost Confusion and Excitement, impossible to describe."

Lord Lucan was unquestionably in the right; nevertheless, the Bench failed to commit O'Malley for disrespect, and worse followed; by a writ of *supersedeas*, the authorities removed both Lord Lucan and St. Clair O'Malley from the commission of the peace, for contempt of court.

Lord Lucan's fury and disgust were intense. Here was a man who had become a magistrate only because he was agent for Castlebar, who had been ignominiously dismissed from the agency for incompetence, who was, moreover, head over heels in debt and only at liberty by license from his creditors; yet he, George Bingham, Earl of Lucan, was to be publicly coupled with and punished with such a man. He wrote angrily to the Lord Chancellor of Ireland, he bombarded authorities in London. Were they aware of what Mr. O'Malley's conduct towards him had been, that at this moment O'Malley was walking the streets of Castlebar, "my own town," declaring that he, George Bingham, Earl of Lucan, dared not show his nose outside Castlebar House, knowing the thrashing which was waiting for him?

He gained no satisfaction; his letters received only formal acknowledgment, and he was not restored to the magistracy. Yet he would not submit, and carried his grievance to the House of Lords. On August 10, 1843, he moved for papers to enable him to vindicate his conduct. Three heated debates followed on the action of the Lord Chancellor of Ireland in removing the Earl of Lucan from the commission of the peace for Mayo. On August 21, however, the Duke of Wellington, exerting his enormous prestige and his matchless common sense, settled the question. Lord Lucan, he said, had written to him asking him to speak in the House of Lords as to his military character, but this he had been unable to do, as he had not been present on that day. Then he went on to remind the Lords that facts were in question. The Earl of Lucan, with whom he sympathised, and whose high character in the Army was well known to him, had made use of an expression which amounted to contempt of court, under the provocation of being grossly insulted, certainly, but nevertheless it was contempt of court. This, he understood, the noble Earl himself admitted. It was clearly impossible for a magistrate who was guilty of contempt of court to continue in the commission of the peace, so Lord Lucan had, rightly, been removed. The Duke was, as usual, unanswerable, and the matter dropped.

But Lord Lucan had not yet come to the end of his resources. Very well, if the laws were such, he would do without the laws. Richard Bingham, his ancestor, had been granted his lands with manorial rights, and, in the sixteenth century had dispensed justice in his own manorial court. He, George Bingham, third Earl of Lucan, would revive that court and establish it at Castlebar —he owned the town and he owned the country for miles around. No more petty sessions should be held on his property; he would do justice himself in his own court. The scheme pleased him immensely, and he wrote to his lawyers to enquire how he should proceed and how far his powers would extend—hardly, he supposed, to matters of life and death. It was with redoubled fury that he read an apologetic letter in which his lawyers informed him that, unquestionable though the rights had been, they were now extinct. Eminent legal authorities, including the Lord Chancellor of England, were called into consultation, but their opinions were unanimous—the Earl of Lucan could no longer set up his own court, he must be amenable to the common law of the land.

The consequences of the O'Malley affair were serious. There was bad blood between Lord Lucan and Castlebar at a most unhappy juncture. The country was approaching a terrible crisis. Reasons far graver than any mismanagement by the O'Malleys lay behind the unsatisfactory condition of the estates at Castlebar, and not only the estates at Castlebar, but throughout Ireland. The economic structure of the country was such that a frightful catastrophe was inevitably approaching.

In 1844 Ireland presented the extraordinary spectacle of a country in which wages and employment, practically speaking, did not exist. There were no industries; there were very few towns; there were almost no farms large enough to employ labour. The country was a country of holdings so small as to be mere patches. The people inhabited huts of mud mingled with a few stones, huts four or five feet high, built on the bare earth, roofed with boughs and turf sods, without chimney or window and destitute of furniture, where animals and human beings slept together on the mud floor. In 1843 the German traveller Kohl pronounced the Irish to be the poorest people in Europe. He had pitied, he wrote, the privations endured by the poor among the Letts, Esthonians, and Finns, but compared to the Irish they lived in comfort. "There never was," said the Duke of Wellington, himself an Irishman, "a country in which poverty existed to so great a degree as it exists in Ireland." And yet, in spite of misery, the population swarmed. "The population of Ireland," said Disraeli in the Commons on February 15, 1847, "is the densest of any country in the world; the population as regards the arable area is denser even than in China."

Until the last half of the eighteenth century the population of

Ireland had been inconsiderable; then abruptly, mysteriously, an extraordinary and fatal phenomenon occurred, and the population began to increase at a rate unknown to history. The accepted increase for the years 1779 to 1841 is 172 per cent, and many authorities put the figure higher. This increase was linked with the adoption of the potato as the staple, indeed the sole, food of Ireland. The people, in their desperate poverty, lacked land, implements, barns. Potatoes require only one-third of the acreage of wheat, flourish anywhere, need the minimum of cultivation, can be stored in the ground and shared with fowls and pigs. As Ireland became a potato country, the shadow of starvation lifted slightly and the character of the people made itself felt. The Irish people were religious, their family affections strong, their women proverbially chaste. Early marriages became invariable: girls were usually married before they were sixteen, but religion and ignorance combined to make birth control unthinkable, and by their early thirties women were grandmothers. Thus the population spread with the rapidity of an epidemic. For these people, swarming in the cabins and the fields, there was no employment, no means of earning wages, no possibility of escaping starvation, except the land—and land became like gold in Ireland. Farms were divided and subdivided until families depended entirely for existence on a plot the size of a suburban garden. Potatoes vary in quality, and the Irish came to live on the "lumper" or "horse potato," the largest, coarsest, most prolific variety known. They grew the huge, coarse potatoes by strewing them on the top of beds six feet wide and covering them with earth, this method of cultivation, the "lazy bed," requiring only a spade. They ate this potato boiled, and they ate nothing else. Over great tracts of Ireland any form of cooking beyond boiling a potato in a pot became unknown—greens were unknown, bread was unknown, ovens were unknown. The butcher, the baker, the grocer did not exist; tea, candles, and coals were unheard of. The miserable cultivation of the horse potato occupied only a few weeks, and through the dark, wet winters the people, wrapped in rags and tatters, crouched over the turf fire. "Not a bit of bread," said a tenant of the Marquis of Conyngham in 1845, "have I eaten since I was born; we never taste meat of any kind or bacon . . . the common drink to our potatoes is pepper and water."

It was human existence on the lowest scale, only to be paralleled in its isolation and privation, said observers, among the aborigines of Australia and South America. As the population increased, the continual subdivision of farms into patches brought the landlord higher and still higher rents, and the potato patches of Ireland first equalled what the rich farmlands of England fetched in rent, and then went higher. Men bid against each other in desperation, and on paper the landlords of Ireland grew rich; but the rents were not paid—could not be paid. Castlebar was only one of hundreds of estates in Ireland which, prosperous on paper, were sliding into hopeless confusion. "If you ask a man," reported the Devon Commission in 1844, "why he bid so much for his farm, and more than he knew he could pay, his answer is, 'What could I do? Where could I go? I know I cannot pay the rent; but what could I do? Would you have me go and beg?' "

By 1845 the population of Ireland had swollen to eight million, and the enormous majority of these people were living exclusively on the potato, were feeding such animals as they possessed on the potato, were consuming fourteen pounds of potatoes per head per day. The structure of the country, crazily rising higher and higher, was balanced on the potato. And the potato was treacherous: over and over again it had proved itself to be the most uncertain, the most dangerous, the most unpredictable of crops.

In 1739 the potato harvest had failed, and again in 1741, when deaths had been so numerous that the year was named the year of slaughter. In 1806 the crop partially failed, and in the west of Ireland it failed in 1822, 1831, 1835, 1836, and 1837. In

1839 failure was general throughout Ireland. In 1838 the Duke of Wellington, speaking on the Poor Law in Ireland, said in the House of Lords, "I held a high position in that country [Ireland] thirty years ago, and I must say, that from that time to this, there has scarcely elapsed a single year in which the Government has not, at certain times of it, entertained the most serious apprehension of famine. I am firmly convinced that from the year 1806 down to the present time, a year has not passed in which the Government has not been called on to give assistance to relieve the poverty and distress which prevail in Ireland."

The solution, the only possible solution, was to reduce the number of potato patches, to throw the small holdings together into farms, and give the people work for wages. But how was this to be done, where were the people to go, helpless, penniless, and without resources as they were? The Irish peasant dreaded the "consolidating landlord"—and prominent among consolidating landlords was the third Earl of Lucan.

He was, in fact, far in advance of most of his contemporaries. The Land Commission of 1830 had stated that in their opinion the poverty and distress of Ireland were principally due to the neglect and indifference of landlords. Large tracts were in the possession of individuals whose extensive estates in England made them regardless and neglectful of their properties in Ireland. It was not the practice of Irish landlords to build, repair, or drain; they took no view either of their interest or their duties which caused them to improve the condition of their tenants or their land. "All the landlord looks to is the improvement of his income and the quantity of rent he can abstract." "Regard for present gain, without the least thought for the future seems to be the principal object which the Irish landlord has in view," wrote an English observer.

Lord Lucan was exceptional in being prepared to invest in the land, to forgo and reduce his income, to tie up capital in barns, houses, drainage schemes, and machinery, in order to establish prosperity in the future. But it was impossible for him to succeed. Between the Irish tenant and the Irish landlord not only was there no hereditary attachment, there was hereditary hatred.

Ireland was a country the English had subdued by force, and Irish estates were lands seized from a conquered people by force or confiscation. But Ireland had refused to acknowledge herself conquered, religion had prevented assimilation, and down the centuries rebellion succeeded rebellion, while underground resistance, assassinations, secret societies, anonymous outrages had never ceased. Moreover, the English, normally kind, behaved in Ireland as they behaved nowhere else; the Irish had earned their undying resentment by persistently taking sides with the enemies of England.

The laws of Ireland were laws imposed by a conqueror on the conquered, and the conditions under which an Irish peasant leased his land were intolerably harsh.

In Ireland alone [wrote John Stuart Mill] the whole agricultural population can be evicted by the mere will of the landlord, either at the expiration of a lease, or, in the far more common case of their having no lease, at six months' notice. In Ireland alone, the bulk of a population wholly dependent on the land cannot look forward to a single year's occupation of it.

The power of the landlord was absolute. Lord Leitrim, for instance, passing by a tenant's holding, noticed a good new cabin had been built, and at once ordered his bailiff to pull it down and partially unroof it. James Tuke was told in 1847 that his Lordship used to evict his tenants "as the fit took him." Only in Ulster had a tenant any rights. In Ulster a tenant could not be evicted if he had paid his rent, and when he left his farm he had a right to compensation for any improvements. Elsewhere in Ireland the tenant had no rights. All improvements became the property of the landlord without compensation. Should a tenant erect buildings, should he improve the fertility of his land by drainage, his only reward was eviction or an immediately increased rent, on account of the improvements he himself had laboured to produce.

Sir Charles Trevelyan, a far from sympathetic observer, wrote of Ireland in 1845 ". . . what was the condition of the peasant? Work as he would, till and rear what he might, he could never hope to benefit. His portion was the potato only, shared, it may be said, with his pig." No ordinary amount of hard work, no thrift or self-denial could bring a better life to the Irish peasant.

And, in all Ireland, the county which, said the Poor Law commissioners, stood pre-eminent for wretchedness was Mayo, where Lord Lucan held his estates. Mayo, with Sligo, Roscommon, and Leitrim, made up the province of Connaught, and Connaught had a history which made prosperity and good relations between landlord and tenant impossible.

Connaught had been the scene of great severities under Elizabeth, when the Binghams acquired their estates, and of greater severities under Cromwell. After the massacres of Drogheda and Wexford, Cromwell, in the words of Lord Clare,

collected together all the native Irish who survived the devastation and transported them into the province of Connaught which had been completely depopulated and laid waste. They were ordered to retire there by a certain day, and forbidden to repass the Shannon on pain of death . . . their ancient possessions were seized and given up to the conquerors.

These unhappy people, turned loose to starve in a ruined country, joined with the few survivors of the depopulation to form a population in Connaught which has never yet been able to forgive or forget.

The people were rebellious, the land poor, the country inaccessible. Roads were few, education non-existent—in 1845 at Castlebar only seven people out of 145 could read—and, in addition to the normal evil of subdivision, two deplorable systems of land tenure flourished: rundale, a primitive survival where the land was rented jointly by a group who farmed it in strips; and conacre, where a patch of land was rented only for the growing of a single crop.

To the people of Mayo an Earl of Lucan, a Bingham, was an oppressor, responsible for the cruelties of the past and the misery of the present, automatically to be hated. Between any Earl of Lucan and his tenants history had erected a barrier almost impossible to surmount. The third Earl of Lucan, however, had no smallest inclination to try to surmount it. Though his Irish tenants might cherish an hereditary hatred for him, he cherished an equally powerful contempt for them. From the bottom of his heart he despised them, swarming, half-starving, ignorant, shiftless, and Roman Catholics into the bargain. It is doubtful if he considered the Irish as human beings at all.

And yet it was not an ignoble vision which the third Earl of Lucan cherished; and for it he was prepared to forgo his immediate comfort. The Irish countryside was to be remade, sound cottages were to replace mud cabins, machinery succeed the spade, trim furrowed fields were to appear in place of "lazy beds," herds of dairy cattle and fat pigs supplant the lean and miserable animals who shared their owners' bed and board. But to make that vision real it was necessary to be relentless—the miserable hordes of the half-starved must disappear. Evictions became numerous, and it began to be said in Mayo that he possessed "all the inherited ferocity of the Binghams."

Fear of the third Earl bit deep into the consciousness of the people, and he still survives as a bogey in Castlebar. Tales are told of the fierce Earl galloping through the town, the hoofs of his great black horse striking sparks from the cobble-stones, bringing terror to his tenants' hearts. When least expected he suddenly appeared, for though he gained the credit of being a resident landlord, he seldom stayed in Castlebar more than a few days—it was his custom to swoop down a dozen times a year. On one occasion, believing him to be safely in England, the inhabitants of Castlebar were burning him in effigy on the Mall when suddenly the sound of the great black horse was heard and the Earl galloped into the midst of the crowd, shouting as they scattered in terror, "I'll evict the lot of you."

Honours might come to him from England—he was elected a Representative Peer of Ireland in 1840, in 1843 he had the satisfaction of refusing to be restored to the Bench, in 1845 he was made Lord Lieutenant of Mayo. But on his estates the antagonism between Lord Lucan and his tenants became acute. He brought in Scottish farmers, particularly detested in Mayo, to manage his farms. Irish bailiffs could not be trusted, he said: turn your back for a moment, and hovels were allowed to spring up again on the newly cleared land. Asked for mercy, he declared that he "did not intend to breed paupers to pay priests"; for his part he would be only too glad if he did not have a single tenant on his estates in Mayo. On June 21, 1845, a meeting of protest was held at Castlebar and a resolution unanimously passed and forwarded to the Earl of Lucan. It condemned the inhumanity of his declaration, "worthy only of the days of persecution and oppression of which it so forcibly reminds us." During the next few years men were to look back and say with a shudder that the Earl's angry words had drawn down a curse on Mayo.

In 1844 it was reported that the potato crop had failed in North America, but no apprehension was created in Ireland, for the country was occupied with her own concerns. That year was a restless one: rents were at their highest, evictions numerous, secret societies active, and more than one thousand agrarian outrages occurred.

In September, 1845, the early potato crop was dug, and proved to be exceptionally abundant. The main crop, on which the food of the people depended, was not dug until December, and there was every sign that this, too, would be remarkably good. Potatoes lifted at the end of November were matured in good condition and the plants were prolific. A few weeks later the crop was dug, and found to be tainted with disease. The news came like a thunder-clap: failure was totally unexpected throughout the three kingdoms. Once the disease had appeared, it advanced with fatal speed, part of the crop rotting at once, and what was stored swiftly rotting in the pits. Within a month the whole was lost.

Dire distress followed. In January Parliament in London repealed the duties on the importation of foreign corn, the "corn laws," and an attempt was made to replace the potato by supplies of Indian corn, unknown as a food in the United Kingdom. A start was made, too, towards establishing a system of public works to provide the people with money with which food might be purchased, since wages in Ireland were almost unknown. It was at this juncture that the Duke of Norfolk suggested that the Irish should substitute curry powder for the potato and nourish themselves on curry powder mixed with water.

Nevertheless, hope ran high in 1846: the Irish had a tradition that when the potato crop failed next year's crop was exceptionally abundant. The growing of crops other than potatoes was not attempted, because the people had no implements, no seeds, and no knowledge of how to cultivate anything else. Once again almost all Ireland became a potato field.

The plants came up strong and sturdy. May and June gave every promise of a bountiful harvest, and through the first weeks of July the plants bloomed richly, and the weather was good. Then disaster struck.

Father Mathew, the famous Temperance reformer, travelling from Cork to Dublin on July 27, saw the "plant blooming in all the luxuriance of an abundant harvest." Five days later he travelled back to find "one wide waste of putrefying vegetation." At the edge of their decaying patches the people sat weeping and wringing their hands.

In Clare, Captain Mann, R.N., senior Coastguard officer "passed over thirty-two miles, thickly studded with potato fields in full bloom." A day later "the whole face of the country was changed; the stalk remained bright green, but the leaves were all scorched black. It was the work of a night."

The disease appeared first in the form of a small brown spot on the leaf, the spots spread, the foliage withered, and the stem snapped off. In two or three days all was over, and the fields were covered with blackened plants, giving off a sickening smell of decay. The potato tubers if lifted, were hard, withered, and the size of walnuts.

In England, too, the potato crop failed partially, and potatoes became a luxury. In France, Belgium, Holland, and Italy both potato and rye crops entirely failed. Prices rose steeply, freight charges more than doubled and such supplies of grain and other foods as were available, instead of being sent to relieve Ireland, were diverted to the Continent.

Famine began in earnest. The magnitude of the disaster was almost inconceivable. The people of Ireland had no food, no money, were in any case entirely unaccustomed to buying food; in the west of Ireland no organisation existed, no corn factor, miller, baker, or provision dealer, through which to bring food to them. The evils of subletting and subdividing now disclosed themselves with frightful effect. Captain Mann quotes a typical case of a landlord occasionally resident, who let his land to a middleman at 10 shillings an acre. The middleman also re-let it. It was again and again re-let, until the price received for a quarter of an acre was £1 10s. In 1846 the landlord, by no means a hard-hearted man, applied to the Society of Friends for food for his starving tenants. He calculated that he had about sixty to provide for and was "terrified" to receive over six hundred applications. He had never inspected his farms.

All over Ireland famished multitudes, whose existence was utterly unsuspected and unknown, rose like spectres from the ground, demanding food.

The Government of Great Britain regarded the starving multitudes with the utmost apprehension. Distress and starvation in Ireland—the very words, woefully familiar, evoked hopelessness. Was the Government to tie the frightful burden of responsibility for the support of eight million people round the neck of the British tax-payer? It was decided to proceed with great caution. Extravagant action, large Government purchases of food from abroad, for instance, would inevitably upset the normal course of English trade. To preserve the normal course of English trade became the first object. No orders for supplies of food would be sent by the Government to foreign countries; they would rely on private enterprise to find food for the starving multitudes. No Government depots for the sale of food were to be established, except in the west of Ireland, where dealers were unknown. Wages were to be earned through the relief works, and new roads were to be made; but works for the improvement of the land were not to be undertaken, through a fear of favouritism and corruption.

The winter of 1846 was exceptionally severe. Wages paid by the relief works, eightpence to tenpence a day, were insufficient, and women wept as their men brought home insufficient money to buy food. The Irish peasant was accustomed to spend the cold, wet winter crouching over his turf fire, and the half-starved multitudes caught cold and died. An officer of the Board of Trade said he was ashamed to require men in such an emaciated condition to work. In any case works were slow in starting, and many districts had no relief. By December, 1846, cholera had appeared. On December 17 a Mr. Nicholas Marshal Cummins, J.P. wrote a letter to the Duke of Wellington describing a visit to Skibbereen. He found the village apparently deserted, but on entering one of the cabins he discovered

. . . six famished and ghastly skeletons, to all appearance dead, huddled in a corner, their sole covering what seemed to be a ragged horse cloth, and their wretched legs hanging about, naked above the knees. I approached in horror and found by a low moaning that they were alive,

124

they were in fever—four children, a woman and what had once been a man. . . . In a few minutes I was surrounded by at least 200 of such phantoms, such frightful spectres as no words can describe. By far the greater number were delirious either from famine or fever. . . . Within 500 yards of the Cavalry Station at Skibbereen, the dispensary doctor found seven wretches lying, unable to move, under the same cloak—one had been dead many hours, but the others were unable to move, either themselves or the corpse.

Josephine Butler, as a young girl, was in Ireland during the famine years.

I can recollect [she writes] being awakened in the early morning by a strange noise, like the croaking or chattering of many birds. Some of the voices were hoarse and almost extinguished by the faintness of famine; and on looking out of the window I recollect seeing the garden and field in front of the house completely darkened by a population of men, women and children, squatting in rags; uncovered skeleton limbs protruding everywhere from their wretched clothing, and clamorous though faint voices uplifted for food and in pathetic remonstrance against the inevitable delay in providing what was given them from the house every morning. I recollect too, when walking through the lanes and villages, the strange morbid famine smell in the air, the sign of approaching death, even in those who were still dragging out a wretched existence.

In poverty-stricken and backward Mayo the famine was at its most severe. Starving and dying, the people came into Castlebar and roamed the streets, begging for food. William Forster, the Quaker, who made his headquarters at Castlebar, particularly remembered the children, with "their death-like faces and drumstick arms that seemed ready to snap." It was a common occurrence when the front door of a house was opened in the morning, to find leaning against it the corpse of some victim who had sunk to rest on the doorstep and died during the night. Dead bodies lay by the side of the roads leading into Castlebar, men and women who had fallen by the wayside were seen struggling in vain to rise until, with a low moan, they collapsed in death, while in remote hamlets, unknown to the outside world, every soul was found to have perished—the people had become too weak to fly from death.

To the Earl of Lucan famine horrors were so many convincing demonstrations of the urgent necessity of clearing the land. The land could not support the people, could never support the people; so the people must go. He did not consider it was his responsibility, any more than the British Government considered it was their responsibility, to arrange how the people should go and where. He was getting nothing from his estates, all his rents and a great deal more were being put back into the land and on one farm alone he spent £8,000; he was doing his share, and more than his share. To bolster up a hopelessly false economy, to pour out money, badly needed to improve the land, on paupers who could never be anything but paupers, was criminal sentimentality. A large part of the population of Ireland must disappear.

Evictions became wholesale on the Earl of Lucan's estates. Ten thousand people were ejected from the neighbourhood of Ballinrobe, and fifteen thousand acres cleared and put in charge of Scotsmen. A relieving officer told Sir Francis Head, an English observer, that the destitution caused by Lord Lucan was "immense." Pointing to an eminence enclosed by a capital wall and in a good state of cultivation, he said, "That was a densely populated hill called Staball. All the houses were thrown down." Several populous villages in the neighbourhood of Castlebar completely disappeared, farms being established on the sites. Behind Castlebar House the Earl of Lucan established a large dairy farm; the yard and buildings of this farm, which covered three acres, were cleared in the town of Castlebar itself—whole streets were demolished, and the stones from the walls used to build barns and boundary walls.

Terror seized Mayo. The people, ignorant, starving, and terrified, clung desperately to the land. They could not be got rid of —turned out of their cabins, they took refuge with neighbours, or crept back in the night and hid in ditches. It was necessary to forbid any tenant to receive the evicted, on pain of being evicted himself; it was necessary to drive them out of the ditches; finally it was necessary to organise gangs known as "crow-bar brigades," to pull down cabins over the heads of people who refused to leave them. The Bishop of Meath saw a cabin being pulled down over the heads of people dying of cholera; a winnowing sheet was placed over their bodies as they lay on the ground, and the cabin was demolished over their heads. He administered the sacrament for the dying in the open air, and since it was during the equinoctial gales, in torrents of rain.

Sick and aged, little children, and women with child were alike thrust forth into the cold snows of winter [writes Josephine Butler], for the winters of 1846 and 1847 were exceptionally severe and to prevent their return their cabins were levelled to the ground . . . the few remaining tenants were forbidden to receive the outcasts. . . . The majority rendered penniless by the years of famine, wandered aimlessly about the roads and bogs till they found refuge in the workhouse or the grave.

In addition to the crow-bar brigade, a "machine of ropes and pulleys" was devised for the destruction of more solid houses. It consisted of massive iron levers, hooks, and a chain to which horses were yoked.

By fixing the hooks and levers at proper points, at one crack of the whip and pull of the horses the roof was brought in. By similar gripping of the coign stone the house walls were torn to pieces. It was found that two of these machines enabled a sheriff to evict as many families in a day as could be got through by a crow-bar brigade of fifty men. It was not an unusual occurrence to see forty or fifty houses levelled in one day, and orders given that no tenant or occupier should give them even a night's shelter.

Imprecations and curses were hurled at the Earl of Lucan as village after village was blotted out. He was called the "Exterminator." It was said that he regarded his tenants as vermin to be cleared off his land. But he held relentlessly to his view. There was only one solution for Ireland—a large part of the population must disappear.

Meanwhile, in London the Government became seriously disturbed. The number of persons on relief was increasing with terrifying speed: by January, 1847, half a million men were employed on relief work on the roads, and more than two million were receiving food; and each day added fresh tens of thousands. There was apparently no end to the helpless starving multitudes of Ireland. Moreover, the relief works were unsatisfactory; for a variety of reasons persons not entitled to relief were receiving it, the attraction of wages was so strong that the fields were being deserted for the roads, and the construction work was so badly done that the new roads were useless.

Parliament turned angrily on the Irish landlords. How had they ever allowed this state of things to come about? What had they done to prevent or to remedy the disaster? The Irish landlords had come forward with no plan, they had provided the Government with no information, they had assumed no responsibility, the miserable hordes perishing on their very doorsteps had been callously ignored. All they had done was to "sit down and howl for English money."

On February 15, 1847, Lord Brougham attacked the Earl of Lucan in the House of Lords. In Mayo six thousand processes had been served, four thousand of which were for rent.

The landlord in Mayo had thought it necessary to serve his tenants with notice to quit in the midst of one of the most severe winters that had ever been known, in the midst of the pestilence too which followed, as it generally did, in the train of famine. He had turned out these wretched creatures when there was no food in the country and no money to buy it.

Six thousand evictions might involve more than forty thousand people, as the average Irish family consisted of seven persons. What, asked Lord Brougham, was the result of this wholesale clearance? A great flood of Irish paupers had begun to pour across the Irish Channel into Liverpool and Glasgow. At Liverpool in the last five days 5,200 paupers were landed, without possessions of any kind, in an advanced state of starvation, and with the cholera among them. They did not come to emigrate, because they had no money and the emigration season did not begin until the end of March or the beginning of April. They came to be fed. Large numbers of these people had come from Mayo.

Lord Lucan's defence was irritable. Anyone who knew anything about Ireland knew that processes were not evictions. The trouble at the present moment was that people made themselves heard who knew nothing about Ireland. Processes were actions for recovery of rent brought usually by middlemen, and he challenged the figure of six thousand.

Lord Brougham informed the House that the figure was an official return quoted in the House of Commons by the Chancellor of the Exchequer. It appeared that a new system of clearing land was being adopted in Mayo and that the processes now before the courts were novel in Ireland. There had previously been a right of levying a distress on goods and chattels for rent, but this year in Mayo there were no goods and chattels left, so the person of the debtor was to be attached—that is, he was to be imprisoned. The husband and father was to be removed, and the wife and children were to be left to fend for themselves. It was usual in Ireland to allow three months' grace for payment of rent, but this year in Mayo no such period was allowed. The landlords had calculated that these processes would have all the efficiency of evictions, and they had been proved right. The people were distracted by the loss of their potato crop, feared the land would never produce a similar crop again, were terrified by the evictions all round them, were starving and in despair. Before the processes could be heard, people by the thousand abandoned their holdings and fled. Yet when, said Lord Brougham, he connected the poverty now inundating the ports of England with the legal processes carried on in Mayo, he excited the indignation of his noble friend, and he was told he knew nothing about it.

The Marquess of Westmeath rose to observe that it ought to be known that the people who had so left the country had omitted to give up possession of the tenements they held. The very circumstances of having acted in that way showed great dishonesty of principle. What could be more so than for individuals to leave the country still holding possession—a procedure which threw a great deal of trouble on the injured party in obtaining possession of property thus deserted.

The noble Marquess's complaint did not strike the House of Lords as unreasonable. Was not the starving condition of the peasantry involving the landlords of Ireland in immense losses, and was it not the duty of the peasantry to realise their responsibility and do everything in their power to minimise these losses? No one rose to comment on the Marquess of Westmeath's statement, and the debate on the distress in Ireland came to an end.

Early in 1847 William Forster, a member of the Relief Committee of the Society of Friends, visited Castlebar. The suffering, he noted, was very severe. About 1,200 were being relieved daily in Castlebar by the charity of the townspeople, and some clothing had been made; but the work was stopping for want of funds. Outside Castlebar, out of 460 persons examined, 364 were completely destitute. Nothing, he commented, seemed to have been attempted in the way of relief on the Connaught side of the Shannon, and he cited the case of the Castlebar Union Workhouse. The Castlebar Union was capable of taking 600 to 700 persons, but the gates had been closed by order of the chairman of the Board of Guardians. The chairman was the Earl of Lucan.

Huge and forbidding, the Castlebar Union had opened its doors in 1841. Built from blocks of grey stone, surrounded by high walls, standing outside the town on bare and treeless land, and appearing half fortress and half prison, it was regarded by the people of Mayo with dread. Within were stone walls of great thickness, immense wards with wooden platforms where the paupers lay on straw, bareness, chill, inhuman emptiness. But there was food, however revolting, however meagre, and the Union was besieged. Starving mothers dragged their children to the Union doors and besought that they at least should be taken in; whole families made their painful way from the wild lands and collapsed moaning in the courtyard when they were refused.

On February 15, 1847, Viscount Duncan asked a question in the House of Commons. It had been reported in the newspapers that the Earl of Lucan, Lord Lieutenant of Mayo and chairman of the Board of Poor Law Guardians of the Castlebar Union, with twelve other magistrates, had been dismissed by the Poor Law commissioners for not performing his duties. Was that statement correct?

Viscount Duncan produced facts from the Report of the Assistant Poor Law Commissioners. The Castlebar Union workhouse had been built to hold 600 to 700 persons, but had never contained more than 140. After the potato failure, when distress became acute, its doors were closed and all relief refused. The inmates still in the workhouse were neglected and starved and commonly left without food or attention for twenty-four hours at a time. Very many died, and since there were no coffins, their bodies were left to rot in the dead house. On October 26, 1846, the Earl of Lucan, chairman of the Board of Guardians, had declared the workhouse bankrupt, and, in spite of vehement protests from the Poor Law Commissioner, ordered the Castlebar Union to be entirely closed down. At that time over £1,000 of poor rate were owing, one of the principal debtors being the Earl of Lucan himself. It was customary, when money was urgently required, to "strike" a new rate, that is, to make a fresh assessment and a fresh collection, but this the Earl of Lucan had refused to order. As a result of suspending relief and shutting the doors of the workhouse, upwards of one hundred persons had died of starvation in its immediate vicinity, and a protest had been made by the coroner who held the inquests upon the corpses.

On February 16, 1847, the Earl of Lucan defended himself in the House of Lords. He was not a man to evade his obligations; though harsh and pitiless he was not one of the landlords who contributed a penny in the pound from their Irish rents to famine relief and continued to enjoy themselves on the other side of the Irish Channel. It was repeatedly, and unwillingly, admitted in the House that his energies were devoted to improving his Irish estates, and that he spent far more on them than the income from his Irish rents. But, inflexibly determined to get rid of the old system, he allowed no mercy to temper his ruthlessness.

He was very angry. He told the House of Lords that anyone who knew anything about Ireland was aware that the organisation of the country had entirely broken down. The Castlebar Union was not warmed because the fuel contractor had failed to fulfil his contract. He, Lord Lucan, had ordered his own agent to produce fuel, but the reply was that in the present state of the country none could be got. The same situation obtained for bread. The supply failed, a fresh supply was ordered, but none was forthcoming. In September he had been requested to come to London to make a representation to the Government on the state of Ireland. On his return, on September 28, he took the chair at a meeting of the Board of Guardians. He was then informed that all the contracts for the supply of provisions had expired, that not one single fresh tender had been received by the Board, and even if tenders were received there was not one farthing of money to pay for them. The question at that moment was not merely of closing the workhouse for the future, but of putting out those who were actually in it. He then volunteered to keep the workhouse open at his own expense, and this he had done for four weeks. He would like to know what would have happened if he had not come forward.

He entirely denied that he was a debtor for rates. All the rates for which he was responsible were punctually paid. What happened was that when his tenants did not pay he was debited, and for those rates he declined to be liable. As for striking a new rate, it was ridiculous and unjust to strike a new rate while so large a proportion of the old rate was still outstanding, and, in any case, owing to the high proportion of very small holdings in

Mayo, striking a rate took too long to be efficacious. Distresses should be levied, and those who owed rates should be forced to pay. He observed that he had been favoured with many declarations about the horrors of starvation, but no practical suggestions.

No man was ever more certain of being in the right. But was he justified, was there nothing to be done for the miserable beings lying down to die as the gates of the workhouse were shut in their faces? The House resented his inhumanity, and the subject was not allowed to drop: the Earl of Lucan and the Castlebar Union were brought up again and again in the Commons, while in the Lords, Lord Brougham, the scourge of Irish landlords, pursued the subject of evictions in Mayo. Within a few weeks, however, the Earl of Lucan was no longer present to reply; he had gone back to Ireland, where a fresh tide of misfortune was sweeping over the Irish people.

Every effort to keep in check the numbers on relief had failed. By March, 1847, more than three-quarters of a million men were working on the roads; and three million persons were on relief. Since January, in eight weeks, an extra million and a quarter persons had thrown themselves on the Government for support, and on February 19 it was announced in the House of Commons that fifteen thousand persons were dying every day in Ireland. From uneasiness, the Government passed to alarm. The public works were sliding into chaos, and peculations and false returns were reported from all sides. When the Government felt that England was being "drawn into what threatened to become a gigantic system of permanently supporting one portion of the community at the expense of the remainder," drastic action was taken. The public works were closed. On March 20, 20 per cent of the workers on the roads were struck off, successive reductions of 20 per cent following until all had been dismissed. At the same time the method of distributing relief was changed and tightened up. Uncooked food was not now to be distributed. Eminent doctors had been consulted, and the daily ration was fixed at one pound of maize meal and rice steamed solid so that it could be carried away, or a quart of soup thickened with meal, along with a pound and a quarter of bread. This ration was to be collected each day in person by everyone except the sick, the aged, and young children, and, with a few rare exceptions, there was an additional and severe condition—no one occupying more than a quarter of an acre of land was to be entitled to relief.

That spring the roads to the ports of Ireland became thronged with people flying from certain death. Not half the land had been sown with any kind of crop: the people were accustomed only to a primitive method of potato culture, and though the Government had sent round lecturers to teach them to sow wheat, they had not been able to understand what was said. In some districts the starving peasantry had received pamphlets containing extracts from Adam Smith's *Wealth of Nations*. There was want of everything: implements, manure, seed, knowledge, and, after a year's starvation, energy. Above all, there was a fatal want of goodwill. "If only," wrote William Smith, an English engineer in charge of public works, "the people had been treated with a little kindness." As the year advanced, it became evident that the harvest of 1847 had completely failed, and the throng on the roads steadily grew. The "quarter-acre" clause proved fatal, and thousands who had clung to their patches were forced to give them up to obtain food. The food was not enough, and women wailed as they carried it home to their children; and a coroner's jury in Connaught, holding an inquest on a woman found dead of starvation, brought in a verdict of wilful murder against the Prime Minister, Lord John Russell. Once the patches had been given up, the landlords would not let the people stay: a new race of beggars must not be allowed to grow up on the land. Flight or death was the choice. The people tramped to the ports, for as little as half a crown were transported across the Irish Channel, and the destitute and starving came into the industrial towns of England like an avalanche. Between January 13 and November 1, 278,000 Irish poured into Liverpool, 90,000 into Glasgow, while in Manchester outdoor relief was given to 4,000 a week. Nineteen relieving officers and thirty Roman Catholic priests caught the cholera and died.

The dearest wish of these people was to emigrate, to Canada, to Australia, above all to the United States, but the English Government decided not to undertake any scheme to assist emigration. It was felt that "a burden would be transferred to the tax-payers of the United Kingdom which would otherwise be borne by those to whom it properly belonged, owing to their interests being more immediately concerned." Considerable Irish emigration had already taken place, however, and those Irish already established assisted their relations and friends with extraordinary generosity. In New York the sum required for a family would be made up from small subscriptions, often from strangers, given by the Irish labouring poor. Between £4 and £5 was charged for the passage, the emigrants providing their own food. The English Government did not inspect or regulate the ships, and the greed of the speculator was subject to no control. Inconceivable miseries were endured on the long voyage across the Atlantic, made in small sailing-ships. The low fare charged resulted in only the worst kind of vessels being used, and in hundreds of cases ships, known as "coffin ships," which were notoriously unseaworthy were cheaply hired by speculators. The emigrants were crammed in regardless of health, safety, or decency; they were in the last extreme of misery and poverty, often had been unable to provide themselves with adequate supplies of food, often had the cholera upon them. Of 89,738 persons who emigrated to Canada during 1847, 15,330 perished.

The winter of 1847 was again exceptionally severe, with heavy falls of snow, sleet, and gales of icy wind. But when spring came, a change had taken place. The demolishing machine and the crow-bar brigade were no longer needed—the period of mass evictions was over. Thousands had died, thousands had fled, thousands were still dying and fleeing, and the problem was solved—the people had disappeared. In Mayo alone it was estimated that 100,000 acres lay without a single tenant. The harvest of 1848 proved a good harvest, and the famine was over.

On November 16, 1849, *The Times* published a long letter which was reprinted next day as a leading article. The writer of the letter, the Rev. and Hon. Sidney Godolphin Osborne, had just travelled through Mayo as *The Times* correspondent and special commissioner. A fearless, indeed a bellicose, philanthropist, he was later to be one of Miss Nightingale's chief supporters and lieutenants in the hospitals at Scutari. Lord Lucan was "utterly unknown to him," and they did not meet when Sidney Godolphin Osborne was at Castlebar, because Lord Lucan happened to be in England.

Lord Lucan is [he wrote] eminently a practical man; that which he determines to do he sets about at once, suffering no expense of pocket or popularity to interrupt him. He is one of the few landlords left in the West of Ireland who reside on and perseveringly endeavour to improve their property. He has been one of those who, finding their estates occupied by masses of small tenants, the majority of whom could not pay rent or taxes, and were in fact paupers, looked the matter in the face and saw that he had the option either of allowing them to remain, and thus to self confiscate his whole property, or of removing them by legal process, and have at least the forlorn hope that should better times arrive he might have this property prepared for a more wholesome system of occupation. I, it is true, have heard him called by very hard names; he has earned himself the character of "a great exterminator" . . . I saw sufficient remains of his exterminating system, in the shape of roofless cabins and roofless villages, which I was informed were on his property, to make my heart bleed for the suffering these evictions must have created. . . . But if I saw this, I saw also, what is not often seen in Ireland, the so-called exterminator giving his every effort, at any cost, to lay the foundation of a system of cultivation which should give to a future generation, if not to this generation of peasantry, comfortable dwellings, with fair wages for fair work as farm servants, in place of the precarious livelihood that had been the peasant's lot as an occupant of the land himself. . . . I could have wished and prayed from my heart that the stern law of necessity had not driven him, and many other landlords, to the defence of their property by a course which has wrung the hearts and kindled the worst feelings of hundreds of their fellow creatures. . . . I can believe that had Providence not blighted the potato . . . the system of extermination would not have been carried out in the hurried manner it latterly has been, and the transition of the peasantry from the condition of small owners to that of hired labourers would have been attempted with more deliberation. Three successive years of famine, however, brought the struggle between poverty and property at once to a crisis. . . .

Now, Sir, if a Landlord is to be found resident . . . cultivating large tracts of land in the best possible manner . . . he does appear to me to deserve no little credit. . . . It matters not whether he is a popular or an unpopular man, what his creed, what his station; there he is, having weathered so far the storm, always called up by one who, careless of present odium, aims at a given end however painful the means of its attainment, and halts not until he has attained it.

Sidney Godolphin Osborne was genuinely a philanthropist, but how little he felt for the Irish people! He was genuinely a liberal, but how little he foresaw! He felt no more responsibility for the fate of the doomed and wretched masses of Ireland than the Earl of Lucan. The population of Ireland had to be reduced, that was clear, and as a humane man he felt regret that an unavoidable necessity should also be painful, but he felt no more. What happens to the rabbits when the warren is cleared? What happens to the rooks when the trees are cut down? Somehow, somewhere they disappear—and so must the Irish.

No faintest apprehension of the fatal result crossed the minds of landlords, statesmen, and philanthropists. As the "coffin ships" made their slow voyage across the Atlantic, a voyage said by men who had experienced both to transcend in horror the dreaded middle passage of the slave trade, they bore with them a cargo of hatred. In that new world which had been called into being to redress the balance of the old there was to grow up a population among whom animosity to England was a creed, whose burning resentment could never be appeased, who, possessing the long memory of Ireland, could never forget. The Irish famine was to be paid for by England at a terrible price; out of it was born Irish America.

In the opinion of Kinglake, the historian of the Crimean campaign, it was Lord Lucan's conduct in Ireland, his ruthlessness, energy, disregard for sentiment, and contempt for public opinion which decided the Government to select him for a command in the Crimea. He had, however, also developed other qualities less desirable in a commander.

During his years in Ireland, detested, execrated, and, according to his genuine conviction, criminally misunderstood, he had become combative to an extraordinary degree. He came to every discussion in an antagonistic frame of mind, took it for granted that he would be opposed and unappreciated, resorted to browbeating when no brow-beating was necessary. His impatience had increased, and his irritable temper, sharpened by a sense of injustice, expressed itself in habitual discourtesy. Officials in Ireland complained bitterly. "It is not often," wrote the secretary to the Poor Law Commission in 1849, "that the Commissioners receive from any individual, however humble his station in life, letters so unofficial and so offensive as your Lordship has deemed it becoming to address to them." His Lordship was requested in future "to adhere to the ordinary rules of courtesy by which official correspondence in this country is usually conducted."

His temper affected the success of his farming operations,

for he quarrelled with his tenants, and lawsuits between the Earl of Lucan and the occupants of his farms became frequent. Some of the most capable tenants left, and it was not easy in any case to let farms cleared during the famine. At Ballinrobe, where evictions on the largest scale had taken place, the land lay vacant and was turned into a race course.

And life ran no more smoothly at Laleham. Soon after Lord Lucan succeeded, he fell out with the rector over the family sittings in Laleham Church. In Lord Lucan's opinion these were inadequate, and in 1843 he brought down an architect from London, who got out plans to alter the church to suit his convenience. It was proposed that it should be rebuilt entirely, "since the building is so old, having a Norman character. A clean sweep can then be made and the view of the church will not be obstructed by Norman pillars." However, the rector would not agree, in spite of the fact that Lord Lucan was prepared to sweep away the Norman features at his own expense. Whereupon Lord Lucan flew into a passion, consulted ecclesiastical authorities, and came forward with an assertion of his absolute right to do what he pleased with what he called the "Manorial Chancel." The chancel of the church had in mediæval times been the private chapel of the Lord of the Manor, and Lord Lucan stated that since it was "still kept up out of the Lord of the Manor's private funds," he had as Lord of the Manor an absolute right to do what he pleased in it.

I consider [he wrote] I have exclusive and entire control over the Manorial Chancel, may exclude even the minister from passing through and may occupy it in any way I prefer. . . . I cannot be debarred from so arranging the Manorial Chancel, my own private property, as would allow it to accommodate us. . . . I claim exclusive power and control over the Manorial Chancel, and consequently a right to close up the door when or how I may think right. What course I shall adopt on the subject I have not yet had time to consider and decide.

Year after year, even during the famine, whenever Lord

Lucan paid one of his flying visits to Laleham he found time to harry the rector on the subject of the "Manorial Chancel." Nor was the rector his only problem: there were trespassers, there were unpunctual farm hands, above all, at Laleham there were swans. Swans in an open and common river belong to the Crown: they are royal fowls, marked as royal property by the Royal Swanmaster; but they are also truculent, destructive, and untidy, possessing an extraordinary aptitude for fouling fields; and the Queen's Swans had a special fondness for the water meadows of the Earl of Lucan at Laleham. On December 8, 1853, he wrote furiously to the Lord Chamberlain:

Sir, I have within the last hour seen more than, if not quite, 70 swans on my fields. I can and will submit no longer to so intolerable a nuisance. I therefore and hereby give you notice that unless the swans are removed on or before Friday 16th instant, I shall myself shoot 6, leaving them on the ground, and shall cause 6 to be shot every following Friday, until they are reduced to the number of 6. I have too patiently suffered this nuisance to be inflicted on me and I will rid myself of it.

The result of this protest is not known, but time has brought the swans victory over the Earl. Today the traveller crossing the Thames by ferry from Laleham will almost certainly see to his left a concourse of swans, more swans, in all probability, than he has ever seen together in his life before. Waddling on the grass, tearing it up, preening their plumage, dropping their feathers, sleeping peacefully in the sun, the swans are in undisputed possession of what were once the meadows of the Earl of Lucan.

Having regard to Lord Lucan's character, his irascibility, fidgetiness, restless energy, his domestic life could not be expected to run smoothly. He was, however, singularly fortunate in his children. His heir, George, Lord Bingham, leaving Rugby in 1847, brought away glowing testimonials to his amiability, good conduct, and sweet temper when corrected—only one point needed attention: he was sadly ignorant of Old Testament history, which he seemed "unaccountably to have neglected." His daughter Lavinia united the good looks of Brudenells and Binghams, and was described as "the most beautiful girl in fashionable life." His Countess, however, the sister of Lord Cardigan, though described as a tyrant herself, found Lord Lucan too tyrannical to live with. She came very seldom to Ireland, it was said that she detested Castlebar, and while Lord Lucan was struggling with his farms, her name was to be found in "fashionable intelligence" as a guest at London parties. In 1847, in the midst of the famine, a second son was born, but by 1854 the Earl and Countess of Lucan had parted. There were, it was admitted, faults on both sides.

Perhaps as a result of this separation, the enmity between the two brothers-in-law, the Earl of Cardigan and the Earl of Lucan, became generally known. According to *The Times* it was common gossip in the clubs, and a contemporary memoir states that the Duke of Wellington was called in to try to smooth matters out.

It is said that Lord Cardigan considered his sister to have been disgracefully treated, sacrificed to Lord Lucan's farming mania, kept short of money, and deprived of suitable enjoyments. In 1824 he had challenged and fought a young man who, in his estimation, had treated one of his sisters badly; but, perhaps thanks to the intervention of the Duke, no duel was fought with Lord Lucan and no public recriminations took place. After the parting Lady Lucan spent a great deal of time at Ryde, in the Isle of Wight; as a family the Brudenells were fond of the sea, and Lord Cardigan kept a yacht at Cowes.

For the next few years the lives of the two men divided. At Deene Park, or Portman Square, or in his magnificent yacht *Dryad*, or in Paris, Lord Cardigan was living in princely splendour, spending very little time with the 11th Hussars. He remained parted from his wife and had acquired an inseparable companion in Mr. Hubert de Burgh, a celebrated man about town, who had married one of his wife's sisters. Mr. de Burgh, described by William Howard Russell as an "unlovely gentleman," had a whim for wearing country clothes in London and was nicknamed by the world of clubs, race courses, and gambling hells "the Squire." Lord Cardigan depended on him, and in negotiations of delicacy "the Squire" frequently acted on his behalf.

Meanwhile, Lord Lucan, indifferent to splendour, was living austerely in a few rooms in Castlebar House, hurrying between Ireland and Laleham, absorbed and relentless, always with a dozen disputes on his hands, still clearing his estates in Mayo amid the lamentations of the tenantry, and still doing battle with the rector, the trespassers, the farm hands, and the swans of Laleham.

Both were now elderly men, and the course of their lives seemed set for the rest of their days. Then suddenly fate intervened. Russia, the ally of Britain during the Napoleonic wars, abruptly transformed herself into a menace to the peace of Europe, and overnight, it seemed, Europe was on the verge of war.

Russia, desiring naval power and access to the Mediterranean, had long cast envious eyes on Turkey in Europe; and the Turkish Empire, sprawling helplessly on her very doorstep, unwieldy, corrupt, and decaying, invited attack. In a famous phrase the Czar Nicholas christened Turkey "the sick man of Europe," and remarked to the British ambassador that it would be a great misfortune if one of these days he should slip away before all necessary arrangements were made. For his part, the Czar made the necessary arrangements by building a great naval base at Sebastopol, from which Constantinople was menaced by the guns of the Russian fleet. British statesmen began to have nightmares of Constantinople in Russian hands and Russian warships dominating the Mediterranean. There was nothing for it but an alliance with the French.

The British detested Napoleon III, who had just seized the throne by means of a bloody *coup d'état*. They were horrified by the spectacle of the French nation once more intoxicated with imperialism and joyfully submitting to a despot. Only a menace to their sea power could have induced them to enter into an alliance with France.

Meanwhile Nicholas was looking out for an excuse to attack Turkey, and in the summer of 1853 he found his excuse at Bethlehem. The Church of the Nativity there, traditionally built over the stable where Christ was born, was the scene of violent clashes between monks of the Orthodox Church, supported by Russia, and monks of the Roman Catholic Church, supported by France; and since Palestine was in the Turkish Empire, the police in the church were Turkish Mohammedans. The Orthodox denied the right of the Roman Catholics to place a silver star over the manger and to possess a golden key to the church door, and this summer of 1853 a serious riot took place; the Roman Catholics succeeded after a prolonged struggle in placing their star over the manger, but not before several Orthodox monks had been killed. The Czar instantly asserted that the Turkish police had deliberately allowed the Orthodox monks to be murdered, and marched into the Danubian provinces of Turkey, proclaiming himself the protector of the Orthodox Christian subjects of the Sultan from Turkish persecution. By October, 1853, Turkey and Russia were at war.

England remained neutral. But when on November 30, the Russian fleet sailed out of Sebastopol, took the Turkish fleet by surprise at Sinope, and wiped it out, the English were transported with rage, and angry mobs paraded the London streets. By the end of January, 1854, war was plainly inevitable.

For the Earl of Cardigan and the Earl of Lucan, now fifty-seven and fifty-four years of age, it was an extraordinary moment. The opportunity they had longed for all their lives had arrived at last; dreams forty years old were coming true, trumpets were shrilling, squadrons gathering, courtyards ringing to the tramp of armed men. Military glory beckoned them at last.

If, rather surprisingly, they had no doubts as to their suitability for command in the field, no qualms, no inertia held them back. In February Lord Lucan wrote to Lord Hardinge, Commander-in-Chief since the death of the Duke of Wellington in 1852, and offered his services. He did not ask for a senior command, since he supposed no considerable force of cavalry would be employed, but he suggested that he might usefully take out a brigade of infantry; having campaigned in the Balkans, he was accustomed to foreign armies and to living with foreign officers.

At the same time Lord Cardigan applied to Lord Raglan, the former Lord FitzRoy Somerset, who had just been appointed Commander-in-Chief of the British Expeditionary Army to the East. They were old family friends; indeed, earlier *The Times* had accused Lord Raglan of using his official influence to shield the Earl of Cardigan. Certainly during the period of disturbances in the 11th Hussars, Lord Raglan, then Military Secretary at the Horse Guards, had intervened on Lord Cardigan's behalf. For the moment, however, Lord Cardigan did not receive a favourable answer to his application.

On January 28, 1854, *The Times* commented on the elderliness of the generals of the British Army. There was not a single lieutenant-general, it was asserted, who did not secretly feel himself unfitted by age to undergo the exertions and hardships of active service. Lord Hardinge, Commander-in-Chief, was sixty-nine, Lord Raglan sixty-five; of the major-generals, Lord Lucan, at fifty-four, was one of the two youngest. Yet the Duke of Wellington when he finished his active military career at Waterloo was only forty-five. *The Times* quoted Chatham's comment on the officers appointed to command in the American war: "I do not know what effect these names have on the enemy, but I confess they make *me* tremble."

In February it was announced that, should war be declared, a cavalry force would accompany an expeditionary army; and on the 21st Lord Lucan was appointed to command the cavalry division.

Meanwhile an extraordinary bellicosity had seized on the nation. Grave doubts were entertained in well-informed quarters on the wisdom and the probable outcome of the war—the Prime

Minister, Lord Aberdeen, was against it, *The Times* was against it, the Queen and the Prince Consort were uncertain. But the people were intoxicated. Memories of past victories went to their heads, the names of Waterloo and Trafalgar were on every lip, crowds paraded the streets delirious with excitement, inflated with national pride. "When people are inflamed in that way they are no better than mad dogs," wrote Cobbett; and so in March, 1854, shouting, cheering, singing, the nation swept into war.

On March 27 the Queen's message of war was read in the Commons, and next day war was declared. The precise causes and objects of the war remained obscure. It was puzzling to find the British nation fighting on the side of Mohammedans against Christians, even if Palmerston was right when he said that that had nothing to do with the question. Mr. Disraeli's explanation did not seem much more satisfactory: he remarked that he thought we were going to war to prevent the Emperor of all the Russias from protecting the Christian subjects of the Sultan of Turkey. And John Bright told the House of Commons that he could see no adequate reason for the conflict. The voice of the people, however, found expression in a less distinguished member, a Mr. John Ball, who assured the House that the real justification of the war was vast, high and noble: "the maintenance in civilized society of the principles of right and justice."

On the somewhat sinister date of April 1, Lieutenant-Colonel the Earl of Cardigan was gazetted brigadier-general in command of the Light Brigade of Cavalry, and the cavalry appointments were completed by giving the Heavy Brigade to Col. James Scarlett of the 5th Dragoon Guards, who at fifty-five had been on the point of retirement. With the exception of Lord Lucan, whose Balkan experience had occurred twenty-six years previously, not one of the three cavalry generals had any experience of active service. Yet England, in spite of forty years' peace in Europe, was fortunate enough to have a superb list of cavalry officers who had done brilliant service in the field and were in the prime of life—but their services had been in India. The caste system which kept "Indian" officers down was so powerful that not one man from the list was given a cavalry command.

Lord Cardigan received his appointment as brigadier-general with chagrin—he wished to command, not to obey. Above all, not to obey Lord Lucan. In London clubs the news of the two appointments was received with "cynical amusement." It was "notorious in every circle acquainted with them both that the state of feeling which had long existed between them was likely to lead to unpleasant results."

At this point Lord Cardigan was allowed to get a fatal idea into his head. He was, he said, given to understand by Lord Raglan that the cavalry command was to be, in practice, divided. He would be junior in rank to Lord Lucan, certainly, but he would operate separately and on his own account: there would be no question of carrying out Lord Lucan's instructions or of obeying Lord Lucan's orders. He, Cardigan, would give the orders and instructions to the Light Brigade, which would be a separate command. Soothed and animated by this belief, he plunged enthusiastically into preparations for war.

Bulletins began to appear in the newspapers issued from the headquarters of the 11th Hussars. One announced that Mr. Lamprey, "an eminent Irish cutler from Limerick," had been hired to sharpen the swords of the 11th; another that the officers of the 11th were having pieces of black leather sewn to the seats of their cherry-coloured trousers the better to withstand the additional friction incidental to active service.

The Times commented on the style of these announcements, which were exclusive to the 11th Hussars, and on April 22 ridiculed the uniform of the 11th. "The splendour of these magnificent light horsemen, the shortness of their jackets, the tightness of their cherry-coloured pants" were "as utterly unfit for war service as the garb of the female hussars in the ballet of Gustavus, which they so nearly resemble." The Earl of Cardigan rushed into print. "In the 11th the men's jackets are longer and their overalls [trousers] looser than almost any other cavalry regiment in the service." An acrimonious correspondence followed in which Lord Cardigan accused *The Times* of "petty and paltry slander," and in this way the cherry-coloured pants of the 11th became famous. The Duke of Newcastle, Secretary for War, writing to Lord Raglan on April 28 on clothing for the troops, assured him, "I am not going to write to you about the colour and tightness of Cardigan's cherry-coloured pants."

The first orders of the cavalry were for the Balkans: the British and French armies were to relieve Silistria, in Roumania, then a Turkish province, which was besieged by the invading Russians. Varna in Bulgaria was to be the port of disembarkation, and Scutari, a large village opposite Constantinople on the Asian shore of the Bosphorus, the British base.

By the end of April, when Lord Cardigan left England, Lord Lucan had already reached Scutari, taking with him as his aide-de-camp his son, Lord Bingham.

8

The cavalry have always regarded themselves as socially superior to the remainder of the British Army. They have been the most expensive arm of the service, the most aristocratic, and the most magnificent. Exempted from the more irksome duties of war, marches, gradual encirclements, retreats fought painfully inch by inch, and reserved for brilliant feats of arms, they have preserved the primitive pride of the horseman riding while other men trudge in the dust.

Cavalry superiority was a doctrine in which British military authorities long acquiesced, and down to modern times a surprisingly large proportion, sometimes even a preponderance, of the generals of the British Army have been drawn from the cavalry. Yet the British cavalry has seldom been successful. The Duke of Wellington remarked that the cavalry of other European armies had won victories for their generals, but his cavalry had invariably got him into scrapes. Gronow reports the celebrated French cavalry commander, Excelmann, as saying,

Your horses are the finest in the world and your men ride better than any Continental soldier; with such material the English cavalry ought to have done more than has ever been accomplished by them on the field of battle. The great deficiency is in your officers . . . . the British cavalry officer seems to be impressed by the conviction that he can dash or ride over everything; as if the art of war were precisely the same as that of fox-hunting.

The dash of British cavalry officers was never greater than at the opening of the Crimean campaign in the spring of 1854. These aristocratic horsemen were, in the idiom of the day, "plungers," "tremendous swells." They affected elegant boredom, yawned a great deal, spoke a jargon of their own, pronouncing "r" as "w," saying "vewwy," "howwid," and "sowwy," and interlarded sentences with loud and meaningless exclamations of "Haw, haw.' Their sweeping whiskers, languid voices, tiny waists, laced in by corsets, and their large cigars were irresistible, frantically admired, and as frantically envied. Magnificently mounted, horses were their passion; they rode like the devil himself, and their confidence in their ability to defeat any enemy single-handed was complete. Cavalry officers were saying in London drawing-rooms that to take infantry on the campaign was superfluous; the infantry would merely be a drag on them, and had better be left at home.

The unpleasant truth was that they were completely ignorant of the art of war, had no experience, no education, and no ability. Throughout the British expeditionary army which sailed to war in the spring of 1854 the qualifications for command were rank, influence, and privilege.

Good Heavens! [wrote Lord Wolseley]. What Generals then had charge of England's only Army and of her honour and fighting reputation! They were served to a large extent by incompetent staff officers, as useless as themselves; many of them were "flaneurs about town," who knew as little of war and its science as they did about the Differential Calculus. Almost all our officers at that time were uneducated as soldiers, and many of those placed upon the staff of the Army at the beginning of the war were absolutely unfit for the positions they had secured through family and political interest. . . . They were not men whom I would have entrusted with a subaltern's picket in the field. Had they been private soldiers, I don't think any colonel would have made them corporals.

THE PLUNGER IN TURKEY.

"I SAY, OLD FELLAH!—DO YOU THINK IT PWOBABLE THE INFANTWY WILL ACCOMPANY US TO SEBASTOPOL?"

This state of affairs had arisen for an extraordinary reason. The British Army was now paying the price for the supreme military genius of the Duke of Wellington. The Duke had been an aristocrat, a reactionary Tory, an upholder of the purchase system and the privileges of rank. He had, for instance, strictly adhered to the practice which was later to bring down a Parliamentary storm on Lord Raglan's head; he would recommend only staff officers, who usually had aristocratic connections, for decorations and distinctions, passing over regimental officers who were usually of a lower social class—though the regimental officers had in fact done the fighting. But the all-important fact was that the Duke had been a military genius, perhaps the greatest in history, and unsurpassed as a military administrator; and, beyond this, he had possessed a force of character and a power over men which transcended even his military genius. Under the Duke the system had worked, but he had died in 1852, and the British Army was now to experience what it was like to fight under the system but without the Duke.

The nation seemed to believe that the Duke was still with them. The high military authorities in charge of the British Army had been brought up at his feet—Lord Hardinge, the Commander-in-Chief at home, and Lord Raglan, Commander-in-Chief of the expeditionary army, were two of his most intimate friends, and for this reason their arrangements were accepted by the nation with childlike faith. The mantle of Wellington had fallen upon them, and they could do no wrong. But, alas, in tireless attention to detail, minute scrutiny of transport and commissariat, power to grapple with the endless problems that harass the commander of an army like gad-flies, the Duke's disciples were fatally unlike the Duke. The heroes of battles long since past, called back from an age now dead, the generals of the British Army confronted the infinite complications involved in high command with a weariness natural to their years. Difficulties were felt to be too great; supply was ignored, intelligence was ignored, transport was left to chance. As so often in the history of the British Army, all was flung on to the known, the extraordinary fighting quality of British troops. The quality of the troops would compensate for everything. The men were magnificent, the officers recklessly brave; they would "go over the Russians like grass." "Our men," wrote a lieutenant in the 8th Hussars, "are splendid fellows; it is a privilege to fight with them; if we were to meet an Army two or three times our size we should lick them."

In this spirit, thirsting for military glory, filled with confidence and excitement, as if, indeed, going to a fox hunt, the British Army embarked for war.

The embarkation had the gay informality of a picnic. Officers took their wives with them, some took their mothers, there were several young brides. Lady Errol, wife of a captain in the 2nd battalion of the 60th Rifles, was accompanied by her French maid and sailed wearing a habit with long, trailing skirt and a swallow-tailed coatee with rows of shining buttons. She had permission to share a tent with her husband on the campaign, but it proved to have only one bed. Years later one of her grandchildren asked her if the bed was comfortable. "I don't know, my dear," she replied; "his Lordship had the bed, and I slept on the ground." Captain Duberly, of the 8th Hussars, was accompanied by his vivacious, daring young wife, a splendid horsewoman who brought her favourite mount with her. It was all such an adventure, she wrote. Cases of wine, baskets of hot-house fruit, bouquets of flowers were handed up the sides of transports, and the general hope was that the war would not be over before the Russians had a taste of British quality. Unfortunately a rapid termination was thought likely. It was common gossip that the Russian soldier was a poor fighter, had to be driven by his officers on to the field at pistol-point, and was wretchedly armed—it was said that in many cases Russian rifles had been proved to be wooden dummies.

To a critical mind, however, the arrangements, especially in the case of the cavalry, appeared inadequate. The transport of troop horses presents great difficulties: horses, being bad sailors, are nervous and suffer severely from confinement at sea. The obvious course was to send the cavalry in steamers, but steamers were not yet in universal use, and there was difficulty in collecting sufficient of them. It was decided that sailing ships should be used, four or five to each regiment. But as steamers reached the East in from ten to twelve days, while sailing ships took as much as sixty to seventy, it would have been quicker to keep the cavalry in England until sufficient steamers had been collected. The holds of the sailing ships were small, stifling, and horribly foul. When Mrs. Duberly went down to see her horse, she burst into tears. No proper arrangements had been made for securing the horses, there were head ropes only, and when gales blew in the Bay of Biscay the animals endured a martyrdom. Lieutenant Seager wrote from the sailing ship *Henry Wilson* on May 12:

We had all the men standing at their horses' heads, although some were so sick that they could scarcely stand. The scene below during the whole time was dreadful and one that I hope never to see again. As the vessel rolled from one side to the other, it pitched all the horses forward off their feet against the manger, they were absolutely frantic, the stamping of their feet on the boards, their screams together with the shouts of the men trying to pacify them, were something awful. Horse after horse got down, and as soon as one was, with great difficulty and danger got up, others went down. Some were in the most critical position with their bodies lying under the other horses who were kicking and plunging upon them, and to get them out of these positions was a very dangerous and difficult affair. Our men worked well and were ably seconded by some of the sailors. Such a fearful scene I never wish to witness again, 85 horses all mad with fright, trying to break loose from their fastenings and I am surprised they did not succeed, for when the vessel rose on one side, all the horses on that side, 43 in number, dashed forward simultaneously against their mangers with all their force, and this occurred every five minutes during the night.

In the Mediterranean it being unseasonably hot, a number of horses went mad in the heat and had to be shot, and Mrs. Duberly's died.

Meanwhile the Earl of Cardigan, by permission of Lord Hardinge, the Commander-in-Chief, was travelling independently of his brigade to the seat of war. Accompanied by an aide-de-camp, he left London for Paris on May 8, gave a dinner party at the Café de Paris on the 10th, was entertained by Napoleon III and the Empress Eugénie at the Tuileries on the 11th, and left Marseilles in a French steamer on the 16th. On May 21 he arrived at the Piræus, spent a couple of days sight-seeing in Athens, and on May 24 anchored off Scutari, the British base, and went ashore to call on Lord Lucan, "Looking as usual highly important," wrote young George Higginson of the Guards.

The intense dislike the two brothers-in-law cherished for each other was well known to the Army, and trouble was considered inevitable. "If they do not clash 'tis passing strange," wrote Captain Calthorpe, nephew of Lord Raglan and on his staff. Letter after letter went home speculating on the probable result of appointing two men notoriously hard to get on with, and known to be estranged in private life, to a command requiring the closest co-operation and cordiality. "When the Government," wrote William Howard Russell, war correspondent of *The Times*, "made the monstrous choice of Lord Cardigan as Brigadier of the Light Cavalry Brigade of the Cavalry Division, well knowing the private relations between the two men, they became responsible for disaster." However, on the night of May 26 the two men dined together without incident. Lord Lucan was fully aware of the difficulties which lay before him—he had been warned by everyone in London, he wrote, of the difficulty of commanding Lord Cardigan. He was nevertheless Lord Cardigan's commander, and he was determined to command Lord Cardigan, who on his side, however, had no faintest intention of being commanded. If Lucan relied on his position as general commanding the cavalry division, Cardigan had as firm a faith in the promise of a separate command which, he was convinced, Lord Raglan had made him in London.

Lord Cardigan lost no time in asserting his independence. On

May 28 the first portion of his brigade, part of the 8th Hussars and 17th Lancers, sailed in on their way to Varna, the port in Bulgaria selected as a base for the Balkan operations which opened the war, and he instantly took steps to escape from Lord Lucan. He applied for permission to join his troops at Varna, and he went over Lucan's head, the head of his immediate superior, and applied direct to Lord Raglan. Lord Raglan, very curiously, did not refer him back, but granted permission, and Cardigan proceeded on his own authority to make arrangements for embarking himself and his staff. Meanwhile Lord Raglan sent Lucan a note informing him that Cardigan was about to proceed to Varna, and "as his Lordship wished to leave next day, arrangements for his embarkation should be made forthwith." Lucan then discovered that Cardigan had already issued the necessary orders on his own account.

It was a situation which would have been intolerable to an even-tempered man, and Lord Lucan notoriously possessed the temper of a tiger. But well aware that he must not be provoked, he managed to restrain himself.

True, he cancelled Lord Cardigan's embarkation arrangements and substituted his own, but he made no official complaint to Lord Raglan, nor did he raise any objection to his brother-in-law's departure. On June 2, however, he wrote an unofficial protest.

MY DEAR CARDIGAN

. . . It is obvious that the service cannot be carried on as it should be, and as I hope in my division it will be, if a subordinate officer is allowed to pass over his immediate and responsible superior and communicate direct with the General Commanding in Chief of the Forces, or with any of his departmental officers. . . . I write privately, as though I consider the error deserving and requiring notice, I wish this, like all other communications between us, to be of the most friendly nature. I hope that the arrangements I made for your embarkation were, as I intended them to be, as agreeable and convenient as they could be made.

Yours very truly,
LUCAN

Lord Cardigan, as was his custom, neither acknowledged nor answered the letter. He sailed next day, and by June 7 had joined his brigade at Varna.

It was Lord Lucan's opinion that he had not received proper support from the Commander-in-Chief in this incident, nor was the licence permitted to Cardigan his sole source of irritation with the Commander-in-Chief. With the 8th Hussars had arrived the lively Mrs. Duberly. Lord Lucan strongly disapproved of her presence, and though she asserted that she had sailed with the permission of the Horse Guards and had accommodation provided by the Admiralty, she had, in fact, no permission to be on board a transport. He sent an aide with a message that unless she could produce an official permit she was to disembark, and at the same time he informed Lord Raglan of her presence, which he considered highly undesirable. Lord Raglan, however, told Mrs. Duberly that he had "no intention of interfering with her," and she sailed on to Varna.

Lord Cardigan had made a poor impression at Scutari. On the voyage out he had not been well—he suffered from chronic bronchitis—and one of Lucan's aides noticed that "though a great swaggerer" he looked "very old," and added that his Lordship did not seem to have "the bodily activity for the job."

The bodily activity of Lord Lucan, on the other hand, was too great: he was leading his staff "a terrible life," rising every morning at four, never pausing for a moment during the day or allowing anyone else to pause. Kinglake, who accompanied the Army, found it impossible to believe that "this tall, lithe, slender, young looking officer" was fifty-four years of age. He enjoyed perfect health, saw like a hawk, and pursued his duties as commander with a "fierce tearing energy" and a dramatic intensity "rare among English men." When issuing orders his face would "all at once light up with a glittering, panther-like aspect, resulting from the sudden fire of the eyes, and the sudden disclosure of the teeth, white, even and clenched." Orders poured from him in a stream; no detail was too small to escape his all-seeing eye, no trifle too insignificant to receive his meticulous attention. For example on May 29:

The Major General calls upon Brigadier Generals and officers commanding corps to insist on their officers being properly dressed. When the officer is wearing any part of his uniform, the uniform must be complete; when in plain clothes the Major General hopes that officers will not appear in fantastical foolish dresses, but will appear like gentlemen, as they do in their own country.

On May 30:

The Major General observes that officers do not wear their gold sword knots as prescribed by regulations. It is to be observed that a gold sword knot has always been considered, in the English and foreign armies, as one of the distinctive marks of a commissioned officer. The officers comprising the cavalry division are to wear their regulation sword knots and no others.

Then on June 2:

The Major General finds it necessary to observe on the hair and beard of both officers and men. Long hair on the head is most objectionable; on service the hair cannot be well kept too short. Moustachios and whiskers are to be allowed to grow, but no officer or private will be allowed to wear a beard. Below the mouth there is to be no hair whatever, and the whisker is not to be worn more forward on the chin than the corner of the mouth.

Again:

Women belonging to the different regiments of cavalry under his command are doing washing in the troughs near the fountains—the Major General is surprised that such a thing should be tolerated.

And he observes too that great difference prevails in the different regiments under his command in the time given in the different sounds preparatory to turning out for the field, and he considers it most important in this, as in every other part of the service, that strict uniformity should be established.

Day by day and twice a day the stream poured forth—on the composition of squadrons, the picketing of horses, and their marking, the care of baggage animals, horse nails, heel ropes, packing of valises, carriage of ammunition, reports, tents, spy glasses, boots, trumpet calls, watch setting, marching, drill, pipe clay, and polishing. Alas, as in his early days, all effort, meticulousness, strenuousness were doomed to come to nothing. Lord Lucan was always trying to catch up, always entangled in the midst of a thousand problems. Everything took longer than he anticipated, matters gave birth to other matters, reeled themselves out interminably. "However good a plan my Lord may make overnight, by the time he has done half a dozen things he is sure to be behind time," wrote one of his aides.

For such a man to have his authority flouted, his orders ignored, was not to be borne, and that, as soon as Brigadier-General Lord Cardigan was safely in Varna, was just what he proceeded to do; he ignored his divisional commander, Lord Lucan, completely. Things were not going well for the cavalry at Varna. The horses had suffered even more severely from the voyage than had been anticipated, the arrangements for landing them from the ships were ludicrously inadequate, and many were injured. "Anything more mismanaged can hardly be conceived," wrote Major Cresswell of the 11th Hussars. Forage was in short supply, and water was dangerously insufficient. More serious still, a cholera epidemic had broken out. Varna was a half-savage Balkan town, as primitive as it was picturesque. The armies of England and France descended upon it without any sanitary precautions being taken, and within a week cholera and dysentery were ravaging the troops.

Lord Cardigan, however, was not much involved with the difficulties of his brigade. He was suffering from bronchitis, and had found himself a house across the bay at Devna, built over a stream and shaded by a tree. As the heat was terrific, he stayed indoors all day, nursing his bronchitis, eating fruit and issuing a stream of orders, "giving everyone as much trouble as he possibly can," wrote Lieutenant Seager. "No end of reports, returns and official letters, even more than at home." An order particularly annoying to officers and men forbade patrols to carry their cloaks to wrap round them at night; the days might be scorching, but the nights were cold. "The practice was to be discontinued, as the Brigadier-General considered it effeminate."

Though Lord Cardigan exacted reports and returns, he forwarded none of them to his divisional commander. As far as Lord Lucan was concerned, the Light Brigade had vanished into thin air, taking with them the Horse Artillery, which had now reached Varna and come under Cardigan's command.

Lord Raglan was also at Varna. He had established his headquarters there on May 11, and once more he was permitting Lord Cardigan to deal with him direct, acquiescing in—indeed, seemingly, encouraging—a brigadier in deliberately and consistently going over his immediate superior's head.

Lord Lucan was left behind at Kulali, outside Scutari, separated from his division, more than 150 miles away across the Black Sea, with no orders, with nothing to do but, boiling with fury, to watch transport after transport going up to Varna. Every day the situation became more infuriating. During the first week in June part of the Heavy Brigade arrived and went on to Varna; and since Lord Cardigan was senior brigadier, it came under his command. He was now not merely attempting to exercise a separate command, he was in practice actually taking his divisional general's place, and with the consent of the Commander-in-Chief. On June 11 Lucan wrote Raglan a letter seething with indignation.

The Commander of the Forces takes the field with the main body of his army, and with the larger part of my division, and I am to be left behind. The whole of the horse artillery, and the whole of the cavalry present, full half of what is expected, and composed of troops of the two brigades, are to be in the field with the headquarters of the army under a brigadier (Lord Cardigan), whilst I am to be left behind without troops, and for all I can see without duties. . . . When I was appointed to the command of the cavalry division, it certainly occurred to very many, that the great difficulty would be to command Lord Cardigan. I apprehended no difficulty of the sort, confident that I should receive from Lord Raglan that support which a divisional commander may fairly expect to receive from the Commander of the Army; I never doubted that, commanding with judgment and tact, I could maintain my position. . . . I trust I shall be found entirely submissive to the will and wishes of my commander: I must require, though perhaps to a smaller extent, submission from my subordinates; from Lord Cardigan I can scarcely hope to receive it if his lordship is allowed to continue in the opinion he is well known to entertain, that the position of a brigadier is one of independence towards his divisional superior.

At the same time he sent a severe official reprimand to Lord Cardigan. Would the brigadier-general kindly note that, as was customary and proper in the service, all returns and reports were to be sent to himself, the divisional general, and not to the Commander-in-Chief? Upon this Lord Lucan received an immediate and agitated call from Lord de Ros, the quartermaster-general, an appointment corresponding to the modern appointment of chief of staff. Lord de Ros had little military experience, very pleasing manners, and a number of amiable eccentricities—he was one of the first practitioners of sun bathing. He hastened to assure Lord Lucan, with all the persuasiveness at his command, that he was perfectly mistaken. Lord Raglan had not the smallest intention of shelving him; indeed, Lord Raglan was expecting him at Varna. The position had now been made absolutely clear to Lord Cardigan; all misapprehensions in that direction had been corrected, and of course Lord Lucan must go up to Varna whenever he wished. But—the letter must be withdrawn.

Lord Lucan allowed himself to be persuaded, and it was withdrawn. After tremendous and exhausting exertions to clear everything up—"we missed the boat, of course," wrote one of his aides—he arrived at Varna on June 15.

The cavalry were no longer there. Cholera was raging, the state of the town and the bay had become "disgusting," and the cavalry had been moved. The Heavy Brigade was a couple of miles outside Varna, the Light Brigade and the Horse Artillery were at Devna, about nine miles away, where Lord Cardigan had his house. No one seemed to expect Lord Lucan at Varna. He called at headquarters and found that Lord Raglan was away, but he saw Sir George Brown, commander of the Light Infantry Division, one of Lord Raglan's intimate friends and trusted counsellors who acted as his second in command. Were there any orders for him? Lord Lucan asked. None whatever, Sir George answered.

It was a horribly humiliating position. Where was the fulfilment of the promises, the fine words, with which he had been cajoled before he left for Varna? But Lucan's obstinacy was iron; he was not going to let Raglan break him; he was general in command of the cavalry division, and in command he would remain. He took up quarters at Varna and turned his attention to such troops as he could put his hands on. Part of the Heavy Brigade was accessible, and the 4th Light Dragoons, a regiment of the Light Brigade, arrived late, and was kept at Varna. It was the first time that he had been in actual contact with his division, the first time he had been able to handle the troops under his command. Even a small force was better than nothing, and he was eager. Field days were ordered, and there was to be a review before the Turkish Commander-in-Chief. The result was disastrous. Seventeen years had passed since Lord Lucan had handled a regiment on the parade ground, and in the interval cavalry drill had been changed, in particular, the words of command had been completely altered. Neither officers nor men understood what Lord Lucan meant. His words of command were obsolete, and at the review he "clubbed" the 5th Dragoon Guards—got them into confusion. "It was as if one of the cavalry commanders of the Thirty Years' War had risen from his grave to take command after the fashion of his day," wrote Anthony Bacon, that old enemy over whose head he had bought the command of the 17th Lancers in 1826.

Lord Lucan's method of solving the problem was characteristic: the troops were to discontinue using the new drill and return to the old. "With sternness of will," wrote Lord George Paget, who commanded the 4th Light Dragoons, "instead of bending to the new order of things, he sought to unteach his troops the drill which they had been taught, and to substitute for this the drill which in his time was in vogue." In practice the change he ordered proved impossible: the officers could not teach the men because there was no way of teaching the officers. Lord Lucan obstinately insisted on the old method, however, and his officers became apprehensive.

With the 4th Dragoon Guards, now a major, was William Forrest, who had prudently exchanged out of the 11th Hussars in 1844. He had no confidence in Lord Lucan, he wrote from Varna in August:

. . . for he and Cardigan would be certain to have a row immediately. Lord Lucan is a very clever sharp fellow, but he has been so long on the shelf he does not even know the words of command . . . he has had a lot of field days which we only hope may have taught him and his staff something, for certainly nobody else has learned anything. If he is shown by the drill book that he is wrong, he says, "Ah, I'd like to know who wrote that book, some Farrier I suppose." . . . Officers who drill under him are puzzled to know what he means when he gives a word of command. . . . I write all this to you in order that if any mishap should occur to the cavalry, you may be able to form a correct idea how it happened.

Meanwhile General Scarlett of the Heavy Brigade, finding all authority assumed by Lord Lucan, remarked to William Forrest that he was "nobody here," and wisely went up country.

By this time Lord Cardigan, at Devna with the bulk of the cavalry, had received Lord Lucan's reprimand of June 11 and, on June 15, in a towering rage wrote off a reply.

I consider that being sent forward in advance of the Army, and not being very far distant at the present moment from the enemy, that my command may be considered as a separate and detached command, and that I am not bound to anybody except the general officer in command of the forces in the country in which the brigade under my command is serving. . . . I beg to state that it is my intention to take an early opportunity of submitting an appeal to General Lord Raglan upon the subject for his decision.

It was a letter no subordinate officer could reasonably expect to write to his military superior and survive, and Lord Lucan instantly forwarded it with a formal complaint to Lord Raglan. At this point, in the opinion of William Howard Russell, *The Times* correspondent who was with the Army, Lord Raglan should have understood that it was impossible for the two men to work together, and removed one of them. However, Lord Raglan preferred to overlook Lord Cardigan's behaviour and directed his adjutant-general, General Estcourt, a man renowned for tact in difficult negotiations, to smooth things over with Lord Lucan once more.

I am directed to say, [wrote General Estcourt to Lord Lucan on June 20] that the misapprehensions which Lord Cardigan has entertained of the nature of his command, have already been rectified by private communication from me, written by Lord Raglan's desire. Lord Cardigan, I am sure, will quite understand now, that you may call for what returns you think necessary to inform yourself of the condition of the cavalry belonging to your division, and that you may and ought to visit detached parties, and look to their efficiency in every respect for which you are responsible to Lord Raglan. I have not returned you an official letter in answer to yours because the misapprehension being corrected it is better to consider the question as never having arisen in a formal shape.

Lord Lucan received the letter with indignation. On June 22 he wrote to General Estcourt that he was very far from satisfied with the treatment accorded to Lord Cardigan.

Though Lord Cardigan may now better understand his position, he has written a very insubordinate letter to his commanding officer, and secondly has appealed to the Commander of the Forces *direct* against the official act of his commanding officer and not through that commanding officer, as is required by the regulations of the Army.

Lord Raglan nevertheless still preferred to overlook and

soothe; and, instructed by him, General Estcourt merely wrote in reply that Lord Raglan thought all that was essential had been done when it was explained to Lord Cardigan that he had taken a wrong view of his command.

However, I am directed to add, now, that no departure from the regular and usual channel of communication will be permitted in this Army; and therefore the point which you urge ought to be noticed as an irregularity of Lord Cardigan's will be the subject of a letter to him, but it will be a *private* communication, as indeed all the correspondence on this occasion has been.

Nothing, in fact, was to be done. Lord Cardigan remained as he was, Lord Lucan continued to be superfluous, furious, and ignored.

On June 24 Lord Lucan, finding his position intolerable, wrote again imploring Lord Raglan to allow him to leave Varna. There was nothing for him to do, the majority of the cavalry had long since arrived, he had called on Sir George Brown and been told there were no orders for him: "I beg that I should not be any longer totally separated from the division to which I have been appointed, and which I shall be supposed to command." He was refused. It was Lord Raglan's special wish, wrote Lord de Ros, that Lord Lucan should remain at Varna; certain detachments of cavalry had still to arrive, and Lord Raglan wished Lord Lucan "to inspect each troop carefully before it disembarks."

Meanwhile in the delightful surroundings of Devna, a beautiful valley like an English park, with trees, streams, banks of wild flowers, and a profusion of wild grapes, Lord Cardigan had recovered his health and thirsted for action. Very little hope of action seemed to lie before him; his brigade was occupied in nursing its horses back to health, cholera was rampant, supplies short; nothing was thought of but difficulties relating to water, food, forage, and sick nursing. Suddenly came a surprising sound: on June 21 and 22 a cannonade was heard, and on the

23rd a startling rumour reached the camp. The siege of Silistria had been raised.

On the 25th the rumour was confirmed: Silistria was free. The Turks under the command of British officers from the Indian Army had driven off the Russians unaided; the task which the British Army had come to Bulgaria to perform had been executed before they had struck a blow. Now the Russian army was retreating across the Danube.

Without troubling to inform Lord Lucan, Lord Raglan sent written orders to Lord Cardigan to make a reconnaissance; he was to proceed to the banks of the Danube and discover "if the Russian Army was still on this side of the Danube." On June 25, with 121 troopers of the 8th Hussars and 75 of the 13th Light Dragoons, Cardigan vanished into the interior. It was an opportunity after his own heart; a swift, daring, brilliant exploit. Only the minimum of food and forage was taken, and no tents; speed was to be the object; the pace was to be as rapid as was humanly possible. The little force reached the banks of the Danube on June 29 and found that the Russians had already retreated across the river. Lord Cardigan, however, on his own responsibility patrolled the banks of the river, returning by Silistria and the ancient fortress of Shumla. No close observation was kept on the enemy and no information of military usefulness was gained, though he observed with interest many decaying monuments of antiquity. From the further bank of the Danube the Russian General Luders through his glasses watched with interest the English horsemen galloping about and, though they were within range of his guns, forbore to fire.

But though no casualties were inflicted by the enemy, Lord Cardigan's patrol took a fearful toll of the unfortunate horses. Heat, overwork, want of forage and water resulted in piteous and, in the opinion of the army, unnecessary suffering. Mrs. Duberly saw the patrol return on July 11, "and a piteous sight it was—men on foot driving and goading the wretched, wretched, horses; three or four of which could hardly stir. There seems to have been much unnecessary suffering, a cruel parade of death." An *araba*, a Turkish cart, brought in men who had collapsed. They had slept on the ground, lived on salt pork, and never taken their clothes off for seventeen days.

Five horses had dropped dead, seventy-five were dying; besides this total loss, many would never be fit again for anything but light work, through fever in the feet. The net result of Lord Cardigan's patrol, christened by the army "the Sore-Back Reconnaissance," was the loss to the Light Brigade, already short of horses, of nearly a hundred of their best chargers. Four days later it was necessary to send a second reconnaissance to cover the same ground; twelve mounted artillery men, with pack saddles, tents, and baggage animals, went out under one officer. Men and animals returned safe and sound with valuable information as to the dispositions of the enemy.

Lord Cardigan, however, was more than satisfied; he had led the patrol, "borne it well," eaten "almost the same food as the men," and only changed his clothes once. On July 20 he was promoted major-general. It was a triumph.

His return to Devna was followed by a fresh outburst of activity, and the Light Brigade, grumbling and sulky, was drilled, polished, pipe-clayed, oiled as if Devna Camp were a smart cavalry station. "Our doings . . . will make you laugh," wrote Major Cresswell of the 11th Hussars. "The Major-General amuses us by giving us regulation Phoenix Park Field days —such a bore he is—comes round stables just as if he were Colonel, instead of Major-General." Lieutenant Seager of the 8th wrote, "That *mighty* man Cardigan is annoying everyone; he does all he can to knock up both horses and men before the work begins in earnest."

Unhappily something infinitely more serious than the irritating and exacting ways of Major-General Lord Cardigan was wrong at Devna. Had the commanders of the British Army enquired from local inhabitants, they would have been told that the beautiful valley, with its foliage, its fruits, and its cool, refreshing streams, was known as the valley of death; cholera stalked there, and the Turks shunned it. The number of cholera cases rose by leaps and bounds. The harsh routine of polishing, blacking, pipe-claying, became inexpressibly gloomy, and the men, discontented and resentful, growled that they had come out to fight, not to die.

All this time Lord Lucan, stranded at Varna, was doing his best to revenge himself on Cardigan by harassing him, criticising and correcting him and curtailing his authority. He demanded returns and reports of the most detailed kind, issued minute directions for hobbling troop horses and drawing baggage carts, for greasing and oiling, for burnishing and watering, and requested assurances that the directions were carried out. He sharply and frequently put Cardigan in his place: no appointments were to be made by Lord Cardigan within the brigade and no courts martial were to be held without permission from his superior officer, Lord Lucan. Small matters received Lucan's unremitting attention: a constant subject of correspondence was the loss of five kits from the transport *Shooting Star*. Cardigan retorted by sending down returns which were incomplete or unsigned, never supplying explanations, and ignoring requests.

At the end of July Lord Lucan suddenly discovered that the Light Brigade had vanished again. Though he had not been consulted or informed by either Lord Raglan or Lord Cardigan, the Light Brigade had been moved up country to a village called Yeni-Bazaar, twenty-eight miles from Devna.

Yeni-Bazaar was a high, bare, treeless plateau "like an immense race-course," with a valley in the middle. It was hoped to leave cholera behind at Devna, but the troops brought cholera with them. Deaths became so numerous that military funerals were discontinued; the Dead March in Saul sounded so incessantly over the camp that an order went out that it was not to be played, and cholera victims were buried silently at night.

Yeni-Bazaar, hot, shadeless, and infinitely remote, was detested by the troops. Lord Cardigan, however, made himself comfortable. There was a little oasis near the camping ground, with a spring, called a fountain, and two large trees, the only shade within miles. Here he pitched his camp, occupying two large marquees, one for dining, the other for sleeping; his staff, cooks, grooms, and valets took up the rest of the shade.

Now at the fountain there was a good supply of water [wrote Sergeant Mitchell of the 13th Hussars], quite enough to have supplied the whole brigade for cooking purposes, had we been permitted to use it; but a sentry was posted on it night and day to prevent any man taking any. . . . Instead of being able to get water at about 100 yards, we had to go upwards of a mile, and climb a steep hill on our return loaded.

In spite of the heat, protected by the shade of his oasis and on a diet of "tough meat and excellent champagne," Major-General Lord Cardigan preserved his energy, and the brigade continued with drill after drill and field days twice a week. But the spirits of the troops daily sank lower. "I would rather do anything than continue here," wrote Lieutenant Seager of the 8th Hussars. "No one knows what we are here for or what we are going to do," wrote Major Cresswell. Captain Maude of the Horse Artillery christened the British army in Bulgaria "the army of no occupation." Captain Robert Portal of the 4th Light Dragoons noticed "the men and officers getting daily more dispirited and more disgusted with their fate. They do nothing but bury their comrades; they have no excitement to relieve the horrid monotony of their camp life. . . . There is nothing in the world to do but listen to growls and grumbling from all sides, from the highest to the lowest, of the dreadful mortality that is decimating our once magnificent Army."

Down at Varna Lord Raglan was saying openly that he wondered why more officers who could get away remained in such a vile country. He had been brought up in a period when British officers of aristocratic regiments, though brave as lions, did not, and were not expected to, take readily to discomfort. Gronow relates an experience in the Peninsula with a young officer of the Hussars who joined his regiment with a stud of blood-horses, three grooms, and two carriages, one of which carried his plate and linen. On being ordered to outpost duty and required to leave his comforts behind, he remarked that campaigning was not for gentlemen, and went home.

All this misery occurred in the pause following the relief of Silistria. It was a pause of uncertainty; while the army waited and drilled and grumbled and died, their fate was quivering in the balance. The commanders of the French and British armies were nerving themselves to take an all-important decision; should they or should they not invade the Crimea? Though the ostensible aim of the war was to protect the Turks in the Danube provinces from the invading Russians, the real object, frankly avowed in the press, was to destroy Sebastopol and end Russian naval power in the Mediterranean. But nothing had gone according to plan. The difficulties with transport, with commissariat, above all, the cholera, had had frightening results, and the British army was now in very poor shape.

The Guards Division, for instance, was so enfeebled by sickness that the men could march no more than five miles a day, and that only if their packs were carried for them; moreover, which to a few observers appeared even more serious, the defects in the organisation of the British Army were serious and disquieting. What might not happen, they asked, if that organisation was subjected to the strain of mobile operations and a protracted campaign? But—and this was very present in Lord Raglan's mind—none of these unpleasant facts were known at home. They were not known because Lord Raglan had not mentioned them. The nation was expecting every morning to read the news of the fall of Sebastopol, and the Government, anxious for a victory to justify the sums expended on the expeditionary force, was pressing the Commander-in-Chief to invade.

In the end a decision of the utmost recklessness was taken. The British Army, riddled with cholera, deficient in transport, in baggage animals, in supplies of all kinds, was to be landed on a hostile coast, in an unknown country—the only reconnaissance of the Crimea had been some observations taken from the sea at a distance. And it was to attack a fortress of extraordinary strength defended by the most numerous army in the civilised world. The coast had not been blockaded, and the strength of the garrison was perfectly unknown. It might be, said Lord Raglan, that fifty thousand men would oppose the invasion, it might be a hundred thousand.

Preparations began at the end of July, and the final decision was taken at a council of war held at Varna on August 24. Lord Raglan asked Sir George Brown for his opinion, and it happened that Sir George kept a note of his reply, which he later handed to Kinglake.

You and I [he told Lord Raglan] are accustomed, when in any great difficulty, or when any important question is proposed to us, to ask ourselves how the Great Duke would have acted under similar circumstances. Now I tell your Lordship that without more certain information than you appear to have obtained with regard to this matter, that great man would not have accepted the responsibility of undertaking such an enterprise as that which is now proposed to you.

It was observed that, after this incident, Lord Raglan did not ask Sir George for his opinion as frequently as before.

The Army received the decision with delight. It meant movement, action, escape from the sickening alternation of boredom and death. Confidence returned. The Crimea was painted as everything that was healthy and salubrious, "the Isle of Wight of Russia"; the stories disparaging Russian troops, of dummy rifles, of regiments driven into battle at pistol point, were revived. Bets were laid that a representation of the victorious storming of Sebastopol by the British Army would be the show piece at Astley's Circus at Christmas.

Throughout this period Lord Lucan was at Varna. He might

just as well have been in England. He received no instructions, he was neither consulted nor informed; and now he learned that part of the Heavy Brigade, in addition to the Horse Artillery, had been sent up to Yeni-Bazaar to be under Lord Cardigan's command. While he, Lucan, had no troops at all, Cardigan was commanding the greater part of the cavalry division. It would have been impossible not to feel resentment, and Lord Lucan's resentment was devouring. He became a man with a grievance. The grievance took possession of him. The favour shown to Cardigan became an obsession. For him the important issue of the war was not so much to gain victory over Russia as over Lord Raglan and Lord Cardigan.

On August 25 the troops began to move in earnest, and on the 27th Lord Lucan received instructions at last, but of the most electrifying nature. The Light Brigade and the Heavy Brigade were to be prepared to embark at shortest notice, but he, Lord Lucan, the divisional general, was to play no part in the preparations; all arrangements, including those for embarkation, were to be taken entirely out of his hands, nor did he receive any instructions to proceed with his division. When the cavalry division sailed on active service, its divisional general was to be left behind.

9

The key to this extraordinary situation lay in the strange and contradictory character of Lord Raglan. At first sight he appeared all benevolence; "Lord Raglan has arrived—kind-looking old gent," Lieutenant Seager had written from Varna. Nobly handsome, his presence radiated graciousness and serenity, while in personal relationships he exercised an almost irresistible charm. His staff adored him. "I never met a man who had the power to please so completely whomsoever he chose," wrote one of his aides. His personal courage was astonishing: he was both utterly indifferent to danger and stoical under pain. After his right arm was amputated, without an anæsthetic on the field of Waterloo, he called out, "Here, don't take that arm away until I have taken the ring off the finger!"

And yet, as the commander of an army, as a general directing troops in battle, there was something disturbing about Lord Raglan. Without the military trappings, the uniform, the gold lace, one would never have guessed him to be a soldier. His beautiful face looked like the face of an ecclesiastic—a cardinal of the Renaissance, perhaps—urbane, subtle, diplomatic. Ruthlessness, determination were wanting.

In fact, he had hardly been, in the ordinary sense of the word, a soldier at all. True, his career had been a military career, and he had attained very high rank, but he had risen not as a leader of men, but as a diplomatist. The work of his life had been to make himself the second self of the Duke of Wellington. From 1808 until Wellington's death in 1852 he had stood at the Duke's right hand, interposing between him and the world, softening, with the happiest results, the harshnesses, the acerbities, the occasional ferocities which formed part of that great man's extraordinary character. He had performed a work of immense and far-reaching importance, but it had been work of such a nature as absolutely to unfit him for command. For more than forty years he had been subservient to one of the most powerful minds in the history of the world. He had never taken decisions, he had never conceived plans, he had executed them. For more than forty years it had been his function to take second place, to depend, to admire, to look up. He had never stood alone.

His experience of personally handling an army on active service was non-existent. His career had been on the staff. He had never commanded so much as a battalion in the field; he had never led troops into battle in his life.

He cherished, moreover, beneath the urbanity, the gracious charm, ideas of the most rigid, the most reactionary description. His principles were fiercely aristocratic; his attachment to his family connections and his class was religious in its intensity. Liberalism, democracy, he strenuously opposed. Rank was of overwhelming importance to him, talent of little consequence.

But the final, the hopeless disability was the fact that he was sixty-five years of age. Though his appearance was physically youthful, his mind was tired, "schooled down by long, flat years of office life," and it was impossible for him to learn anything new. Moreover, he hated to be bothered. When Sir John Adye joined Lord Raglan's staff, he was advised, "Never to trouble him more than absolutely necessary with details. Listen carefully, anticipate his wishes and make light of difficulties."

As old men do, Lord Raglan lived much in the past, and the glorious days of the Duke and the Peninsula were always in his mind. Frightful embarrassments were the result. He could not recollect how totally the situation had changed, and he covered his staff with confusion by forgetting that the French were now his allies and invariably talking of "the French" when he meant "the enemy."

It was an evil chance which placed such a man in command of Lord Cardigan and Lord Lucan. To be calm, to be reasonable, to adjust, to compromise were ideas whose meaning they could not remotely conceive. Lord Raglan's policy had been to preserve peace by keeping the two apart; according to his present plan, Lord Lucan, though left behind at Varna, was to console himself with the fact that he did, after all, command the cavalry division; while Lord Cardigan, though subordinate in rank, was to have the satisfaction of a chance to distinguish himself on active service.

It was a plan which had not the faintest chance of success. Lord Lucan, obsessed with the furious conviction that Lord Raglan was favouring Lord Cardigan, was the last man to accept the position proposed for him, and it was undeniable that Lord Raglan did have a personal regard for Lord Cardigan. He had given Cardigan permission to write him private letters, and on August 20, at the very moment when Cardigan had appropriated the fountain and the shade at Yeni-Bazaar for his exclusive use, he wrote, "I am very sorry I never see you now. My consolation is that you are doing your duty like a man."

On August 29, the day after receiving Lord Raglan's instructions, Lord Lucan wrote him an unanswerable letter which ended any hope that he would consent to be conveniently shelved.

My Lord—Last evening I received a memorandum, instructing me to direct "that the regiments of the Light Cavalry Brigade be held in readiness to embark at shortest notice under the Earl of Cardigan" and another memorandum stating that "the internal distribution is left to the direction of the general officer commanding." Brigadier-General Scarlett had already informed me that your Lordship had stated to him that the Heavy Brigade would be embarked at a later period under his command. I find myself left, as on former occasions, without instructions regarding myself, the commander of the division, except, as I read them, not to accompany the Light Cavalry Brigade and not to interfere with their embarkation. . . . I cannot conceal from myself, what has not been concealed from the Army—that during the four months I have been under your Lordship's command, I have been separated, as much as it was possible to do so, from my division; being left at Kulali when the force was at Varna, and at Varna when it removed to Devna, and I have been left to discharge duties more properly befitting an inferior officer; whilst to Lord Cardigan has been intrusted, from the day of his arrival, the command of nearly the whole of the cavalry, having under his charge the Light Brigade, half the Heavy Brigade and any horse artillery attached to the cavalry.

If my position has been little consonant with my feeling, my duties have been difficult, having to provide for circumstances and occurrences not under my control, and distant. Though naturally unwilling to divest myself of any responsibility which ought to belong to a divisional commander, I have often felt that I could not in fairness be considered responsible for cavalry always out of reach of me, and under the command of an officer like Lord Cardigan, who, as your Lordship is aware, began to repudiate my authority altogether, and who has, consistently with that view of his position, left me as ignorant of the stationing of the troops under his command, their duties, efficiency and discipline as he could. I believe I can affirm that Lord Cardigan has never, on any one occasion, voluntarily offered information on any one of these points, or on any other which a periodical return would not divulge. The commander of the division was left in entire ignorance of the marching of his Lordship's patrol, its return, and of everything connected with it: again, of the movements of the cavalry to Yeni-Bazaar etc. etc.—in short of everything.

It is a subject of remark that I do not command the division; it is said it is not left to me, to prevent any collision between Lord Cardigan and myself. Now, as I happen never to have come into collision, or had a disagreement with a single officer during the very many years I served in the Army, and during the twelve years I commanded a regiment, no apprehension of the sort should be entertained of me, but of Lord Cardigan, whom it might be supposed was not to be controlled by any superior authority. It is surely unfair, on that account, to make his Lordship independent of his immediate commanding officer, and to confide to him duties which the custom of the service properly gives to the divisional commander.

The issue was now in the open—Lord Raglan must choose between Lord Cardigan and Lord Lucan. But the Commander-in-Chief had no choice—in fact, had never had any choice. Lord Lucan had been appointed to the command of the cavalry, and if he insisted, command them he must. Raglan had done his best for Cardigan, but if Lucan chose to insist on his rights, the Commander-in-Chief was helpless and Cardigan must make the best of it.

Lord Raglan went to see Lord Lucan. Lord de Ros was ill—sun bathing in the glare of Bulgaria had brought on fever—and Raglan conducted the interview himself. He made one last effort to effect a compromise. Would not Lord Lucan remain behind until the Heavy Brigade, who were sailing later, embarked, instead of sailing with the Light Brigade? Lucan refused. It had, he pointed out, been laid down by the Duke during the Peninsular campaign that a divisional general might accompany any part of his division he thought fit. The Duke's ruling was conclusive, Lord Raglan gave way, and Lucan obtained everything he wished for, and more. He was to sail with the Light Brigade in the steamship *Simla;* Lord Cardigan was to have it made clear to him beyond any possibility of doubt that he was to be commanded by and that he was to obey Lord Lucan; and finally, to establish the position of Lord Lucan more firmly, he was to be promoted from major-general to lieutenant-general. The appointment was gazetted a week later on September 6.

The Commander-in-Chief made one condition—the letter, the unanswerable letter—must be withdrawn. Lucan consented, and once more one of his letters became officially non-existent.

Meanwhile Lord Cardigan was moving down from Yeni-Bazaar in high spirits. The separate command was in his grasp: he was, he had been semi-officially informed, to be recognised as responsible only to headquarters. Captain Wetherall, one of Lord Raglan's aides, who brought up the order to proceed to Varna for embarkation, had told him that he was to go to the Crimea in sole command of the Light Brigade: he had been named at headquarters as commanding officer of the Light Brigade on active service in the Crimea, and Lord Lucan was to be left behind. Lucan was to busy himself with returns and stores, while he, Cardigan, independently commanded the fighting portion of the force.

He arrived at Varna to have his hopes dashed. Everything he had been told previously was contradicted. He was not to proceed to the Crimea in sole command of the Light Brigade, Lord Lucan was sailing with him, Lord Lucan would be in command, and he would be subordinate to Lord Lucan.

It was a bitter blow. "From this date all pleasure ceased in the command which remained to me," he wrote in his diary. "I had been actively employed, almost from the day of landing at Scutari on the 24th of May, and had been sent forward in command of the Light Cavalry Brigade, and had had the Horse Artillery attached to me, and two or three of the Heavy Dragoon regiments placed under my command"; but from the moment of arrival at Varna "my position in the cavalry was totally changed."

Nevertheless, in spite of the record in his diary, Cardigan was very far from accepting his fate. He possessed the type of mind which by brooding on facts is able to transform them. He was the kind of man who talks incessantly of what is on his mind, repeats hundreds of times and in the same words his own version of events, ignores his adversary's point of view, and so ultimately is able to convince himself that what has happened has not happened, and that black is white.

He brooded, he talked, he complained; the determination to command separately crept back. Presently he was able to view what had occurred in a very different light. He then had an interview with Lord Raglan, and came away in the belief that

Raglan had assured him once again that there would be no interference by Lord Lucan. Lucan would sail with the Light Brigade certainly, but the Light Brigade was to remain Cardigan's command. When Cardigan embarked for the Crimea, he was as inflexibly determined as ever not to be commanded by Lucan. Nor did he let any small opportunity of annoying his brother-in-law slip. Mrs. Duberly, who had become friendly with Lord Cardigan at Yeni-Bazaar, was now in Varna hoping to go on with the army to the Crimea. Lord Lucan, however, declared that she was to go no further: he "absolutely declined" to allow her to proceed on active service with the Light Brigade. Cardigan interceding with Lord Raglan on her behalf, received a snub—Mrs. Duberly was certainly not to sail. When Cardigan himself brought her Raglan's answer, she burst into tears, upon which Cardigan, "touched," told her "Should you think it proper to disregard the prohibition, I will not offer any opposition to your doing so." A plot was devised, and while Lord Lucan was pacing up and down the quay, determined to stop Mrs. Duberly should she attempt to get on board, she managed to have herself smuggled on Lord Cardigan's transport the *Himalaya* disguised as a Turkish woman and sitting in a native cart. Lord Lucan, she wrote triumphantly, missed her because he was looking for a "lady."

The embarkation of the army was a scene of utter confusion, since the lack of space which caused so much hardship on the way out had not been rectified. A typical case was the *Simoon*. Into this vessel, an old screw man-of-war with the guns removed, but otherwise not adapted for the transport of troops, were marched 1,300 men. Below decks became packed, and the men overflowed on to the deck; 200 were removed, but the ship was still so full that the men could not turn round.

In order to pack the army somehow into the transports, sanitary requirements were disregarded, and men were crammed in wherever there was an inch of space. But still it proved impossible to accommodate both the army and its equipment. The order being given to strip everything to the bone, tents, medicine chests, and ambulances were carried ashore. Animals had to be left behind, including the baggage animals which had been collected with infinite difficulty in Bulgaria; cavalry officers were parted from their chargers and Lieutenant Seager had to leave his favourite "Jerry." At the last moment a depot was hastily formed where 1,200 officers' horses and 4,000 baggage animals were left. Most of these, including Jerry, starved to death.

As the first transports were about to sail, a mob of weeping, screaming women rushed on to the quay. The hundreds of soldiers' wives who had come with the army to Varna had been forbidden to follow to the Crimea, but no kind of provision had been made for them; they had neither food, shelter, money nor any means of getting away from Varna. There was nothing for it, late though it was, but to cram them also into the transports.

On September 4 Lord Lucan sailed in the *Simla* and on the 5th Lord Cardigan followed in the *Himalaya,* a converted P. & O. steamship, and the largest of the transports, carrying 700 men and 390 horses. The transports were to rendezvous with the fleet in Balchik Bay, fifteen miles south of Varna, and be convoyed to the coast of the Crimea.

With thankful hearts the army turned their backs on Bulgaria. But cholera embarked with them, and cholera had raged in the fleet as it waited in Balchik Bay. The disgusting sights of the bay at Varna were repeated at Balchik. Men who died of cholera were flung into the sea with weights at their feet, but the weights were too light; as the bodies decomposed they rose to the surface, the weights kept them upright, and they floated head and shoulders out of the water, hideous in the sun. At Varna the dreadful spectres had bobbed about the transports as if watching their comrades embark; at Balchik they seemed to be waiting for the army to arrive. Cholera was soon rife in the crowded transports, and at night splash after splash told of fresh bodies adding to the horrors of the bay.

By September 7 all transports had arrived, and at 4:30 A.M.

a fleet of more than six hundred vessels sailed out of Balchik
Bay. The ships were formed into lines, half a mile apart and four
to five miles long; each steamer towed two sailing ships, and
each line was led by a man-of-war.

On September 8 the British fleet kept a rendezvous with the
French fleet off the mouth of the Danube, upon which both fleets
hove to, and, inexplicably, paused. All through the 9th and the
10th the immense and conspicuous collection of vessels remained
at anchor, boats went to and fro, visits were paid, and Lord
Cardigan and Lord Lucan quarrelled. On the 8th Cardigan had
issued an authority for a court martial, and was sharply reminded he had no right to do so—"The Lieutenant-General alone
has the right." On the heels of this message came a memorandum
reminding Major-General Lord Cardigan that immediately on
landing he would be required to submit embarkation returns to
Lieutenant-General the Earl of Lucan. Cardigan lost his temper
and wrote a furious letter.

I beg that the Lieutenant-General will intimate to me the exact
position which I hold in this expedition. I beg to state that the Commander of the Forces, Lord Raglan, previous to leaving Varna, informed
me in the most distinct terms, that Lieutenant-General the Earl of
Lucan had distinctly informed his Lordship that, though he accompanied the expedition, he did not in any way intend to interfere or
deprive me of the command of the Light Cavalry Brigade of this
division.

Since no immediate reply came from Lucan, Cardigan sent
over a further letter—it was "impossible for him to carry out his
duties with any satisfaction until his position in the expedition
was defined." Lucan instantly seized the opportunity to put
Cardigan in his place.

To circulate a memorandum that disembarkation returns would be
required immediately on landing [he wrote], a memorandum which has
been circulated to all senior officers, is not an irregularity, still less disrespectful or any encroachment on your authority and Lord Lucan
much regrets that you should entertain what his Lordship considers a

great misconception. In reference to the rest of your letter, the Lieutenant-General instructs me to add, that whilst he knows his own authority he equally respects yours; and that your position as a Major-General commanding a brigade in the Cavalry Division, will not, so far as depends on him, differ from that held by the other brigadiers, of whom there are so many in the six divisions of this Army.

As Lord Cardigan received this letter, thé fleet sailed again.

The pause at the mouth of the Danube had, in fact, an explanation, extraordinary beyond the wildest guess. The army had been embarked before it was decided where it was going. The Crimea was to be invaded, certainly, but the point at which the invasion was to take place was by no means agreed. Some weeks earlier Sir George Brown had sailed along the coast of the Crimea and through his field-glasses had picked out a likely bay, but he was notoriously short-sighted, and the French now asserted the bay was too small; a second bay selected by Sir George was known to be fortified, and no landing could take place without enormous loss. It was decided that the fleet must wait while the commanders of the French and British armies personally examined the coast of the Crimea. At 6 A.M. on the morning of the 9th Lord Raglan's steamer, the *Caradoc* with the *Agamemnon* and two French vessels sailed away from the fleet. Sebastopol was reached on the morning of the 10th and approached so closely that Russian officers could be seen in front of their troops, looking through their field-glasses at the generals in brilliant uniforms on the deck of the *Caradoc*. The British officers thereupon saluted, "which courtesy was returned with an air of restrained formality."

When the *Caradoc* returned early in the morning of the 11th, it had been decided to land at a bay near Eupatoria, bearing the ill-omened name of Calamita Bay.

On the afternoon of the 11th the fleet began to sail towards Eupatoria. As on the voyage out, great suffering was being endured by the horses. After the hardships of the voyage from England, they had been kept short of forage and water and worked hard in the burning sun; now they were once more shut up into foul airless holds and horribly overcrowded. On the *War Cloud*, which followed the main fleet on September 25, one hundred horses were packed into space designed for fifty-six, and no proper head collars for tying up were provided. When the ship ran into one of the sudden gales common in the Black Sea, seventy-five of the horses perished.

The troops were not much more fortunate. Three days was the time allowed for crossing the Black Sea, but the troops who had embarked earliest were at sea for seventeen days. Fresh provisions were exhausted, and for the last five days the rations were salt pork and biscuit; water ran short; and worst of all, the crowded, stinking transports were a hot bed of cholera.

The main cause of all these difficulties was the incompetence of the staff. Lord Raglan had surrounded himself (but, then, the Duke had also surrounded himself) with his aristocratic connections. Five of his nephews held appointments on his staff, and the staffs of other generals were almost without exception similarly composed of relatives or friends. Though the Senior Department of the Royal Military College, Sandhurst, precursor of the Staff College, had been in existence for more than sixty years and was designed to train officers of promise for the performance of staff duties, only 15 of the 221 officers who held staff appointments in Lord Raglan's army had passed through the Senior Department. Against "Indian" officers Lord Raglan's prejudice was very strong. The fact that "Indian" officers were the only men who had recent experience of war weighed nothing with him, and from the moment of first preparing for the campaign instructions had been issued that "Indian" officers were to be discouraged from joining the expeditionary army.

On the eve of embarkation a change of great importance took place on the staff: Lord de Ros, a victim of sun bathing, was invalided out, and his place was taken by General Airey. Richard Airey was fifty-one years of age, and had achieved a distinguished military career, without, however, seeing active service. He had entered the Army at eighteen, risen by purchase to be lieutenant-colonel at the age of thirty-five, and had then been attached to the staff at the Horse Guards. After holding several important appointments, he was in 1854, at the outbreak of war, Military Secretary to the Commander-in-Chief, Lord Hardinge. The Duke of Wellington had thought very highly of Richard Airey, who had worked closely with Lord Raglan to whom he was devotedly attached. Indeed, he had been Lord Raglan's first choice for Quartermaster-General, but had declined, as he wished for duty in the field and had obtained a brigade of the Light Infantry Division. However, after Lord de Ros's collapse Lord Raglan pressed the appointment on him with the greatest urgency, and he accepted.

Richard Airey was a man of formidable character, ardent, urgent, imperative. Though the greater part of his life had been spent in administrative posts, he had had experience of a very different nature. With the Duke of Wellington's permission he had spent several years on the immense remote estates, almost territories, of his cousin, Colonel Talbot, famous in his day as the "recluse of upper Canada." Here he had built his own log house, lived for years in the wilderness cut off from civilisation, and established his authority over the wild, reckless inhabitants of his trackless forests.

His dominating characteristic was a desire for action; hesitation was unknown to him, and his capacity for taking instant decisions was backed by an impatient eloquence. No other man of anything approaching his quality was to be found on Lord Raglan's staff, and it was inevitable that he should swiftly gain an ascendancy, not only over his colleagues and subordinates, but also over Lord Raglan himself.

Yet though energy and decision were sorely needed by Lord Raglan, the part played by Richard Airey was not altogether approved by the Army. It was felt that he went too far, that his desire for action led him, devotedly attached to Lord Raglan though he was, to take too much on himself, that at times he absolutely put the words into Lord Raglan's mouth.

With him as aide-de-camp he brought a brilliant young cavalry officer, Capt. Lewis Edward Nolan, as energetic and decisive as himself. It was thought to be an admirable appointment. Captain Nolan was a "lion" in cavalry circles; indeed, Lord Cardigan had been anxious to have him on his staff, and no faintest foreboding of disaster crossed anyone's mind as Captain Nolan joined. It was in fact a fatal moment. This officer, brave, brilliant, devoted, was destined to be the instrument which sent the Light Brigade to its doom.

Lewis Edward Nolan was a romantic character. He had been brought up in Milan, where his father, Major Nolan, an Irishman of good family, was British vice-consul, and he had shown from childhood an extraordinary aptitude for riding. His father placed him in the Military Academy at Milan, and, before he was fourteen, he was famous as a prodigy of horsemanship. One of the Austrian imperial archdukes was struck by his feats, and, when Nolan was seventeen, he presented him with a commission in a crack Austrian cavalry regiment.

Nolan, highly intelligent, fanatically devoted to his profession, became a celebrity in cavalry circles. British cavalry officers on their travels made a point of visiting him, and presently he was urged not to deprive his own country of his talents—it was his duty to serve in the British cavalry. He left the Austrian army and obtained a commission in the 15th Hussars, where he was allowed to act as riding master, to break horses according to his own method, and to suggest many improvements. In 1852 he became a captain without purchase, and, in the following year, after visiting Russia, France, and Germany to study cavalry systems, he published two books which created a sensation in military circles—*Cavalry, Its History and Tactics* and *Nolan's System for Training Cavalry Horses*. It was his belief that, properly led, cavalry could do anything, even break infantry squares, but he maintained that British cavalry were wrongly led and wrongly trained, especially as regarded the horses. The root of his system for training horses was kindness. Young horses should never be punished or startled, but made confident in their riders. "Teach them that acquiescence will be followed by caresses. There must be sympathy between man and beast." He asserted that in less than two months under his system young horses could be prepared for the field. Both his books became textbooks for the cavalry, and his system of training horses was adopted by the American cavalry.

In manner, though he possessed great charm, Nolan was not English: the Irishman brought up in Italy was voluble, mercurial, dramatic. His enthusiasm knew no bounds, his whole heart and soul were bound up in his profession. As the transports slowly crossed the Black Sea, he was devoured by impatience, straining at the leash for the moment to come when the British cavalry would be in action and show what they could do. That great things would be accomplished he never doubted for a moment.

On September 11 news spread through the fleet that the landing would be made very shortly. Spirits rose, and the troops, who had been miserably silent, began to joke. The *Himalaya* forged ahead, trying to lead the fleet—"we conclude Cardigan is at the bottom of this, it looks like a piece of his silly vanity," wrote one of Lord Lucan's aides. At dawn on the 12th a dark line was visible on the port side. Everyone who could do so rushed on deck. The light brightened. The dark line was the coast of the Crimea.

In the *Himalaya* Mrs. Duberly noticed that the officers gazed at the future battle-ground quietly and silently, with the exception of Lord Cardigan, who was highly excited. "He begins to be all eager for the fray, and will be doing something or other directly he has landed I fancy." Throughout the 12th the fleet ran along the coast of the Crimea, and at noon on the 13th anchored off the pretty little town of Eupatoria. Then a party of officers went ashore with a summons to surrender, and the governor instantly submitted; his garrison, he said, consisted of two hundred invalids. He insisted, however, on performing his duties by fumigating the summons, in accordance with the sanitary regulations of the port, and he informed the officers of the party that when the army landed it must consider itself in strict quarantine.

The fleet then sailed on to Calamita Bay and began preparations for disembarkation. No effort was made to conceal its presence. Sunset guns reverberated from the cliffs, the sound of cavalry trumpets and infantry bugles floated across the water, and as night fell mast-head lights and lanterns shone from every ship, producing a strange effect of festivity.

The men were ordered to leave their packs behind in the transports, for dysentery and colic, in addition to cholera, had so ravaged them that in the opinion of the medical officers they had become too weak to carry their packs; they were to wrap up what they could in their blankets. Both men and officers were to land with three days' ration of cold salt pork, three days' ration of biscuit, and their canteens filled with water. Officers were to land in full dress with sword.

At eight o'clock on the morning of the 14th disembarkation began in golden sunshine. No enemy was in sight. The Russians might have sent down their field artillery and shelled the troops as they landed, since they could not fail to be aware of the operation in progress, but they did nothing. Presently, however, an officer with a troop of Cossacks appeared on the top of the cliffs at a distance of about a thousand yards. English officers, watching the officer eagerly through their field-glasses, observed that he wore a dark green uniform with silver lace, and rode a fine bay horse. "With great coolness," he proceeded to take notes and make sketches in a memorandum book, but though he was within rifle range the English did not fire.

The army disembarked in silence. The quiet of the bay, the absence of the enemy, the coolness of the watcher on the cliff top had an intimidating effect. Officers and men began to apprehend that the invasion of the Crimea was not merely bold, but rash. The British army had alighted on the shore of the Crimea like a flock of birds, but without wings to fly away. They had no transport, no ambulances, no litters, no food; they knew nothing whatever of the country ahead of them; they had no base. Within an easy march must be a Russian army, equipped with artillery and accompanied by Cossacks, but of the size and whereabouts of that army no one had any idea.

In the afternoon the weather suddenly changed, the sky became dark, the sea rose. Further disembarkation, including the disembarkation of the cavalry, had to be postponed. At sunset rain began to pelt pitilessly down. Water had been so short on board the transports that the men drank the rain like animals, scraped the water up from puddles, and struggled to fill their water bottles. There were no tents, and the men, almost all suffering from diarrhœa and dysentery, lay in rows on the wet ground behind the beach, wrapped in their soaking great-coats. Officers and men shared an equal misery. Sir George Brown lay under a cart, the Duke of Cambridge under a gun carriage. Hundreds of men were taken ill during the night; many died and the others were taken back to the beach, where they lay in rows waiting for the sick transports.

The French were slightly more fortunate. Though in Bulgaria they had been ravaged by cholera even more severely than the British, their arrangements were a little better. Their troops had not been packed quite so tightly into the transports, and every man had with him a small tent. These *tentes d'abri* or, as the British called them, dog tents, saved them from the rain.

Dawn brought a fierce burning sun. In an hour or two every trace of moisture had disappeared and the British were as short of water as they had been on the transports. Only one spring of fresh water was discovered to serve the whole army. A lake from which much had been hoped proved salt, and wells dug at General Airey's orders were without exception brackish.

During the morning of the 15th the cavalry disembarked,

Lord Cardigan, whose sympathy with his horses was not great, remarking on their poor condition. Next morning, nevertheless, Lord Raglan ordered him to proceed on an expedition into the interior. With a force of 250 cavalry, 250 infantry, and 2 guns from the Horse Artillery, he was to reconnoitre and bring in supplies. The expedition was a dismal failure. The condition of horses and men was so poor that they were unable to perform the work required of them, many of the infantry collapsed from dysentery and cholera and had to be brought back in *arabas*, the horses returned hardly able to stand. No information was obtained and only a few country carts brought in. Want of water, wrote Cardigan in his diary, was responsible for the condition of the horses. They had been short on board ship and there was none for them near Calamita Bay. The wells were a failure and all the rivers and streams in the neighbourhood were brackish.

No similar expedition was ever again ordered. One of the important functions of light cavalry is to sweep the country and bring in supplies. But supplies and information had both to be relinquished for Lord Raglan dared not run any risk. His position with regard to cavalry was deplorable.

Yet the Crimea was perfect cavalry country. Beyond the British position stretched a grassy steppe, without tree or shrub, rolling endlessly away into the distance. The Russian cavalry, including the famous and dreaded Cossacks, were an enormous force, and it must surely have been obvious from the first that cavalry would play a leading part in the Russian plan of campaign. Yet the Allies, though by invading the Crimea they had chosen to fight in cavalry country, had left themselves incredibly short of that arm. The French, practically speaking, had none; the English had only one division, and out of that the Heavy Brigade was not present—it had not yet left Varna. True, the small force of English cavalry was brilliant, the troops were of splendid quality, superbly disciplined and drilled, but they had

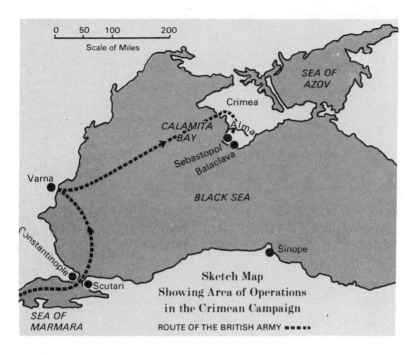

Sketch Map
Showing the Progress
of the British Army
in the Crimea

suffered severely from illness, and their once splendid mounts were "miserable in the extreme." If only a few more men and horses were lost, the cavalry would become ineffectual, and upon cavalry the success of the whole expedition might well depend.

Lord Raglan determined that his cavalry must be conserved, and in a phrase that ran through the army he declared that he would "keep the cavalry in a band-box."

And yet this shortage had not passed unobserved. Months ago it had become plain that the want of cavalry was highly dangerous, and Lord Raglan had been pressed to allow irregular cavalry to be raised. In India it had been proved over and over again that there were Englishmen who possessed the ability to discipline and lead Oriental troops, and such a man had come forward and placed himself at Lord Raglan's disposal. This was Colonel Beatson, who after joining the Bengal Army of the East India Company at the age of sixteen, had had a brilliant and adventurous career. In 1835, during the first Carlist war, he received permission to serve in Spain and rose to command a regiment. Returning to India he commanded the cavalry of the Nizam of Hyderabad, raised the Bundelkund, and by 1854 had received the thanks of the Government of India fourteen times. In 1853 he volunteered once more and was now in command of the Bashi-Bazooks. From "the fierce, devout and temperate Moslem horsemen of the Turkish provinces," whose hatred of Russia was traditional, Colonel Beatson proposed to raise a contingent of cavalry. Lord Raglan angrily refused. Firm believer in orthodoxy and discipline as he was, the very suggestion of irregular troops was vile to him, nor did he find Colonel Beatson's Indian career any recommendation. Colonel Beatson then offered his services to Lord Raglan in any capacity whatever, and was refused; he then made a similar application to Lord Lucan and was refused. General Scarlett of the Heavy Brigade, however, took him on his staff.

Meanwhile, through the 16th and 17th, the army waited at Calamita Bay, growing more and more impatient. "What the devil are we waiting for? Has the Czar caved in?" demanded a young officer of William Howard Russell. The lamentable truth was that fresh difficulties appeared every hour. The shortage of transport was desperate. It had been thought that pack animals could be collected from the country round, but animal life seemed to have disappeared from the Crimea. The beach became a scene of confusion. Stores were landed, but no wagons waited and there was nowhere to put them; sometimes they were piled on the beach, sometimes carried back to the ships. Cholera advanced with deadly strides—besides those who died, 1,500 men were sent down to the sick transports in twenty-four hours. When men woke in the morning, their first action was to enquire if the friends with whom they had talked the previous evening were still alive.

On the 17th the tents were landed and laboriously dragged up the beach, and the men slept in them that night. Next day Lord Raglan came to a decision; to wait longer was useless; for better or worse the army must push on. Stores must be abandoned, the troops must take what they could carry and march. Another three days' ration of salt pork and biscuit was to be prepared and water bottles filled. At 6 A.M. next day tents would be struck and the march begin.

On the morning of the 19th the British camp was in confusion. There was no transport for the tents, and they had to be dragged down to the ships again; men who had sickened with cholera during the night had to be taken to the transports; the corpses of those who had died had to be buried; there was difficulty in cooking the salt pork and the men had to take it raw; it was impossible for the whole army to fill its water bottles at the single spring. Meanwhile the French impatiently drummed and tootled, and sent over to enquire why the British delayed. Finally at 9 A.M. the Allied armies marched.

The spectacle was magnificent. Sixty thousand men marched in two great double columns, bands playing, colours flying. The French, since they had no cavalry, marched on the right, their

flank protected by the sea and the fleet. The British army was preceded by an advance guard of the 11th and 13th Hussars under
Lord Cardigan, covered on the left flank by the 8th Hussars and
17th Lancers under Lord Lucan, and in the rear by the 4th Light
Dragoons under Lord George Paget. Two dense columns, on the
left the Light Infantry Division and the 1st Division of Guards
and Highlanders, on the right the 2nd and 3rd Divisions, were
protected by a line of Riflemen, in front, rear and flank. The 4th
Division, to its disgust, was left to clear up the camp and follow
later. At the head of the army rode Lord Raglan, surrounded by
his staff.

It was a day of brilliant sunshine, the sky cloudless, the sea
as calm as a lake. The country, said the men, reminded them of
Salisbury Plain, downland, empty, rolling, and bare. The turf,
short and springy, gave out an odour of wild thyme, larks sang
overhead, hares started up and were halloa-ed down the line.

As the masses of troops, in wave after wave, breasted the
slopes to the sound of martial music, the neighing of horses and
the rumble of artillery, they seemed the incarnation of the
majesty of war. The lines glittered in the sunlight, rays darting
from epaulettes and buttons, from the brass ornaments on shakos
and pouches, from helmets and bayonets and lances. Uniforms
were brilliant—scarlet and green and royal blue, the scarlet
slashed with the dazzling white of cross-belts, whose effect was
to increase the height and formidable appearance of the British
soldier. The Guards marched in their bearskins, Hussars and
Horse Artillery displayed furred pelisses laced with gold, many
regiments wore plumes. Everywhere colour and brilliance caught
the eye, the richness of scarlet and gold, the shimmer of polished
steel. Round this splendid host circled the cavalry, most magnificent of all, men and horses alike splendid in cherry colour and
claret and blue, adorned with silver and gold lace and white and
scarlet plumes.

But it was better not to examine the splendid-looking army
too closely. From the beginning of the march, men, French as

well as British, were falling out from the ranks; many, seized with cholera, flung themselves on the ground and writhed in agony; many more, stupefied by weakness and exhaustion, staggered a few paces away from their comrades, fell prostrate, and refused to be roused—even fear of the Cossacks could not get them to their feet. In the British army the men were tortured with thirst. Great numbers had not been able to fill their water bottles at all, the day was overpoweringly hot, and the salt pork and biscuit which formed the sole ration dried the men's throats.

The bands stopped playing. The army was seen to be toiling. The high spirits of the start had evaporated, and hares were no longer halloa-ed; the columns plodded on under the blazing sun, bathed in sweat, leaving behind a trail of fallen men lying in the short grass. The rear was in utter confusion: men staggered along holding to the sides of such wagons as there were. Lady Errol, who had secured a mule, was festooned with rifles of men of the 60th who had no longer strength to carry them. After less than an hour a halt of fifty minutes was called, and the men flung themselves panting on the ground. When the march was resumed, cries of "Water! water!" were heard; after thirty minutes it was necessary to call another halt, and the men begged on their knees for water.

There was no water in the hot, glittering plain. No water, no shade, no sign of life. No enemy was to be seen and no sign of opposition, save that from time to time one or two Cossack horsemen would appear on a distant ridge, survey the marching host, and silently vanish. The men felt the silence to be sinister and uncanny; the tramp of sixty thousand feet was deadened by the grass, the gun carriages rumbled, from time to time a horse neighed, larks sang unceasingly in the cloudless blue sky —otherwise the army toiled on soundlessly.

Progress was slow: thirty minutes' marching was all that could be accomplished without a halt, and the columns moved spasmodically across the burning downs. As the sun rose to its height, the heat became unendurable and the men began to throw away such equipment as they had brought; and a trail of heavy brass-mounted shakos, mess tins, and overcoats marked where the army had passed. Men staggered from the ranks to fall prostrate in such numbers that the ground, wrote Lord George Paget, resembled a battle-field. His regiment brought up the rear, and he found "men and accoutrements of all sorts lying in such numbers that it was difficult for the regiments to thread their way through them."

At two o'clock the army struggled to the top of yet another ridge to see—water. Below them, in a hollow, glistened a stream, the Bulganek. The men could not be restrained. Discipline was flung to the winds, and, with the exception of the Highland Brigade, who were kept in hand by Sir Colin Campbell, the troops broke ranks and, elbowing each other fiercely, rushed down to drink, dashing into the water knee-deep to slake their torturing thirst. Suddenly the sound of a volley was heard—an engagement was taking place. The enemy had been met with and the cavalry were in action. At last Lord Cardigan and Lord Lucan were face to face with glory.

Unfortunately, from the moment of landing they had been on the worst possible terms. No longer separated, but in daily contact, they were, wrote Lord George Paget, "like a pair of scissors who go snip and snip and snip without doing each other any harm, but God help the poor devil who gets between them." Lord Lucan had adopted a system with regard to Lord Cardigan which was peculiarly infuriating. No smallest operation was to be performed by Cardigan without the presence of what, in his opinion, was a spy from Lucan. When the Light Brigade landed, he received written instructions from Lucan telling him how he was to encamp, and an officer from Lucan's staff remained to see the instructions were carried out; and on the unhappy expedition of September 16 a staff officer from Lord Lucan had accompanied Lord Cardigan.

Only a few hours before there had been an argument between the two men after Lord Lucan had arranged the disposition of the advance guard of cavalry. General Airey, and subsequently Lord Raglan, altered his arrangements sending instructions direct to Lord Cardigan. But Lucan was determined to allow no independence to Cardigan; he reprimanded him and told him that in the future, whatever the circumstances and however great the distance, he was to send an officer to inform Lieutenant-General the Earl of Lucan of every order he received. It was therefore in a state of acute exasperation that Cardigan reached the Bulganek.

The formation of the little valley of the Bulganek was unusual. From the river the land rose, roughly speaking, in three steps: the first small, the second larger but gently sloping, the third so steep as to conceal from anyone below what was on the plateau above. When Lord Raglan reached the top of the ridge above the little river, he saw on the slope opposite him a detachment of Cossacks, who at once withdrew. He then ordered the advance guard of cavalry under Lord Cardigan, four squadrons of the 11th Hussars and 13th Light Dragoons, to reconnoitre. Upon this Lucan promptly rode away from his position in front of the 17th Lancers and joined Cardigan, automatically superseding him as the superior officer and taking command. The four squadrons advanced to the top of the first step, and saw above them, on the slopes of the second step, a body of Russian cavalry about two thousand strong. The four squadrons of British cavalry formed line with beautiful precision, and the Russians halted and, at impossibly long range, fired a harmless volley with their carbines. At this moment Lord Raglan and General Airey, on the brow of the ridge opposite, saw what neither Cardigan and Lucan nor the army in the valley below could see, that the four squadrons were confronted with a far more formidable force than two thousand cavalry: on the plateau above was waiting an overwhelming body of troops, afterwards learned to consist of sixty thousand infantry, two batteries of artillery, a brigade of cavalry, and nine troops of Cossacks.

In the exhausted state of the army a general engagement was

to be avoided at all costs, and Lord Raglan was desperately anxious for his precious cavalry. The four squadrons must be extricated without provoking an engagement and without giving the enemy, with his overwhelming numbers, a chance to fall on them and destroy them as they retreated. A formidable force was ordered up in support—two divisions of infantry, two regiments of cavalry, and two batteries of artillery; and, inexplicably, the Russians allowed these supports to come into place. They were, it seemed, confused by the extraordinary steadiness, the ceremoniously exact formation, of the small force confronting them.

The opportunity for the Russians to annihilate the four squadrons was now lost, and Lord Raglan sent General Airey to tell Lucan to retire the four squadrons. Unfortunately he did not send a precise order: it was the first of the ambiguously worded orders from Lord Raglan which were to cause uncertainty in the future. General Airey arrived to find Lord Lucan and Lord Cardigan arguing. Lucan had been supervising and correcting Cardigan, altering his distribution of his troops; and Cardigan was in a state of irritation, the general impression being that he was itching to charge. General Airey could not wait to reason; he was aware of the overwhelming force within a few hundred yards, of the vital importance of every passing moment. With all the force and decision of his character he spoke for Lord Raglan, giving Lord Lucan to understand that he brought a definite order —the cavalry force was to retire at once. Lucan then gave the order to retreat, and the four squadrons retired with parade-ground precision, but to the sound of derisive jeers from the Russian cavalry.

A number of shells were fired by the Russian artillery, but in face of powerful support no pursuit was attempted, and the enemy withdrew.

The cavalry were furious and humiliated. The nature of the risk was ignored, no one troubled to find out what had really happened, and the jeers of the Russians at the retreating squadrons rankled horribly. The enemy had been met with at last, the first engagement had taken place, and the cavalry had re-treated. It was not to be borne. Had there been a definite order? It was thought that there had been no definite order. The fault was with Lord Lucan: the enemy had been hesitating—and he had turned tail. He should have his name changed, said someone —not Lord Lucan any longer, but Lord Look-on. The name stuck, and to the cavalry he was henceforward Lord Look-on.

After this affair the British army prepared to bivouac for the night by the side of the Bulganek. It seemed inevitable that the enemy would attack very shortly. The Russians were aware, through their Cossack observers, that all had not gone well with the army on the march; they must surely harry the British dur-ing the night and bring a powerful force out from their strong position on the Alma to fall on them at dawn. The British piled their arms and bivouacked in order of battle. Rum was served out, the casks were broken up, and dried weeds and grass gath-ered to light fires; then officers and men lay down on the ground. But, no Russian attack took place; the British army was allowed to pass the night unmolested. Lord Raglan, for his part, sent out no force to reconnoitre. Next day the position on the Alma must be attacked, but of the formation of the ground, the depth and current of the river his army must cross, the position of the enemy's guns and the disposition of his troops, he was perfectly ignorant.

The night was clear, and the British troops could see the watch fires of the Russian army fringing the sky on the heights of the Alma, six miles away. The men knew that a battle was to be fought, but they did not know that in the opinion of the Rus-sians they were doomed. They had been deliberately drawn on; the unopposed landing, the unmolested march had indeed been sinister. The fact was that mere repulse was not enough to satisfy the Russian command: the plan was to inflict a signal and crush-ing defeat. The great position on the Alma, in its opinion, was impregnable. Against those unassailable heights the Allied armies would first of all batter themselves in vain and then, since their supplies must all be brought long distances and with difficulty by sea, at the foot of the heights they would miserably perish. No other steps need be taken to ensure their destruction.

Orders were issued to the Allied troops to march at six, silently, without trumpet or drums; but it was ten before the British army was fully on the move. Cholera had done its work during the night; and again there was difficulty in filling the men's water bottles, for the Bulganek had been trodden into a muddy swamp.

As the columns began to move, Cossacks circled at a distance and plumes of smoke marked burning farms and hamlets set alight by the Russians as they fell back. Once again the day was blazing hot, once again the throats of the men fed on salt pork became parched with thirst, and once again the march was marked by a line of bodies as men staggered from the ranks and fell writhing on the ground. At noon the vanguard of the British army topped a grassy ridge—below them the ground stretched in a flat plain for about a mile, then sank in a slope fringed with orchards and vineyards to a river. On the farther side of the river rose heights, like giant terraces, one above the other in a double line. The army had arrived at the Alma, and at 12:30 a halt was called.

10

The Russians had reason to consider their position on the Alma impregnable, for it was a natural fortification of extraordinary strength. Above the swift river of uncertain depth a range of hills, called the heights, rose abruptly from the plain. In the course of ages the river running along their base had so cut into these heights as to reproduce, on a gigantic scale, the classical defences of military engineering. The river-bank below the heights, steep and in places fifteen feet high, formed a natural escarpment; above the escarpment were bare slopes, smooth and naked as a glacis, the artificial incline which defends the approach to a fortress. The glacis led to a vast terrace resembling a huge parapet, from which a deadly fire could be poured on the slopes below. In the rear the ground afforded protection, rising sharply once again and then rolling away in ridges.

On the north bank of the Alma, however, the bank which the British were now approaching, the formation of the ground was dramatically different. Here gentle grassy slopes fell to the river, bare except for the fringe of orchards and vineyards above the river-bank, and so completely overlooked and commanded by the heights opposite that every man advancing down them must be clearly visible.

Throughout any attack the British must be under heavy fire.

They must make their way down the slopes to the river, cross it, surmount the steep bank, and advance uphill over the naked slope of the natural glacis, while the enemy pounded at them as he would. The final advance must be into the mouths of heavy guns, firing at a distance of a few yards.

The Russian commander, Prince Menschikoff, considered a direct assault on the heights out of the question—no troops could be got to attempt it. Indeed, so confident was he in the impregnability of his position that he had invited a party to come out from Sebastopol to witness, while eating a picnic lunch, the destruction of the Allied armies. Thirty young ladies were on the heights above the Alma, and later British officers were told that as the army came into view the girls went into raptures over the fine appearance of the troops, especially admiring the scarlet coats of the infantry.

At one o'clock the British had advanced far enough for details of the position to be visible to the naked eye. Immediately in front of them rose a hill, somewhat separated from the range of the heights, and of peculiar shape. The lower slopes swelled out into a natural bastion, on which a large earthwork had been thrown up, and this, which contained a battery of twelve heavy guns, was called by the troops the "Great Redoubt"; above it and to the left was a smaller earthwork containing a battery of lighter guns—the "Lesser Redoubt." Every trace of cover, every bush, every tussock had been removed from the slopes, and on the flanks of the two redoubts troops and artillery were massed, sixteen battalions of picked infantry and four batteries of field artillery. The hill, called the Kourgane Hill, was the key to the position and was destined to be the scene of a great feat of British arms.

At 1:30 another halt was called, when the British army had reached the verge of the grassy slopes leading down to the river. A few seconds later a round shot ripped through their lines, followed by a cannonade from the batteries along the length of the heights. The Allies had come within artillery range. The battle of the Alma had begun.

It was a battle forever memorable for the ferocious courage of the British troops and the extraordinary incompetence displayed by the generals on both sides. What has been called the "characteristic insanity" of the Crimean War reached its height at the Alma. Advantages were gained not through superior skill, but as a result of astonishing blunders made by each participant in turn; and the victory, won after a desperate and bloody struggle, was attributable solely to the fighting qualities of the British soldier. In the battle of the Alma the cavalry played no part. Furious and resentful, it was their fate to sit motionless in their saddles, onlookers once more.

The Allied battle plan gave the hardest fighting to the British. The French, assisted by the guns of the fleet, were to lead off with an attack on the extreme right of the position. When the attack had succeeded and they had established themselves on the heights, the British were to storm the great key position of the Kourgane Hill.

A flank attack was apparently not considered by Lord Raglan; his divisions were to be flung straight at well-protected artillery and superior numbers of infantry established in a fortified position of terrifying strength.

Almost at once Prince Menschikoff assisted the Allies by making an astonishing mistake. His position above the river was six miles long, and he had not enough troops to cover it; but where the Alma ran into the sea, on the extreme right of the Allies, the heights ended in cliffs and precipitous slopes, and he got over his difficulty by treating this precipitous ground as insurmountable by troops. Had he examined the ground even cursorily he would have discovered that paths ran down the cliffs and that within half a mile of his troops there was a track which could be used by carts. Using the steepest path, a French force of Light Infantry ascended unobserved; and Prince Menschikoff, taken by surprise, lost his head. After summoning a considerable force and galloping uncertainly to and fro on the top of the cliffs for some time, he withdrew, leaving only two batteries of field artillery to hold the advancing French.

It was now the turn of the French to blunder—they failed to advance. The force which had ascended was waiting for support from another force of infantry and artillery coming up by the cart track, but there was difficulty in getting guns up, and it was a rule of the French infantry never to advance without artillery support—so the attack on the extreme right came to a standstill. At the same time a second attack, launched on less precipitous ground a little to the left of the first, was subjected to withering fire from a concealed battery of twelve guns, and the men wavered. Spirited and courageous as the French troops were, at the moment of the battle of the Alma political scandals and dissensions had destroyed their trust in their commanders.

At three o'clock a French staff officer, greatly excited, galloped up to Lord Raglan: the French position was desperate, the troops were being massacred, and without support they would be forced to abandon the attack and withdraw from the heights. Bluntly put, either the British must attack or the battle would end.

The British troops had now been lying down for an hour and a half, helpless, since their guns could not reach the Russian batteries; and they were suffering frequent casualties as they were pounded by Russian artillery. It was an ordeal dreaded by the troops; and Lord Raglan, with characteristic disregard for danger, had been riding slowly up and down the lines of his staff, conspicuous in his plumed cocked hat, with the object of drawing the enemy's fire.

One of Lord Raglan's qualities as a commander was a power of divining the temper of troops. Desperate as an assault on the position before them must be, without the support of a successful French attack, he knew that the British troops had the heart to attempt it. In spite of sickness and misfortune, morale was astonishingly high.

At about five minutes past three he gave the order to advance; the first line of the British army, the Light Infantry Division and the 2nd Division, rose to its feet with a cheer, and, dressing in a line two miles wide, though only two men deep, marched forward towards the river.

Under terrific fire—forty guns were trained on the river, and rifle bullets whipped the surface of the water into a bloody foam —the first British troops began to struggle across the Alma, the men so parched with thirst that even at this moment they stopped to drink. Everything was confusion: the advance on the two-mile front was obscured by dense clouds of smoke, the Russians had fired a village on the British left after stuffing it with straw, and on the slopes before the Great Redoubt piles of brushwood were set alight. Men could not see each other, could not see their officers. During the terrible crossing of the river, formation was lost, and it was a horde which surged up the bank and, formed by shouting, cursing officers into some ragged semblance of a line, pressed on up the deadly natural glacis towards the Great Redoubt.

It seemed impossible that the slender, straggling line could survive—huge columns of Russian infantry raked it with fire, heavy guns in the Great Redoubt poured round shot, grape, and canister into it at a distance of a few hundred yards. Again and again large gaps were torn in the line, the slopes became littered with bodies and sloppy with blood, but the survivors closed up and pressed on, their officers urging, swearing, yelling like demons.

The men's blood was up. The Light Infantry Division, heroes of a dozen stubborn and bloody battles in the Peninsula, advanced through the smoke, swearing most horribly as their comrades fell. Foot by foot they climbed upwards, wavering as broadsides tore through them, steadying by a miracle, and pressing on—if only one man survived, that man was going to get into the Great Redoubt.

Then, suddenly, unbelievably, the guns ceased to fire. The smoke lifted and the British saw, to their stupefaction, that the Russians, with frantic haste, were limbering up their guns and dragging them away. The Emperor Nicholas had given Prince Menschikoff an order that on no account whatsoever was a single gun to be lost, because he believed, incorrectly, that the Duke of Wellington had never lost a gun.

In the sudden silence a fox-hunting subaltern put his hand to his mouth and yelled, "Stole away, stole away"; the British troops gave a great shout, and in a last frantic rush a mob of mixed battalions tumbled into the earthwork. The Great Redoubt had been stormed.

But the battle was not over. It is a military axiom that the climax of a successful assault is a moment of great peril. It is then that the second line must be at hand to make good the achievement of the first. But here no second line was to be seen.

The Duke of Cambridge, commander of the division which formed the second line, a brigade of Guards and the Highland Brigade, had received orders from Lord Raglan to support the Light Infantry Division, but they had not been clear to him, and he waited for more precise instructions. It was said, perhaps with justice, that the difficulty found by Lord Raglan's generals in interpreting his orders was due to the fact that they had had no military experience—men who had been in battle would have found his meaning perfectly clear; and certainly the Duke of Cambridge had never heard a shot fired in anger in his life. Now he had brought his division to the edge of the strip of vineyards and orchards above the river, and there he halted.

Meanwhile, Lord Raglan himself had taken up a most curious position. At three o'clock, as the first line rose to its feet, he had cantered down, followed by his staff, crossed the river so far on the right that he passed through French skirmishers, and, riding up a sunken lane, had taken up his position on a knoll actually behind the enemy's front line. The Russians made no attempt to interfere with him, because, it was learned later, they were quite unable to believe that he and his staff were alone. Here, separated completely from his army, he watched the long lines of British troops advance to the attack more than a mile away. "Never did Commander-in-Chief take up a more amazing station from which to fight a battle," writes Sir John Fortescue.

After the assault there was utter confusion within the Great Redoubt: regiments were mixed together; men could not find their officers nor officers their men, no one knew who was dead and who alive. Within a few minutes guns from the Lesser Redoubt and batteries on the slopes began to fire into the Great Redoubt, and the British were forced out. Before the Guards and Highlanders could cross the river the Great Redoubt was back in Russian hands and the remnant of the first line was in retreat before overwhelming numbers of Russian infantry.

It was all to be done again, and the task was still frightful. Though the heavy guns of the Great Redoubt were silenced, the guns from the Lesser Redoubt and the batteries on the slopes were still in action, and eight battalions of infantry swept the slope with continuous fire, that fatal slope soaked in British blood and piled with British dead. The second line crossed the river, the Highlanders began to ascend the slopes to the left, the Scots Fusilier Guards became entangled with the retreating remnants of the first line and fell back; but the Grenadiers and Coldstreamers, though under a deadly fire, formed into line with as much precision and lack of hurry as if they had been on the parade ground, and began deliberately to advance up the glacis towards the Great Redoubt.

It was an unforgettable sight. The men marched as if they were taking part in a review. Storm after storm of bullets, grape, shrapnel, round shot tore through them, man after man fell, but the pace never altered, the line closed in and continued "ceremoniously and with dignity," as an eye witness wrote, on its way. An officer, galloping up to Sir Colin Campbell, expostulated, "The Brigade of Guards will be destroyed—ought it not to fall back?" "Sir," said Sir Colin Campbell, "it is better that every man of Her Majesty's Guards should lie dead upon the field than that they should now turn their backs on the enemy."

In fact, while this feat of discipline and endurance was being performed, the tide of battle began to turn. The French artillery had at last emerged from the cart track and gone into action, inflicting great damage; and the British field artillery managed to silence the Russian batteries on the slopes. Gradually the Guards advancing on the Great Redoubt and the Highlanders ascending the slopes on their left were freed from artillery fire. But now a new danger threatened—an attack by infantry in overwhelming numbers. As the line, two deep, advanced slowly up the heights, a huge force of infantry, six columns in all, was seen to bear down on it, four to meet the Guards and two to meet the Highlanders.

The cavalry continued to suffer tortures. They had been posted on the extreme left, opposite a force of four thousand Russian cavalry, and earlier in the day it had been confidently expected the Russians would attack. The officers had eagerly discussed the direction from which the Russian charge would come and the best method of receiving it, but it had never taken place. Prince Menschikoff seemed to have entirely forgotten his formidable arm, and the first order the Russian cavalry received was the order to retreat.

Sitting idle in their saddles, the British cavalry watched the first line storm the Great Redoubt. Officers, beside themselves with impatience, sent messages to Lord Lucan "imploring him" wrote Lieutenant Seager, to "let them come on"; and Lord Cardigan made use of "very strong expressions." Lord Lucan, however, could not move without orders, and he received no orders from Lord Raglan. Furious, frustrated, deprived of the discretion which he felt he ought to exercise, he sat waiting for that order to move which never came. Then as the Guards and Highlanders began their march up the heights, he could bear it no longer, and on his own responsibility, and without orders, he crossed the river with his horse artillery and began to ascend the slopes on the extreme left to protect the flank of the Highland Brigade as they attacked.

It had seemed impossible for that unimpressive line, a mere thread straggling along the hillside, to withstand the formidable mass of infantry bearing down on it, but, as observers watched through their glasses in an agony of anxiety, an astonishing phenomenon took place. The massive columns came on, irresistibly, it seemed, and then, suddenly, the slender line had encircled them, and, in a moment, the columns were wrapped in fire. The fire was deadly. Packed tightly shoulder to shoulder, the men in the dense columns could not aim. But the men in the line free to move had been trained to make every bullet tell. The Russians had watched the advance with amazement. "This was the most extraordinary thing to us," wrote one of their officers, "as we had never before seen troops fight in lines of two deep, nor did we think it possible for men to be found with sufficient firmness of morale to be able to attack, in this apparently weak formation, our massive columns."

But now the great columns were bulging, heaving, and the Guards burst into a cheer—the mass opposite them was giving way. A moment later, with a wild yell, the Highlanders on the left charged the two columns opposite them and broke them. Hurrahing broke out all along the line; right, left, and centre the Russians were losing formation, scattering, breaking, the grey masses seeming absolutely to dissolve. The British dashed forward, the Russians turned and fled. The battalions in reserve tried to steady their comrades, but in vain; in full retreat the Russian army streamed away across the hills. The Guards marched into the Great Redoubt, and there was a shout of triumph so loud that William Howard Russell heard it on the opposite bank—the battle of the Alma had been won.

A French officer turned to Evelyn Wood, later Field Marshal

Sir Evelyn Wood, V.C. "Our men could not have done it," he said.

At this point Lord Lucan with the cavalry and horse artillery appeared on the heights beside the Highland Brigade; and, at Sir Colin Campbell's suggestion six guns of the horse artillery were detached and pursued the flying enemy, causing great loss.

The cavalry were now in a position to inflict terrible execution. They had, though without Lord Raglan's orders, come up on the heights, and were so placed that the enemy was streaming away in disorder absolutely at their feet. Nearly one thousand horsemen, fresh, unexhausted, and wild with eagerness sat watching the enemy retreat; and it is the function of cavalry to turn such a retreat into a rout. And now, at last, the cavalry received their first order. General Estcourt, the adjutant general, brought Lord Lucan peremptory instructions from Lord Raglan—the cavalry were not to attack the flying enemy. The Commander-in-Chief had decided that they were too precious to be risked—the enemy might, indeed, in his opinion almost certainly would, turn and make a stand. No advance was to be made until artillery support had been provided. Lord Raglan's order to Lord Lucan was that the cavalry should escort field guns which were being sent to take up positions in advance. Lord Lucan would escort the guns to the left, Lord Cardigan the guns to the right. "Mind now," finished General Estcourt, "the cavalry are not to attack."

When Lucan and Cardigan were off instantly, galloping far ahead of the guns and taking prisoners, Lord Raglan sent a second order: the cavalry were to return to their duty of escorting the guns. Lucan's eagerness was so great that the order had no effect; he and Cardigan were riding with their troops in formation, inviting, indeed evidently hoping for, an action. Then Lord Raglan sent a third, and most peremptory order: the cavalry were to cease pursuit forthwith and return to their duty. On receipt of this order Lord Lucan, according to an eye witness, "boiled," and in a fury directed that all the prisoners, to their astonishment, should be turned loose, and galloped back to the guns.

On his return Lord Lucan went to see General Estcourt—he wished for a message to be conveyed to Lord Raglan: "Lord Lucan trusted that Lord Raglan had that confidence in him, as commanding the cavalry, that he would allow him to act on his own responsibility, as occasion should offer and render advisable, for otherwise opportunities of acting would frequently be lost to the cavalry." To this message he received no reply.

There was no pursuit after the battle of the Alma. The French refused to go further—the men's knapsacks had been left behind when they advanced, and they must go back for them. Lord Raglan dared not pursue alone. The defeated Russian army was allowed to stream away unmolested, and finally poured into Sebastopol.

The cavalry felt themselves disgraced. Nolan came raging into William Howard Russell's tent: "There were one thousand British cavalry, looking on at a beaten army retreating—guns, standards, colours and all—with a wretched horde of Cossacks and cowards who had never struck a blow, ready to turn tail at the first trumpet, within ten minutes gallop of them. It is enough to drive one mad! It is too disgraceful, too infamous, they [the generals commanding] ought to be d——d."

That night the British army bivouacked among the dead and wounded on the heights. Water was horribly short, and the heights were waterless, but Lord Raglan thought it unwise to bivouac on the river-bank below, in case of surprise. Very many officers and men spent the night fetching water for the wounded and dying, whose agonised cries made sleep impossible. Medical aid was wholly inadequate, amputations were performed on the field in the open air without an anæsthetic, and not one man in five saw a doctor. There was no exultation in the British army that night; reaction followed the madness of battle, and the survivors of the great assaults felt only depression and grief. Lord George Paget in the diary he kept for his wife quoted a saying of the Duke of Wellington, "Next to a battle lost, there is nothing so dreadful as a battle won."

There was one British officer, however, who was neither torn by pity nor lowered by reaction. Major-General Lord Cardigan had managed, although the army was bivouacking on the ground, to secure a tent to himself, and in it he sat drafting a long complaint to Lord Raglan about his treatment by Lord Lucan. He was compelled, he wrote, on September 21, though he regretted extremely to have to do so at the present important moment, to trouble Lord Raglan with the unfortunate details of his present position as major-general commanding the Light Brigade, and he proceeded to bring out the old complaints, as freshly and furiously as if he were setting down his grievances for the first time. He clung to the notion of the separate command; he would not, could not, in spite of all that had happened, relinquish the idea that his command of the Light Brigade was to be independent of Lord Lucan. He had been promised, he reiterated, that though Lord Lucan accompanied the expedition he would not interfere with the Light Brigade. And Lord Lucan had interfered: he had absolutely taken the command away from Lord Cardigan. Why had he ridden with Lord Cardigan at the affair on the Bulganek the day before yesterday? Why had he ridden with the Light Brigade during the recent battle? Why did he insist on seeing all orders Lord Cardigan received from Lord Raglan? Why did he write orders and memoranda to Lord Cardigan as if he, Cardigan, were a junior officer? For page after page the complaints flowed on, ending with a demand that Lord Raglan should intervene at once. It was Lord Cardigan's opinion that reflections had been cast on his character and his professional ability by Lord Lucan's conduct, and he owed it to himself to see that his position was established. Would Lord Raglan kindly inform Lord Lucan that he had no right whatsoever to interfere with the Light Brigade?

For the moment, however, the Commander-in-Chief had no time for the Earl of Cardigan. Terrible considerations were weighing on his mind: he was harassed by difficulties with the French, by frightening shortages in supply, by the unending drain of cholera on his forces; and he had not patience to soothe the wounded self-esteem of the Earl of Cardigan. He did not write until a week later, on September 28, and he then administered a severe snub.

I am bound to express my conviction that the Earl of Cardigan would have done better if he had refrained from making the assertions which he has thought fit to submit for my decision. I consider him wrong in every one of the instances cited. A General of Division may interfere little or much with the duties of a General of Brigade; as he may think proper or fit. His judgments may be right or wrong; but the General of Brigade should bear this in mind, that the Lieutenant-General is the Senior Officer; and that all his orders and suggestions claim obedience and attention.

Lord Raglan finished by making an appeal, a despairing appeal, to reason.

The Earl of Lucan and the Earl of Cardigan are nearly connected. They are both gentlemen of high honour and elevated position in the country independently of their military rank. They must permit me, as the Head of the Forces, and I may say the friend of both, earnestly to recommend them frankly to associate with each other, and to come to such an understanding as that there should be no impression of the assumption of authority on the one side, and no apprehension of undue interference on the other.

In short, Lord Cardigan and Lord Lucan were to kiss and be friends. But any hope, however faint, of agreement between them had now vanished, for between the date of Cardigan's complaint on September 21 and Lord Raglan's reply on September 28, events of the utmost importance had taken place, and in their course Cardigan and Lucan had become even more hopelessly estranged, while to Lucan's resentment against Raglan was added fresh and furious bitterness.

That week between the 21st and 28th of September decided

the fate of the British army. When the Allies invaded the Crimea, the plan had been to march on Sebastopol and take it by a sudden assault, a *coup de main*. The victory of the Alma had in fact opened Sebastopol to the Allies; had they followed up their victory, Sebastopol must have fallen and the war then and there come to an end. But the Allies did not advance—they lingered on the heights burying their dead, carrying their wounded and the daily toll of cholera victims down to the fleet, and fatally disputing about what they should do next. The obvious plan was to attack the northern side of Sebastopol, the side nearest to the Alma. But the French had doubts: there was an important fort on the northern side; the fortifications would prove too strong. The Allied commanders had set up no intelligence service whatsoever, and they were unaware that the fortifications were in bad repair and undermanned, and that Prince Menschikoff had withdrawn the army which had been allowed to escape after the Alma to the south side of the city. The Allies could have walked into Sebastopol on the north almost without firing a shot. The French now urged that, instead of an attack on the north, the Allies should make a flank march round Sebastopol and attack on the south. Lord Raglan was unconvinced, and would not give way. Whether the attack should be on the north or the south was still undecided when, on September 23, the Allies turned their backs on the Alma and at last began to advance.

A curious and disturbing phenomenon was now noticed: vultures were unknown in the Crimea, but after the battle of the Alma they appeared in large numbers, coming it was said from great distances, even as far as the north coast of Africa. And when the British left the Alma, the vultures accompanied them.

Since the country was almost waterless, the army must perforce march from river to river. The first stage was the river Katcha, about seven miles off. All the way the ground was thickly strewn with arms and accoutrements thrown away by the Russians in their flight. The river was reached before noon, and Lord Raglan, encouraged by the signs of panic, was eager to press on. But the French would go no farther, and the two armies halted.

And now an episode occurred which gave warning of the dangers likely to arise from the literal interpretation placed on his orders by Lord Lucan. The next day's march was to the river Belbek, and Lord Raglan ordered Lord Lucan to go ahead with the greater part of the cavalry and the horse artillery and "occupy" a village called Duvankoi, which seemed to stand on the river-bank. Cossacks circled round the British force throughout their march, and when the village was reached, it proved a most dangerous spot. The approach was through a narrow defile; the village itself was huddled on the bank of the river, under high cliffs; precipices overhung it on one side and the river flowed on the other. All the inhabitants had fled.

Duvankoi being, in fact, a natural trap, it might have been thought that Lord Lucan would use discretion in executing his orders, and that since the place was empty and dangerous, he would either refrain from occupying it at all, or would send in a small token force.

But he had been ordered to occupy Duvankoi, and occupy it he would. But to do it he took the greater part of the British cavalry and horse artillery into a position of extreme peril where the enemy could have destroyed them with ease. The Russians, though they knew, through their Cossack observers, where the British force had placed itself, did nothing, for they were in a state of distraction, convinced that the Allied armies were about to attack their weak defences on the north. It was unlikely, however, that Lord Lucan would always be so fortunate.

At dusk, "having," he wrote, "sufficiently fulfilled his instructions," he withdrew from the village, and that night he bivouacked on the heights above.

In the morning he observed a large body of Russian troops between the Belbek and Sebastopol. He had, however, no orders to reconnoitre, and without pausing to ascertain the direction or scope of their movements, he rejoined the main body of the army encamped on the Katcha.

There the Allied camp was in confusion. Two highly important pieces of information had just been received. A line of battleships had been sunk across the entrance to the harbour at Sebastopol, blocking it to the Allied fleet; and at the mouth of the Belbek, the next objective, a powerful covered battery had been placed. To land supplies from the fleet at the Belbek was now impossible, and the line of the French march would be under fire.

Once more the French frantically urged a flank march round Sebastopol and an attack from the south. Lord Raglan still held out, but he was in fact defeated. True, the final decision to attack from the south was postponed, but no attempt to silence the battery at the mouth of the Belbek was planned. It was avoided, and when the Allied armies resumed their march they turned from the sea and marched inland.

That evening, September 24, the armies bivouacked inland. They were now only some four miles from Sebastopol. Signs of panic-stricken retreat were all round them: arms, ammunition, equipment littered the ground, everything had been discarded, even Prince Menschikoff's sumptuously appointed field kitchen. From the ridge above the Belbek the north side of Sebastopol was clearly visible, but at this moment, when, like the Promised Land it lay stretched before the Allied armies, Lord Raglan gave way. The fatal decision was taken. The Allies would turn away from Sebastopol, march round it, and attack from the south.

It was an operation of very great difficulty. There was the great, the alarming risk of being separated from the fleet, from the sole source of supplies, including ammunition. There were also perils arising out of the nature of the country; the region now to be traversed was no longer open, it was covered with brushwood, dense, trackless, and blind.

It was decided by Lord Raglan that the next objective was to be a group of buildings called after some Scottish exile "Mackenzie's Farm," which stood on the high road leading from Sebastopol into the interior.

From such maps as the British possessed there appeared to be a track through the brushwood leading from the valley of the Belbek to Mackenzie's Farm. This track was to be used by the cavalry and the artillery, while the infantry made their way through the wood by compass. Lord Lucan was ordered to lead the way with the cavalry division, supported by a battalion of Rifles; on reaching Mackenzie's Farm he was to remain inconspicuous, watch the road, and send a report on its condition and the use made of it.

The result was farcical. Lord Lucan with the cavalry started off along the track ahead of the army just before 8:30 A.M., but after some miles the track forked. An officer from General Airey's staff who was responsible for planning the route had been sent with Lucan, but no fork was marked on his map. After consultation the larger of the two tracks was chosen, but slowly it degenerated into the merest path, and finally it vanished completely. The cavalry were lost! Compasses were produced, and officers and men began to struggle through the wood in a south-easterly direction. Lucan had a battalion of Rifles with him, and he felt that he must keep his troops together and adapt himself to their pace. Presently it came about that, instead of being at the head of the army, as Lord Raglan imagined, the cavalry was far, far behind.

Meanwhile the infantry were painfully making their way through the brushwood, like beaters making their way through a thick covert. It was overpoweringly hot and stuffy, for no breath of air penetrated the brushwood; briars and thorns lacerated the men's flesh, their clothes and their equipment became constantly and maddeningly entangled and they had to carry their muskets above their heads to prevent them from being torn out of their hands. A large number of men collapsed through exhaustion. Nothing could be done for them—they were left where they fell.

Meanwhile Lord Raglan, having waited to see his infantry disappear into the brushwood, cantered with his staff down the track and did not follow the wrong fork. The track was perfectly clear, and he cantered on until he had almost reached the point where the track debouched on to the great road, expecting every moment to meet a staff officer with Lord Lucan's report on the state of the road. General Airey then asked if he might ride on to see whether the road was clear, and galloped ahead. Suddenly he reined in, and held up his hand in such a way as to convey to Lord Raglan that something very serious had occurred. He had, in fact, almost collided with a Russian wagon train and a powerful body of Russian infantry.

These troops were the rearguard of the force Lord Lucan had seen earlier in the morning, and it was nothing less than Prince Menschikoff's army, the same army which had been routed at the Alma and fled into Sebastopol. Now it was no longer inside Sebastopol, but outside. After sinking the ships at the mouth of the harbour, Prince Menschikoff had sent their crews, more than two thousand men, to man the defences of the city, while he himself marched his army out of Sebastopol, intending to fall on the flank of the Allies when they attacked the northern side of the city, as he was confident they were about to do. Thus the British general, in order to capture Sebastopol, was marching round it, and the Russian general, in order to defend Sebastopol, was marching away from it; the conduct of each was so unlikely that they were able to give each other a surprise.

The Russian soldiers, utterly astonished, stood still and gaped. At this moment the rumble of artillery was heard, and a troop of horse artillery which had not advanced with the cavalry approached down the track. The Russians, thinking perhaps a large force was at hand, hesitated. Lord Raglan and his staff were partly concealed by the brushwood, and the Russian soldiers could not guess that the British Commander-in-Chief, with the whole of his staff, had managed to lose the British army and was alone and defenceless. But in this kind of emergency Lord Raglan was supreme; quietly beckoning up two officers, he told them to go and find the cavalry, while he himself, slowly backing his horse a few paces down the track, reined up and sat calmly facing the enemy.

So great was his tranquility that the Russians were confused. Surely, they thought, this English officer must just have prepared a surprise and be waiting to watch the coming attack. Hurried consultations were held, but no responsible officer seemed to be present; minutes passed, and still no Russian troops moved into the wood. Meanwhile the cavalry were found—they had been blundering about in the brushwood lower down. Led by Lord Lucan, they now galloped furiously down the track towards the Russian force. Lord Raglan was very angry, and as they passed he for once raised his voice. "Lord Lucan," he shouted, "you are late." Lucan galloped on, making no reply.

The sight of the cavalry confirmed the apprehensions of the Russians that a large force must be approaching, and they fled, leaving behind, to the delight of the troops, a quantity of rich booty—furred coats, silk shirts, wine, and silver plate. But though the Russians were retreating in disorder, Lord Raglan sternly forbade the cavalry to pursue.

He was very angry, but not as angry as Lord Lucan. Lucan had been publicly rebuked, shouted at before his officers and men for a mishap which, he considered, had nothing whatever to do with him. He had not asked Lord Raglan for an officer to guide him, far from it, but Lord Raglan had sent an officer whose duty it was to find the way, the way had been lost, and now he, Lucan, was being blamed. His resentment was furious. He would not go to see Lord Raglan; he washed his hands of the whole business and retired into angry silence.

Lord Cardigan, however, presented himself to the Commander-in-Chief, and in his diary he wrote an account of the interview:

Lord Raglan was sitting under the porch at Mackenzie's Farm with General Airey, and he began by blaming me that the cavalry had been too low in the brushwood and not in the right place. I simply reminded his Lordship that I did not command the cavalry.

After this episode Lord Lucan and Lord Raglan became utterly estranged, and when the generals of division were assembled Lucan was not invited. "It was common gossip," wrote Lieutenant Seager, "that Lord Raglan thought the cavalry were being wretchedly handled."

On the 26th the British army reached Balaclava, south of Sebastopol, the city had been circled, and the flank march was complete. Lord Raglan's relief was intense: Balaclava was a port, he was no longer cut off from the fleet, and, by a coincidence, as he stood overlooking the harbour, the *Agamemnon,* the largest man-of-war in the British fleet, steamed in. It must be a good omen, and Balaclava was adopted as the British base.

It was a place of extraordinary beauty. The harbour, all but landlocked, had the appearance of an inland lake, a sheet of silver reflecting the surrounding heights. The village, a favourite summer resort for visitors from Sabastopol, was celebrated for its picturesque charm. Gay little villas with roofs of green tiles were set in carefully cultivated gardens. Roses, clematis, honeysuckle, and vines loaded with large pale green Muscatel grapes festooned every house and fence, orchards stretched up the slopes, vegetable gardens were neatly set out in rows of tomatoes, pumpkins, and lettuce. Overnight the charm vanished. More than twenty-five thousand men, of whom nine out of ten were suffering from diarrhoea, marched into the village. Gardens were trampled into mud, fences smashed, vines dragged down, doors and windows broken, trees destroyed. The lovely little landlocked harbour, only half a mile long and less than a quarter wide, was ridiculously inadequate to serve as the port of supply for an army. Ships crowded in, the water ceased to mirror the surrounding heights, refuse floated everywhere, and soon there was a horrible smell. The French meanwhile established their base on two wide and spacious bays, Kamiesh and Kazatch, ten miles to the west.

However, both the flank march and the selection of Balaclava as a base were hailed with enthusiasm by the authorities in England, and Lord Hardinge, Commander-in-Chief at home, wrote to Lord Raglan on October 9 that he had proved himself a most worthy pupil of his great master the Duke.

Nothing can exceed the universal admiration of all of us, for the judgment, ability and nerve shown by you in all your operations. The flank movement by your left, bringing your Army and siege guns down to a safe harbour at Balaclava and at a short distance from Sebastopol and in communication with the Navy, is a master piece worthy of all praise. . . . It is the greatest operation of modern times.

But, though the Allies were now established on the south of Sebastopol, what were they to do next? The flank march certainly had been accomplished, but Sebastopol still lay untouched before them; how were they to take Sebastopol? Another difference of opinion between the Allies appeared. The British wished to assault Sebastopol forthwith, the French wished to besiege. They were, they admitted, uneasy about the morale of their troops. The French army was discouraged, and should the assault fail, might go to pieces.

The most vigorous advocate of assault was the commander of the British 4th Division, Sir George Cathcart. He was encamped on a hill above Balaclava overlooking Sebastopol, and from his personal observations he declared that he could "walk into Sebastopol almost without the loss of a man." He was right; after the war General Todleben, the famous German engineer who defended Sebastopol, said at that date the city must have fallen if a determined assault had been made.

Unfortunately, Lord Raglan had a personal reason which made him unwilling to be guided by Sir George Cathcart.

The most extraordinary of the arrangements which complicated the conduct of the Crimean campaign was the "Dormant Commission." The Government had issued a secret commission to Sir George Cathcart, appointing him Commander-in-Chief if Lord Raglan died or was killed, although several other generals serving in the army, including Lord Raglan's second-in-command, Sir George Brown, were senior to him in rank. Lord Raglan and Sir George Cathcart were soon on bad terms. Sir George felt that Lord Raglan did not pay him enough attention, and wrote angry letters to the Commander-in-Chief complaining that while Sir George Brown was consulted he was ignored, and warned him in irritating terms that both General Airey and Gen. Sir George Brown were issuing orders to the army in his name and without his knowledge.

Sir George Cathcart's advice was not taken. Lord Raglan decided to agree to the French plan and besiege. On September 29 naval commanders were directed to disembark the siege guns, and the British army prepared to sit down before Sebastopol.

Meanwhile Lord Cardigan was still occupied in attempting to establish a separate command. Admittedly he had been forced to accept Lord Lucan's authority in the field, but he now formed the idea that in all matters relating to the internal affairs of the Light Brigade, domestically, as it were, he was independent. The tents having at last been brought by the fleet, he prepared to encamp his brigade. It was a species of military problem in which he took a special pride, and again and again in Bulgaria he had his exhausted and cursing men moving tents not once, but several times until symmetry was attained. But not even in placing tents was the major-general of the Light Brigade to be allowed independence by his lieutenant-general. Precise directions came down from Lord Lucan, an aide-de-camp remained to see that they were carried out, and Lord Cardigan wrote in his diary on September 27: "Lord Lucan is entirely taking the command away from me."

And yet Lord Raglan, in spite of his recent impatience, still seemed to encourage Lord Cardigan. At the end of September it was camp gossip that Cardigan had scored. The Commander-in-Chief had sent him with a strong detachment on a "particular service" without informing Lucan. He had, rumour said, been sent to make a secret reconnaissance of the defences of Sebastopol for the information of the Allied Commanders during their council of war.

On October 4 Lord Lucan retorted by circulating a memorandum explaining their duties to the Light Brigade. "The chief duties of the Light Cavalry are to ensure the safety of the Army from all surprises. . . . It is not their duty needlessly, without authority, to engage the enemy . . . on no account should any party attack or pursue, unless specially instructed to do so." The memorandum was agreed to have been aimed at Cardigan, and to have infuriated him. However, at the moment he was suffering from the prevalent disease of diarrhœa, and on the 4th he "gave in" and went sick on board the *Southern Star* in Balaclava harbour, where Lieutenant Seager hoped he would "stay and be a nuisance no longer." He was still sick on October 7, and therefore was not present at an encounter which put the final touch to the dissatisfaction of the cavalry with Lord Lucan.

The whole of the cavalry division was now at Balaclava under Lord Lucan's command. The Scots Greys had joined the army during the flank march at Katcha, and the remainder of the Heavy Brigade had disembarked at Balaclava between September 30 and October 3, bringing with them Mrs. Duberly, to whom Lord Cardigan lent a horse. On the morning of October 7 an outlying cavalry picket was surprised by a formidable force of Russians, consisting of a division of cavalry supported by two battalions of infantry and a battery of artillery. The British trumpets sounded "to horse," and the cavalry division formed and advanced, led by Lord Lucan. Meanwhile the Russians manœuvred backwards and forwards in the plain, as if holding a field day, or, as British officers declared, inviting an engagement, and the cavalry settled themselves in their saddles, prepared to charge. At last the moment had come. Here were no woods, no narrow lanes to hamper their movements: the plain stretched before them, open and undulating, the ground was firm, the whole force of British cavalry was present. Everything a cavalry man could desire was theirs—but nothing happened.

No trumpet sounded the charge. Lord Lucan halted; his division, raging and helpless, sat in their saddles while the Russians withdrew, jeering loudly.

The cavalry were unable to contain themselves; Lord Lookon was openly cursed, and between Captain Nolan and Lord Lucan an angry scene took place. Lucan taxed Nolan with the use of improper expressions, and Nolan asserted that he told Lucan to his face that by failing to attack the enemy he had neglected his duty. Lord George Paget, with more restraint, wrote that he feared the cavalry had been "miserably handled": Lord Lucan was much to blame, and Lord Raglan was said to be very angry. Though Lord Cardigan had not been present, his rage embraced the whole division, and his old regiment, the 11th, in particular; he considered that they should have taken the law into their own hands, and he abused the officers of the 11th in violent terms, calling them "a d——d set of old women." Lieutenant-Colonel Douglas of the 11th went to remonstrate with him, and was told for his pains that a lieutenant-colonel had no right to remonstrate with a major-general; however, later Lord Cardigan sent for him and admitted that under the influence of excitement he might have made use of some "nasty expressions," but the affair was disgraceful. "Of course, Lord Lucan was commanding the cavalry," he finished.

On October 12, with rage and contempt for his brother-in-law still fresh, Lord Cardigan returned to duty, and he and Lucan were "hard at it at once," wrote Lord George Paget. Lord Raglan decided they must be separated, and detaching the 11th Hussars and the 17th Lancers, he sent them farther up the heights towards Sebastopol, to form a new cavalry camp under Lord Cardigan. The cavalry were indignant, and Lord George Paget wrote that it was a shame that everyone's plans should be upset and their usefulness spoiled for the sake of "two spoilt children."

However, almost at once a different and very surprising arrangement was made for Lord Cardigan.

On October 13 Mrs. Duberly saw an elegant and fairy-like vessel glide into Balaclava Harbour. It was Lord Cardigan's yacht, the *Dryad*, and it brought out from England not only Lord Cardigan's French cook, but also his great friend, Mr. Hubert de Burgh. Mr. de Burgh landed, went to Lord Cardigan's tent, and was greatly distressed to find him dining off "some soup in a jug, boiled salt pork, and a little Varna brandy mixed with rum." That night Cardigan dined in his yacht, and from October 15, by special permission of Lord Raglan, he dined and slept aboard every night. The distance from the yacht to the Light Cavalry camp was several miles, but Cardigan did not relinquish his command. The Brigade major came down to the yacht every evening, and a stream of orderlies spurred the wretched, overworked horses up and down the precipitous hill, soon knee-deep in mud, that led from the harbour to the heights. The army was outraged. What—was Lord Cardigan to escape the hardship and discomfort, the icy winds, the insufficient food, the vermin, the mud? Was he to be allowed to command the Light Brigade from a luxurious yacht with a French cook, and sleep every night in a feather bed? His friends remonstrated with him, but Cardigan brushed them aside. Lord Raglan had given him permission. That was enough.

The army christened Lord Cardigan the "Noble Yachtsman," and the inseparable companion of the "Noble Yachtsman" was Mr. de Burgh. William Howard Russell described a meeting with the pair.

As I rode down the path between the hillside and the beach, into Balaclava, I encountered two horsemen—one in hussar uniform; the other, an unlovely gentleman, in a flat-brimmed bell-topper, frock-coat, and overalls strapped over patent-leather boots. This first was Lord Cardigan; the second, his friend, Mr. de Burgh, known to the London world as "the Squire." They had just landed from the yacht whence the General commanded the Light Cavalry Brigade. "Haw! haw! Well! Mr. William Russell! What are they doing? What was the firing for last night? And this morning?" I confessed ignorance. "You hear, Squire? This Mister William Russell knows nothing of the reason of that firing! I daresay no one does! Good morning!" They rode on.

The siege guns had now been landed; in spite of infinite difficulties they had to be dragged into position by hand, and the gun platforms constructed out of wood obtained by demolishing houses. The cannonade against Sebastopol began on October 17. It was a failure. It was to open simultaneously from sea and land, but the ships of both fleets were wood, and their fire power was ineffective against fortress walls of stone six feet thick. Early in the day a Russian shell blew up a French magazine with great loss, the explosion of a French ammunition wagon followed. The French became discouraged and ceased to fire. The British continued to pour in shell and red-hot shot, and at three o'clock, with a colossal explosion, a great Russian magazine blew up. The principal Russian fortifications were wrecked, every gun was silenced, the infantry massed to meet an assault showed signs of panic, and General Todleben, in charge of the defences of Sebastopol, thought the end had come, and put on all his orders, so that his corpse might be recognised.

But no assault was made. The French refused, and Lord Raglan would not move without the French. Darkness fell, and at dawn next day it was seen that the Russians had repaired their defences. Through that day, the 18th, the cannonade continued. The defences were again broken up, but again no assault was made. Again during the night, inspired by the genius of Todleben and working with incredible industry, the Russians made good the breaches by dawn.

While firing was in progress Lord Cardigan, accompanied by

his friend Mr. de Burgh, rode up to take a look at the batteries of siege guns. They were joined by a young officer of Engineers and William Howard Russell.

"Ah," said Lord Cardigan, "I see! Those fellows below are our men, and they are firing at the Russians. Those fellows who are firing towards us are the Russians. Why don't we drive them away?" The officer explained that there were certain difficulties in the suggested operation, but the gallant General was by no means satisfied, and insisted on his views with an air of haughty conviction. At last, putting up his glasses and turning to remount his horse, he exclaimed, "I have never in my life seen a siege conducted on such principles, Squire." The Squire assented: he had never seen such a siege either; and they rode back to Balaclava.

Irritating and ignorant though he might be, Lord Cardigan had hit on the truth. Without an assault the cannonade was useless. Huge sums had been blown away in ammunition, time which was of the most vital importance had been lost, and nothing had been gained. What was to be done next?

Meanwhile, since the unhappy episode of October 7, relations between Lord Raglan and Lord Lucan had been growing steadily worse, and on October 14 Sir Colin Campbell, a brigadier of the Highland Division, was placed in command of the defence of Balaclava over Lucan's head. "Lord Raglan would not trust Lord Lucan to defend Balaclava, so sent down Sir Colin Campbell," wrote Captain Maude of the Horse Artillery. Sir Colin, however, took it for granted that he would be under Lucan's orders, since Lucan was a lieutenant-general, and wrote that he would cheerfully execute Lord Lucan's directions. He was told he would be in no way under Lucan's authority—his command was to be a separate command. Upon this Lord Cardigan became indignant. If Sir Colin Campbell could have a separate command, why not he? It was suggested that Sir Colin Campbell, the hero of a dozen hard-fought campaigns, had experience which Lord Cardigan lacked, but to this Lord Cardigan simply replied that both were brigadiers, and therefore equal.

It is to Lord Lucan's credit that he became and remained on

excellent terms with Sir Colin Campbell. But Sir Colin had been brought up in a hard school where men of influence and rank were concerned; it was no new thing for him to find himself subordinate to a man like Lord Lucan. After forty-four years' brilliant service, during which he had distinguished himself at Corunna under Sir John Moore, in the Peninsula under Wellington, in China, in the West Indies, and repeatedly in India, he had attained no higher rank than that of colonel—his promotion to brigadier had taken place only three months ago in June, 1854. The son of a Glasgow carpenter who had married a gentlewoman, he had neither money nor influence and, though acknowledged the finest administrator and soldier since Wellington, had over and over again to endure having men who knew nothing and had never seen a shot fired promoted over his head.

Lord Lucan's position was in fact a horrible one. He was very well aware, wrote his old enemy Anthony Bacon, of the feelings of mistrust and want of confidence with which he was regarded throughout his division. He knew he was derided, he knew he was regarded as unfit to command, and the responsibility for this, as for every other misfortune, he laid at Lord Raglan's door. It was the Commander-in-Chief who had ordered him in no circumstances to attack, who had recalled him from pursuit after the Alma, sending two messengers when he was unwilling to turn back, who had said he was determined to keep his cavalry "in a band-box." He, Lucan, was blamed, despised, even, intolerably, accused of cowardice because he was forced—what else could he do?—to carry out Lord Raglan's orders. At the moment he was being censured for deficiency in generalship in the matter of cavalry patrols. Every day at the same hour a patrol had been sent along a most dangerous road, cut in the side of a mountain, with a thick wood on one side and a precipice on the other. It was a death trap; the patrol had daily expected to be wiped out, and officers and men had grumbled. Then on October 24 Lord Raglan ordered the patrols to be discontinued, and the whole army praised him and blamed Lucan. "It is said," wrote William

Forrest, "Lord Raglan found great fault with Lord Lucan for sending them out." What was the truth? The patrols had been ordered by Lord Raglan. A week before Robert Portal had been told by Lucan that he "considered the patrol a most dangerous one and not fit for cavalry at all, but that it was by Lord Raglan's order, not his, that I had gone."

Nevertheless Lord Lucan set his teeth and determined to carry out every order the Commander-in-Chief might give him, however unreasonable. Raglan was to be given no handle, never should Raglan be able to say that he found him insubordinate. Any order Lord Raglan gave should be executed; if the consequences proved unfortunate, so much the worse for Lord Raglan.

While Lucan thus regarded his Commander-in-Chief with resentment and distrust, the officers of the cavalry division regarded both Lord Lucan and his brigadier, Lord Cardigan, with distrust and contempt.

Nolan thundered against "Lord Look-on and the Noble Yachtsman": William Forrest wrote, "We all agree that two greater muffs than Lucan and Cardigan could not be. We call Lucan the cautious ass and Cardigan the dangerous ass." Robert Portal considered that his brigadier, Lord Cardigan, "has as much brains as my boot. He is only to be equalled in want of intellect by his relation the Earl of Lucan. Without mincing matters, two such fools could hardly be picked out of the British army. And they take command. But they are Earls!" When his family received this letter they were greatly shocked, and wrote scolding him for disrespect to his superiors.

Such was the state of mind of the cavalry division when, on October 18, a large Russian force was seen marching along a ridge, above Balaclava and about five miles away. The British could take no action. The position of Lord Raglan was becoming more difficult every day, sickness was rampant, his army was shrinking, and he had not a man to spare. However, the Russians made no offensive movement, but, emerging from the west and marching in plain sight of the British, established themselves in a village some miles to the east. For the next few days the British could see reinforcements streaming in, and by October 24 an army had collected. Twenty-five battalions of infantry, thirty-five squadrons of cavalry, and thirty-eight guns, twenty-five thousand men in all, had been assembled under the command of a general of formidable reputation—General Liprandi.

It was all too evident that this overwhelming force was about to swoop down on Balaclava.

11

The British had got themselves into a position of extraordinary difficulty at Balaclava. High above on the heights, they were encamped before Sebastopol; far below lay Balaclava, as if at the foot of a castle wall, detached, isolated, an outpost.

Yet Balaclava was not only the base but the sole lifeline of the British army. Every morsel the troops ate, every bullet they fired, every item of their equipment must come through it. There was no other avenue of communication with the outside world. Balaclava was the only port, the only storehouse, the only arsenal.

Had Lord Raglan been able to garrison Balaclava with ten thousand men even then its position would have presented grave problems, but when he chose Balaclava he was already short of men and of guns. Merely a skeleton force could be spared, and the British base, inviting attack, was garrisoned only by the 93rd, now the Argyll and Sutherland Highlanders, 100 men from the Invalid Battalion, and 1,100 Turks.

Some two miles above Balaclava, however, at the foot of the heights, was the cavalry camp.

The main road to Balaclava enters through a gorge, which, about a mile above the town, opens out into a wide space, known as the plain of Balaclava. On this plain the battle was fought.

The extent of the plain is some three by two miles; it is a natural amphitheatre enclosed on all sides by hills, and in addition to mounds and hillocks, which here and there break its surface, it is bisected by a ridge, of the kind called in England a hog's back, which runs from left to right and forms a natural causeway. The British had named the ridge, somewhat ambitiously, the "Causeway Heights," and the two valleys on each side of it were called the South Valley and the North Valley. Both valleys were shut in by hills; indeed, the North Valley was so much enclosed as to be a narrow pocket, fenced on one side by the Causeway Heights and on the other by a broken range called the Fedioukine Hills. The North Valley was the scene of the charge of the Light Brigade.

Strategically, the important feature of the plain was the Causeway Heights, because the only road connecting Balaclava with the camp on the heights ran along the top of the Causeway Ridge. The possession of this road, the Woronzoff Road, was vital to the British; it was their sole line of communication, and, deprived of it, they would have to clamber to and from their camp by rough mountain tracks. Recently an attempt had been made to protect the Woronzoff Road and provide a line of defence for Balaclava by throwing up a half-circle of six redoubts on and near the Causeway Heights. These redoubts contained twelve-pounder naval guns, and were manned by Turks. Though Lord Raglan was forced in his extremity to rely on Turks, his contempt and dislike for them were intense. There were men in the British Army with experience in handling Oriental troops, and in their opinion much might have been made of the Turks; only four months ago, under the command of officers from the Bengal and Bombay Armies of the East India Company, they had fought supremely well at Silistria. However, to Lord Raglan Turks were bandits, and officers of the Bengal and Bombay Armies only one degree more acceptable. The Turkish troops had been treated with contempt, their commissariat arrangements were almost non-existent, they were half-starved, and their morale was low.

At eleven o'clock on October 24 a Turkish spy came to Sir Colin Campbell's headquarters at Balaclava with intelligence that twenty thousand Russian infantry and five thousand Russian cavalry were marching on Balaclava from the east and south-east. Sir Colin Campbell called in Lord Lucan, and they examined the man together and were convinced that the information was correct; the blow was about to fall. Sir Colin wrote an urgent report to Lord Raglan, and it was immediately taken the six miles up to headquarters by Lucan's son and aide-de-camp, Lord Bingham. The Commander-in-Chief being in conference with the French Commander-in-Chief, Lord Bingham gave the letter to General Airey, who received it without comment. Presently, however, Airey went into the conference and showed the letter to Lord Raglan, who remarked "Very well." No acknowledgment was sent to Colin Campbell, but later Lord Raglan happened to meet Bingham, who was still waiting, and told him that "If there was anything new it was to be reported to him."

Unfortunately only three days before precisely similar intelligence had come in from the Turks. The report had been believed, and preparations made to meet an attack; the 4th Division, under Sir George Cathcart, had been marched down from the heights, and Lord Lucan had turned out the cavalry. But the Russians did not attack, the 4th Division was marched up the heights again, arriving, to Sir George Cathcart's fury, in a state of utter exhaustion, and the cavalry divisions were kept at their horses' heads from 5 P.M. until 7 A.M. The night was bitterly cold, and Major Willet of the 17th Lancers died of exposure.

The state of the army before Sebastopol was causing Lord Raglan intense anxiety, for so many were sick that those on their feet were having to do double turns of duty, and he was most unwilling to wear out his troops in another wild-goose chase. The letter from Sir Colin Campbell was put aside.

Before dawn on the next day, October 25, the cavalry were already "standing at their horses," in accordance with Lord Lucan's unpopular practice of turning out his division an hour

Sketch Map

THE BATTLE OF BALACLAVA
Showing the Charge of the Light Brigade

THE HEIGHTS

Lord Raglan

French Chasseurs D'Afrique

EDIOUKINE HEIGHTS

NORTH VALLEY

DIRECTION OF CHARGE

Woronzoff Road

Light Brigade

CAUSEWAY HEIGHTS

AREA OF CHARGE OF HEAVY BRIGADE

SOUTH VALLEY

Canrobert's Hill

93rd Argyle & Sutherland Highlanders

To Balaclava

Scale of Miles

0   1/4   1/2   3/4   1

LEGEND

BRITISH
Cavalry
Infantry
Redoubt

RUSSIAN
Cavalry
Infantry
Guns

before daybreak. It was so dark that Lucan and his staff were hardly visible as they jogged along on their usual morning ride of inspection. As they passed the Light Brigade, Lord George Paget joined the cavalcade—Cardigan slept late in his yacht, and at this early hour Lord George usually found himself in command.

Some distance to the east of the cavalry camp was a hillock called Canroberts Hill, on which the first of the six redoubts had been placed and a flagstaff put up. As they approached, Lord George noticed first that darkness was turning to the first grey light of dawn, then suddenly that in the half-light he could make out something extraordinary—two flags hung from the flagstaff. A conversation followed which, he said, he would remember to the day of his death. "Holloa! there are two flags flying. What does that mean?" "Why that, surely, is the signal that the enemy is approaching." "Are you quite sure?" asked Lord George. As he spoke there was a sudden startling crash, the guns in the redoubt fired, and the battle of Balaclava had begun.

Captain Duberly of the 8th Hussars was on duty at headquarters as Lord Raglan's escort, and sent a note down to his wife, who was living in the harbour in the *Southern Star.* "The battle of Balaclava has begun and promises to be a hot one. I send you the horse. Lose no time, but come up as quickly as you can. Do not wait for breakfast." Mrs. Duberly mounted and hastened to headquarters, and witnessed the battle from the heights.

As daylight brightened, Lord Lucan and Sir Colin Campbell saw that the Russians were advancing towards them in enormous strength; two great columns of Russian infantry with artillery, numbering some eleven thousand men and thirty-eight guns, were converging on the Causeway Heights, and Lucan sent an aide-de-camp to inform Lord Raglan that an attack on the redoubts was imminent. Lord Raglan, however, could do nothing: no assistance could be sent in time, since two hours at least must elapse before a division could be brought down from the heights. Nor could

Sir Colin Campbell or Lord Lucan help: Highlanders and cavalry must be kept for the defence of Balaclava itself. Once the Causeway Heights were carried, only the 93rd Highlanders and the cavalry stood between the Russians and Balaclava. The Turks must be left to do the best they could, and for this unfortunate situation Lucan blamed Raglan.

Lord Raglan not having acted on the communication sent him the day previous by Sir Colin Campbell and myself informing him of the approach of a considerable Russian Army, and leaving us altogether without support, we considered it our first duty to defend the approach to the town of Balaclava; and as this defence would depend chiefly upon the cavalry it was necessary to reserve them for the purpose.

Lucan, however, decided to see if he could accomplish anything by a feint, and, placing the Light Brigade in reserve, he went forward with the Heavy Brigade and the Horse Artillery, "making threatening demonstrations and cannonading as long as my ammunition lasted." The impatience and fury of officers and men of the cavalry division were not to be described. It was their belief that the Russian advance could be checked and, in the hands of a general experienced in war, would have been checked; or at least the Russians would have been worried, harassed, and thrown into confusion. The Russians, not deceived by threats, came steadily on, and in order to avoid an engagement, Lord Lucan was forced, inch by inch, to withdraw.

At this point the 1,100 Turks in the redoubts on the Causeway Heights looked out and saw advancing upon them, without any opposition from their British allies, an overwhelming force of infantry with numerous guns, while from the south-east a battery of thirty guns opened a furious fire on Canroberts Hill and redoubt No. 1. At this moment the British cavalry had just been halted near Canroberts Hill, and presently a crash was heard, "splinters of broken guns, horses' legs etc." wrote Lord George Paget, were seen "shooting up into the air." By ill fortune a shell had fallen into a troop of Horse Artillery; Captain

Maude, its brilliant officer, was desperately wounded, and the troop had to be withdrawn.

The concentrated fire of thirty guns did not take long to silence the twelve-pounders of No. 1 redoubt, and the Russian infantry came on in overwhelming strength—five battalions with six in support, eleven battalions in all, against one battalion of Turks. The Russians flooded across the ditch and over the parapet; there was firing, a moment's suspense, followed by a shout, "By God they've taken Canrobert's Hill!" and the Turks were seen to be in flight, tumbling helter-skelter down the steep slope.

Nevertheless, in this the No. 1 redoubt there had been a stiff resistance—casualties approached 50 per cent—but the spectacle of their comrades being pounded and slaughtered, without a company or squadron being launched in their support, was too much for the Turks in redoubts 2, 3, and 4. Some faint show of resistance was put up in 2, but the defenders of 3 and 4 fled without firing a shot and ran in a rabble towards Balaclava shouting "Ship, ship!"

The Russians had now gained possession of four out of six redoubts, and dismantling No. 4, which was nearest the British, they established themselves in 1, 2, and 3, taking possession of the twelve-pounder guns.

The position of the cavalry division now became highly vulnerable. Not only were they within musket shot of the captured redoubts, but they were directly in the line of fire from the 93rd drawn up before Balaclava. On Colin Campbell's advice, Lucan withdrew the cavalry division along the length of the South Valley and took up a position on the slopes of the Causeway Heights, just beyond the dismantled redoubt No. 4, where he would be able to attack the flank of the Russian force as it advanced. The withdrawal, though necessary and well advised, was not understood by the cavalry division.

Our painful retreat across that plain by alternate regiments was one of the most painful ordeals it is possible to conceive [wrote Lord George

Paget] seeing all the defences in our front successively abandoned as they were, and straining our eyes all round the hills in our rear for indications of support.

The retreat of the cavalry marked the end of the first period of the battle. The situation could hardly have been more serious; the Causeway Heights were lost, the road from the base to the camp on the heights was lost, the Russians were coming on in overwhelming strength, and it seemed as if Balaclava must very shortly be lost too. It was now about half-past nine, and at this point Lord Cardigan, coming up from his yacht, took over the command of the Light Brigade from Lord George Paget.

The chilly, misty morning had now, as happens in autumn, turned into a day of extraordinary brilliance and clarity, and the group of watchers, standing with Lord Raglan and his staff on the verge of the heights, had an astonishing experience. Six or seven hundred feet above the plain they watched the battle as if from a box in a theatre. Alma had been a confused and straggling battle, fought over a wide front and obscured by broken ground and drifting smoke; it had been impossible at the Alma to see the action as a whole; but Balaclava was fought on the enclosed plain with its two valleys as on a stage. Observers were conscious of an extraordinary effect of theatrical unreality. The mountain ridges, the azure sky, the waters of Balaclava harbour flashing in the sun seemed a back-cloth, the wheeling squadrons of cavalry, the artillery, the Highlanders in their kilts and red coats part of a spectacle—impossible to believe that they were in deadly earnest. So still was the air that sounds carried long distances—the champing of bits, the clink of sabres, shouted orders, the yells of the Turks as they fled from the redoubts were audible on the heights. As the cavalry retired, individual officers could be identified through glasses and a clamour broke out. "There's Lord George Paget!" "That's Low!" "Douglas," "Jenyns," "Morris."

There had, it seems, been an idea in Lord Raglan's mind that the advance on Balaclava was a feint and the real intention of the Russians was to sally out of Sebastopol in force and attack the besieging British army. He now had had incontrovertible evidence to the contrary, and all that stood between a Russian army and his base at Balaclava was Sir Colin Campbell with 550 93rd Highlanders, 100 invalids, rather less than a battalion of Turks, who had been rallied during the flight to the harbour from the redoubts, and the cavalry division.

Two divisions of infantry—the 1st under the Duke of Cambridge and the 4th under Sir George Cathcart—were now ordered to descend into the plain. But Sir George Cathcart refused to move. The false alarm only three days ago was fresh in his mind, his men were exhausted, having only just returned from duty in the trenches, and the unhappy arrangement of the Dormant Commission was preying on his mind; he was irritable, suspicious, and considered he should have been consulted earlier. Some time passed before he could be persuaded to move, and it was after ten o'clock by the time both divisions had begun to march down from the heights.

Meanwhile General Canrobert, who was on the heights with Lord Raglan, had ordered two brigades of French infantry to take up a position at the foot of the heights immediately below him, and with them—an important decision—were sent two cavalry regiments of the celebrated Chasseurs d'Afrique, who had recently disembarked at the French base.

It was now evident that an action on a large scale was about to be fought, and Lord Raglan made up his mind that the action must be an infantry action. In face of the enormous superiority in numbers of the Russians, not only in infantry but also in cavalry, it seemed to him inevitable that his small division of cavalry, if engaged, must by sheer weight be pushed backwards into the sea.

The position taken up by Lord Lucan on Sir Colin Campbell's advice was excellent. The cavalry covered the Highlanders, drawn up before the gorge which formed the entrance to Balaclava, and could attack the Russian flank as it advanced. But they would engage the enemy as an independent force, and this Lord Raglan refused to allow: the cavalry must wait and act in conjunction with the infantry divisions marching down from the heights. He ordered Lucan to withdraw to a position at the foot of the heights on the extreme left of No. 6 redoubt. This order, known in the controversy which arose between Lord Lucan and Lord Raglan as the "first order," ran: "Cavalry to take ground to left of second line of Redoubts occupied by Turks."

Lord Lucan received the order with anger and despair. Once again the cavalry was to be immobilised and useless, and—far more important—by removing the cavalry from their covering position, the small force under Sir Colin Campbell, the only defence of Balaclava, was left open to the Russian attack. So reluctant was Lucan to execute the order that he requested the staff officer who had brought it to wait until the movement was carried out, so that afterwards it might not be said that he had misunderstood Lord Raglan's meaning.

Meanwhile a second Russian force with artillery had appeared from the east and established itself on the slopes of the Fedioukine Hills, which fenced the North Valley on the north.

And now, from their point of vantage on the verge of the heights, the watchers witnessed an extraordinary episode. A great square of Russian cavalry, supported by artillery, began to move slowly up the North Valley. On they came, three or four thousand men strong. But the British cavalry took no notice. They sat motionless in their saddles. The mass of Russians came nearer and nearer, approached to within a few hundred yards; still the British were oblivious and, it was borne in on the watchers, the Russians were equally oblivious. The two forces were invisible to each other: they could neither see nor be seen. Only to the watchers above, looking down, did the plain appear flat and the movements of the enemy clear; the troops engaged in the battle had their view obscured by hillocks, by rises in the ground, and, above all, by the ridge of the Causeway Heights. Unless Lord Raglan could put himself in the place of his generals 600 feet below and could perpetually bear in mind when issuing orders that what was clear to him would by no means be clear to them, his position high above the battle was dangerous indeed.

Slowly, formidably, unseen, and unopposed, the Russian force came on. Suddenly a body of some four squadrons detached themselves, galloped over the ridge of the Causeway Heights, and bore down on Sir Colin Campbell's little force barring the way to Balaclava. A moment or two later the main mass slowly swerved to the left and also began to cross the Causeway Heights into the South Valley.

The Russians had now advanced far enough to bring Sir Colin Campbell's force within range of their guns, and they opened fire with considerable effect. Sir Colin had drawn up his force on a hillock at the entrance to the gorge leading to Balaclava, and he ordered his men to lie on their faces in a line two deep on the far slope. Lying helpless under artillery fire is notoriously a strain, and at this moment the four squadrons came into view, bearing rapidly down from the Causeway Heights, while behind them, just becoming visible, was the main body of the Russian cavalry. The sight was once more too much for the Turks; they leapt to their feet, and officers and men fled for the port, again crying "Ship! ship! ship!" As they passed the camp of the Highlanders, a soldier's wife rushed out and fell upon them, belabouring them with a stick, kicking them, cursing them for cowards, pulling their hair, and boxing their ears, and so pursued them down to the harbour.

Five hundred and fifty men of the Highlanders and one hundred invalids were now left to stand between the Russian army and Balaclava, and Sir Colin rode down the line telling them, "Men, remember there is no retreat from here. You must die where you stand."

To the Russian cavalry as they came on, the hillock appeared unoccupied, when suddenly, as if out of the earth, there sprang up a line two deep of Highlanders in red coats—the line immortalised in British history as "the thin red line." Every man in that line expected to be killed and, determined to sell his life as dearly as possible, faced the enemy with stern steadiness.

The Russians were taken aback. Their intelligence service was quite as inadequate as the British; they had no idea of the strength and disposition of the British troops, and they suspected once more that they had fallen into an ambush. Indeed, the gorge ahead would have been perfect for that purpose had the idea of an ambush ever occurred to the British command.

The Russian cavalry checked, halted, and from the thin red line came a volley of the deadly musket fire, every bullet aimed, which formation in line made possible. The Russians wavered, steadied, advanced, and a second volley was fired. Once more the Russians wavered, and such was the eagerness of the Highlanders that there was a movement forward: the men wanted to dash out and engage the cavalry hand to hand, and Sir Colin Campbell was heard shouting sternly, "Ninety-third! Ninety-third! Damn all that eagerness." The British line steadied, a third volley was fired, and the Russians wheeled and withdrew in the direction of the main body of their cavalry. The Highlanders burst into hurrahs. Balaclava, for the moment, was saved.

This episode, however, famous though it became, was only a side action: the important feature of the battle at this point was the movement of the great main body of the Russian cavalry over the ridge of the Causeway Heights. Neither the British nor the Russians had thrown out scouts or kept any look-out, and each side remained perfectly unconscious of the other's presence. They were, however, now to collide.

One of the drawbacks to Lord Raglan's position on the heights was his distance from the action in point of time. After he had given an order, more than half an hour could elapse, depending on the horsemanship of the aide-de-camp concerned, before the heights were descended and the order delivered to the general concerned in the plain. From this fact resulted the first great cavalry engagement of the battle.

When the Russians began to bear down on Sir Colin Campbell's little force, Lord Raglan saw that the Turks were uncertain, and he sent down to Lucan what is known as the "second order." "Eight squadrons of Heavy Dragoons to be detached towards Balaclava to support the Turks, who are wavering." Owing to the time taken to deliver the order, the action of the thin red line was over before the squadrons had moved, but they were now trotting down towards Balaclava with the Causeway Heights on their left; two squadrons each of the 5th Dragoon Guards, the Scots Greys and Inniskillings, followed by two squadrons of the 4th Dragoon Guards, led by their Brigadier-General Scarlett.

Though General Scarlett was bent only on reaching Sir Colin Campbell, his route, as it happened, took him straight across the front of the advancing Russian cavalry. His aide-de-camp gave an exclamation; General Scarlett looked to his left, and there, a few hundred yards away on the slopes of the Causeway Heights, a gigantic mass of horsemen was bearing down on him.

The Hon. James Scarlett, brigadier-general of the Heavy Brigade, was a stout, red-faced gentleman with a large white moustache and large white eyebrows, fifty-five years of age, and as destitute of military experience as Lord Lucan or Lord Cardigan. He had, however, two qualities which his colleagues conspicuously lacked: he possessed modesty and good sense. Conscious of his military ignorance, he had provided himself with men who knew what fighting was, and there was only one place where, at that period, experience in the field could be gained. General Scarlett had two aides-de-camp, or, rather, advisers, on whose recommendations he openly relied, and both these men were "Indian" officers of brilliant reputation. One was the celebrated "Indian" cavalry commander, Colonel Beatson, whose services had been rejected by Lord Raglan, Lord Lucan, and Lord Cardigan. When General Scarlett attached Colonel Beatson to his staff, Lord Raglan and Lord Lucan had strenuously opposed the appointment, and officially Colonel Beatson was without status or recognition. General Scarlett's other adviser, Lt. Alexander Elliot, had served throughout the Gwalior Campaign and had commanded a troop of the Bengal Light Cavalry at the battle of Punniar. At the great battle of Ferozeshah he had successfully led a desperate cavalry charge, and as a reward for his service had been given a command in the Commander-in-Chief's bodyguard and made an honorary aide-de-camp. He had also been brilliantly successful in military administration. He held the rank of lieutenant only because he had been forced to leave India on account of his health and start again from the bottom in the British Army.

In character General Scarlett was brave, good-natured, and unassuming; his men thought themselves fortunate in their commander, and his two advisers were greatly attached to him. Lieutenant Seager, contrasting him with his own commander, Lord Cardigan, wrote, "Good kind old fellow that he is, they are all very fond of him and will follow him anywhere."

General Scarlett, in command of the Heavy Brigade, assisted by his two advisers, was now to perform what has been called "one of the great feats of cavalry against cavalry in the history of Europe."

The Russian cavalry were three to four thousand strong, and the effect of such a body of horsemen in a disciplined mass is overwhelming. They were only a few hundred yards away, and they were on the slope above General Scarlett. Nevertheless, Scarlett gave the order to wheel into line. Though his eight squadrons numbered only about five hundred troopers, he intended to charge the thousands before him, and charge uphill.

On his left, however, were the remains of a ruined vineyard—fallen walls, tangled roots, concealed holes—the worst possible ground for a charge, and he was forced to pause and take ground on his right. At this moment Lord Lucan rode up and ordered him, with the utmost urgency, to do what he was already in course of doing; and charge the enemy. It was Lord Lucan's conviction ever afterwards that he had originated the charge.

By this time the whole body of Russian cavalry had crossed

the ridge; they, too, wheeled into line; trumpets blew, and, shaking the ground as they went, the huge mass, at a measured trot, began to descend the hill.

The British had not yet been able to start their advance. The extremely difficult nature of the ground had broken the troops into two sections, and the line had to be restored.

With extraordinary composure, Scarlett sat in his saddle waiting quietly, the great mass of Russian cavalry descending steadily towards him, while behind him the troop officers dressed and redressed the line with as little sign of haste as if they had been on a parade.

To the watchers on the heights the delay was all but unendurable. Three hundred troopers only formed Scarlett's first line, and they were occupied moving a few feet this way or that while a grey torrent of horsemen, appearing all the more irresistible for its deliberate, measured pace, descended upon them. In a moment the line of British troopers must, it seemed, be swept away, helpless as straws before a tidal wave. Suddenly the unbelievable happened once again: Russian trumpets sounded, the great mass of horsemen came to a halt and proceeded to throw out two wings from the central square, with the object of outflanking the British line. Cavalry who receive a charge when halted sustain a far greater shock than when they are in motion, and it is an elementary maxim of cavalry tactics that troops should be in movement when receiving a charge. The astonishing opportunity offered by the Russians must instantly be seized, and Lord Lucan ordered his trumpeter to sound the charge. But the line was not yet accurately dressed, and the charge was sounded twice again before the troop officers were satisfied and ready to advance. After the war Russian officers said that the extraordinary unhurried deliberation displayed in the movements of the tiny British force had done much to shake the Russian morale.

Six of Scarlett's eight squadrons were now drawn up in two

lines: the first, two squadrons of the Scots Greys and a squadron of Inniskillings; the second, another squadron of Inniskillings and two squadrons of the 5th Dragoon Guards. Two squadrons of 4th Dragoon Guards and the Royals were coming up but had still some distance to cover. Five hundred yards away was the huge Russian mass, drawn up in a square so dense that to penetrate it seemed impossible, with two wings far outflanking and enclosing Scarlett's little force, waiting to squeeze and crush, like the tentacles of an octopus. Nor was Scarlett's only difficulty the fact that he was fantastically out-numbered. The Greys were on the site of their own camp, and until they were clear of it must advance over ground encumbered by picket ropes and sick horses; moreover, though the Russians were halted, the approach to them was uphill.

However, Scarlett, with his staff and his trumpeter immediately behind him, placed himself in front of his first line, drew his sword, and ordered his trumpeter to sound the charge.

Between the Scots Greys and the Inniskillings, who formed the first line, a traditional friendship existed, and it happened that the last time each regiment had been in action was together at Waterloo. They had galloped side by side in the first line of Lord Uxbridge's celebrated cavalry charge, and, by a further coincidence, the Greys on that great day had ridden, as they were riding now, on the left of the Inniskillings.

For a few minutes the pace seemed intolerably slow, as the Greys picked their way over the camping ground and the Inniskillings held back to wait for them; then they were clear and riding headlong, stirrup to stirrup, up the slope to the Russians. The maddening events of the day—the capture of the redoubts under their very eyes, the retreat of the cavalry without striking a blow, the final delay while their line was dressed with finicking precision—boiled in their blood: they crashed furiously into the Russian mass, and the wild sound of their battle cries floated up to the heights, the Irish yell of the Inniskillings and the fierce growling "moan" of the Scots Greys.

Hard as they had ridden, Scarlett was first. Fifty yards ahead of his first line, he had galloped straight into the Russian mass and disappeared.

And now the watchers on the heights saw an astonishing sight. First Scarlett and his staff, then the three squadrons of the first line, were swallowed up, lost, and engulfed in the great grey Russian mass, and then suddenly they had not disappeared. Red coats were visible, bright specks of colour against the Russian grey: the men of the Heavy Brigade were alive, fighting, their sword arms moving like toys, and through field-glasses individual officers could be distinguished; Scarlett in particular with his red face and big white moustache, fighting like a madman. Now the great Russian square began to heave, to sway, to surge this way and that, but it did not break, and the two great wings began to wheel inward to cut off the three squadrons, close over them, and crush them. "How can such a handful resist, much less make headway through such a legion?" wrote Lord George Paget, who witnessed the charge. "Their huge flanks lap round that handful, and almost hide them from our view. They are surrounded and must be annihilated! One can hardly breathe." But now it was the turn of the second line. Wild with the rage of battle, yelling madly, the second squadron of Inniskillings and the 5th Dragoon Guards crashed into the Russian mass on the left; a few seconds later the Royals, who had come forward without orders, flung themselves in on the right. Once more the great grey square heaved, and up on the heights a roar like the roar of the sea could be heard, made up, said those who were near the battle, of the violent and ceaseless cursing of the British troopers hacking at the thick Russian uniforms—the Russian coats were so thick that they turned the points of the swords, the shakos so stout that they could not be halved with a hatchet. It was an engagement of a thousand hand-to-hand fights; pistols and carbines were not used—men hacked and chopped at each other, cursing at each other. When their swords broke, they tore at each other, streaming with blood. The roar of battle was accompanied by the sharp clatter of sword on sword and sword on helmet, and punctuated by sudden wild yells as the Russian mass, heaving, surging, swayed this way and that, but still did not break.

Meanwhile where was the Light Brigade? They were only 500 yards away from the Russian flank, in full view of the action, indeed looking down on it, chafing, swearing, devoured by impatience, but not attempting to move. Lord Cardigan rode restlessly up and down declaring, "These damned Heavies will have the laugh of us this day"—but to act on his own initiative never occurred to him. He had, he wrote, been "ordered into a position by Lieutenant-General the Earl of Lucan, my superior officer, with orders on no account to leave it, and to defend it against any attack of the Russians; they did not however approach the position." Lord Lucan's version was somewhat different: he had, he asserted, said to Cardigan, "I am going to leave you. Well, you'll remember you are placed here by Lord Raglan himself for the defence of this position. My instructions to you are to attack anything and everything that shall come within reach of you, but you will be careful of columns or squares of infantry." In Lucan's opinion when before Cardigan's eyes the Russian cavalry proceeded to become engaged with the Heavy Brigade, they came within the category of "anything and everything that shall come within reach of you," and should have been attacked.

The intention of Lord Raglan, however, was to keep his cavalry in hand and prevent their becoming entangled in any engagement until the two divisions of infantry should arrive down from the heights. He issued no further order to the Light Brigade, and, swearing and cursing, the Light Brigade remained inactive.

Suddenly from the swaying, heaving mass tightly locked together—so tightly locked that men found themselves paralysed by dead bodies of their enemies falling across their saddles and into their arms—there came a new sound: the sound of British cheers. The mass was no longer surging to and fro, but swaying in one direction, and that uphill: the Russians were almost being pushed back. At this moment Lord Lucan ordered the 4th Dragoon Guards, who had been held back almost dying of impatience, to charge. Wheeling into line, they bore headlong down on the Russian right, crashed in, and went through the Russian force from flank to flank.

The great Russian mass swayed, rocked, gave a gigantic heave, broke, and, disintegrating it seemed in a moment, fled. A great shout went up: from the troops fighting the battle, from the Light Brigade looking on, from the heights, where the watchers hurrah-ed, flung their hats into the air, and clapped their hands; and Lord Raglan sent an aide-de-camp galloping down with the message "Well done, Scarlett." So great had been the tension, and so swift the change, that men who only a moment before had been fighting like madmen steeped in blood burst into tears.

The enemy was now in full flight, streaming away up the ridge of the Causeway Heights to the north; but there was no pursuit. The regiments of the Heavy Brigade, mixed during the battle into confusion, were busy re-sorting and re-forming, men were seeking their officers and officers their men, and though isolated groups made efforts, no organised action was taken. The brilliant victory was not completed: the great host of the Russian cavalry was suffered to escape; and, though the escape was taking place before their eyes, still the Light Brigade did not move.

In the 17th Lancers there was one of those "Indian" officers whom the cavalry generals and their Commander-in-Chief united in despising, and owing to sickness and to the recent death of Major Willet from exposure, he was in command of the regiment. Captain Morris at thirty-four had taken part in three campaigns, and had charged with cavalry in four battles, including the famous battle of Aliwal in 1846; then, returning to England, he had passed with great distinction through the Senior Department of the Royal Military College at Sandhurst. Short, stocky, immensely powerful, nicknamed "the pocket Hercules," Captain Morris was a popular regimental character, who shared Captain Nolan's fanatical enthusiasm for cavalry and was his intimate friend.

Captain Morris was now seen to move out and speak to Lord Cardigan. "My lord, are you not going to charge the flying enemy?" "No," replied Cardigan, "we have orders to remain here." "But, my lord," pressed Morris, "it is our positive duty to follow up this advantage." "No," repeated Cardigan, "we must remain here." In a frenzy Morris implored him to allow the 17th Lancers to pursue the enemy. "Do, my lord, allow me to charge them with the 17th. See, my lord, they are in disorder!" But Cardigan would only repeat, "No, no, sir, we must not stir from here," and in a rage Morris turned to the officers near, "Gentlemen, you are witnesses of my request."

Private Wightman of the 17th Lancers, in common with the rest of the Light Brigade, saw Captain Morris speaking "very earnestly" to Lord Cardigan in front of the Light Brigade and heard Cardigan's "hoarse, sharp" words, "No, no, sir." As Captain Morris fell back, he wheeled his horse in front of Private Wightman's squadron and, slapping his leg angrily with his sword, said loudly, "My God, my God, what a chance we are losing!"

Had Lord Cardigan pursued, the heavy cavalry action at Balaclava might, in the words of a military historian, "have taken its place as a classic in military literature, and the host of the Russian horse might have suffered a discomfiture with few parallels in the history of war." As it was, the Russian cavalry crossed the ridge of the Causeway Heights with their artillery and, unlimbering the guns, established themselves at the eastern end of the North Valley.

At the close of the action Lord Lucan sent Lord Cardigan an angry message by his son, Lord Bingham. He expressed himself as being extremely disappointed at not having had the support of the Light Cavalry Brigade, and he desired that Lord Cardigan would always remember that when he (Lucan) was attacking in front, it was his (Cardigan's) duty to support him by a flank attack, and that Lord Cardigan might always depend upon receiving from him similar support. Afterwards Cardigan hotly denied that he had ever received this message, and the controversy between the two generals was fought out in the columns of *The Times*. Lord Cardigan also denied that he had ever been urged to pursue by Captain Morris. In both these cases independent evidence shows that his recollection was at fault. Though Cardigan was an efficient "drill-book soldier," he was not only without experience in the field, but without the instincts of a cavalry leader. "The tactics of cavalry," Nolan had written, "are not capable of being reduced to rule. . . . With the cavalry officer almost everything depends on the clearness of his *coup d'œil* and the felicity with which he sizes the happy moment of action." Smartly as Lord Cardigan could handle a brigade of cavalry on a field day, these were qualities he did not even remotely possess.

Lord Lucan angrily rejected the suggestion that he might have, and indeed should have, ordered the Light Brigade to pursue. It was the fault of Lord Raglan's order that the Light Brigade remained inactive.

I know [he wrote] that it has been imputed to me that I did not pursue the routed enemy with my Light cavalry as I should have done. To this I will not allow myself to say any more than that they had been placed in a position by Lord Raglan, that they were altogether out of my reach, and that to me they were unavailable.

The charge of the Heavy Brigade ended the second period of the battle. The aspect of the action had been entirely changed by Scarlett's feat. There was no longer any question of the Russians penetrating to Balaclava; they had been pushed away from Balaclava, even out of the South Valley altogether, and at the moment their position presented difficulties. They held the Causeway Heights and the redoubts, and they had infantry and artillery on the Fedioukine Hills on the other side of the North

Valley, but between them the North Valley, one thousand yards wide, was empty of troops. The troops holding the captured redoubts on the ridge of the Causeway Heights had therefore little support, and Lord Raglan saw that this was the moment to recover the redoubts, the Causeway Heights, and, with the Heights, the Woronzoff Road.

The two divisions of infantry ordered down two hours earlier should now have come into action, but though the 1st Division under the Duke of Cambridge was present, the 4th Division under Sir George Cathcart lagged behind. He was still in a bad temper, and as he unwillingly left the heights, General Airey had brought him orders to assault and recapture the redoubts. So! he thought, his division, straight from the trenches and exhausted, was to attack, while the Guards were merely marched in support along the valley below. He refused to hurry.

Lord Raglan's anger was evident; indeed, William Howard Russell noticed that Lord Raglan had lost his usual marble calm and seemed fidgety and uneasy, continually turning his glasses this way and that and conferring with General Airey and General Estcourt. He now sent Lord Lucan a third order, of which two versions exist. The copy which Lord Raglan retained in his possession runs: "Cavalry to advance and take advantage of any opportunity to recover the Heights. They will be supported by infantry, which have been ordered to advance on two fronts." The order as it reached Lord Lucan and was retained by him is slightly different. The final sentence is divided into two. After the word "ordered" there is a full stop and "advance" is written with a capital "A," so that the final words read "They will be supported by the infantry which have been ordered. Advance on two fronts." The change does not affect the issue. Lord Raglan expected Lucan to understand from the order that he was to advance and recapture the redoubts at once without waiting for infantry support, but that infantry had been ordered, and could be expected later.

Lord Lucan read the order in precisely the opposite sense. He was to advance when supported by infantry. Not only did the words of Lord Raglan's order seem to him to have this meaning, but Raglan's treatment of the cavalry throughout the campaign made it highly improbable that he would order an attack by cavalry alone. Again and again, at the Bulganek, at and after the Alma, on October 7, the cavalry had been restrained, recalled, forbidden to take the offensive, prohibited from engaging the enemy. Only an hour or so ago Lord Raglan had withdrawn the cavalry from their position at the entrance to Balaclava, where they were preparing to engage the Russian cavalry, and placed them in an inactive position under the heights. It never crossed Lucan's mind that he was expected to launch an attack by cavalry with the prospect of being supported at some future time by the infantry. He mounted his division, moved the Light Brigade over to a position across the end of the North Valley, drew up the Heavy Brigade on the slopes of the Woronzoff Road, behind them and on the right, and waited for the infantry, which in his own words "had not yet arrived."

Ten minutes, a quarter of an hour, half an hour passed, and the infantry did not appear. Three-quarters of an hour passed, and still Lord Lucan waited. The attack which Lord Raglan wished the cavalry to make appeared to border on recklessness. Redoubt No. 1, on the crown of Canroberts Hill, was inaccessible to horsemen, Nos. 2 and 3 would have to be charged uphill in the face of infantry and artillery. The Heavy Brigade had earlier come within range of the guns in No. 2 and had been forced to retire. However, Lord Raglan, with his power to divine the temper of troops, perceived that the whole Russian army had been shaken by the triumphant and audacious charge of the Heavy Brigade and that, threatened again by British cavalry, they would retire. Conversations with Russian officers after the war proved Lord Raglan to be right. A feeling of depression had spread through the Russian army as they saw their great and, as they believed, unconquerable mass of horsemen break and fly before a handful of the Heavy Brigade. For the moment the British possessed a moral ascendancy, but the moment must be swiftly turned to account, and up on the heights there were murmurs of impatience and indignation as no further action followed the triumph of the Heavy Brigade, and down below Lord Lucan and the cavalry continued to sit motionless in their saddles.

Suddenly along the line of the Causeway Ridge there was activity. Through glasses teams of artillery horses with lasso tackle could be made out; they were coming up to the redoubts, and a buzz of excitement broke out among the staff. "By Jove! they're going to take away the guns"—the British naval guns with which the redoubts had been armed.

Captured guns were the proof of victory; Lord Raglan would find it difficult to explain away Russian claims to have inflicted a defeat on him if the Russians had not only taken an important position, but captured guns as well. The removal of the guns must be prevented, and, calling General Airey, Lord Raglan gave him rapid instructions. General Airey scribbled an order in pencil on a piece of paper resting on his sabretache and read it to Lord Raglan, who dictated some additional words.

This was the "fourth order" issued to Lord Lucan on the day of Balaclava—the order which resulted in the Charge of the Light Brigade—and the original still exists. The paper is of poor quality, thin and creased, the lines are hurriedly written in pencil, and the flimsy sheet has a curiously insignificant and shabby appearance. The wording of the order runs: "Lord Raglan wishes the cavalry to advance rapidly to the front—follow the enemy and try to prevent the enemy carrying away the guns. Troop Horse Artillery may accompany. French cavalry is on your left. Immediate. (Sgd.) R. Airey."

Captain Thomas Leslie, a member of the family of Leslie of Glaslough, was the next aide-de-camp for duty, and the order had been placed in his hand when Nolan intervened. The honour of carrying the order, he claimed, was his by virtue of his superior rank and consummate horsemanship—the only road now available from the heights to the plain, 600 or 700 feet below, was little more than a track down the face of a precipice and speed was of vital importance. Lord Raglan gave way, and Nolan, snatching the paper out of Captain Leslie's hand, prepared to gallop off. Just as Nolan was about to descend, Lord Raglan called out to him, "Tell Lord Lucan the cavalry is to attack immediately." Nolan plunged over the verge of the heights at breakneck speed.

12

Any other horseman would have picked his way with care down that rough, precipitous slope, but Nolan spurred his horse, and up on the heights the watchers held their breath as, slithering, scrambling, stumbling, he rushed down to the plain.

So far the day had been a terrible one for Edward Nolan; even its sole glory, the charge of the Heavy Brigade, had been gall and wormwood to his soul. He was a light-cavalryman, believing passionately in the superior efficiency of light over heavy horsemen—"so unwieldy, so encumbered," he had written—and in this, the first cavalry action of the campaign, the light cavalry had done absolutely nothing. Hour after hour, in an agony of impatience, he had watched the Light Cavalry Brigade standing by, motionless, inglorious, and, as onlookers had not scrupled to say, shamefully inactive.

For this he furiously blamed Lord Lucan, as he had furiously blamed Lord Lucan on every other occasion when the cavalry had been kept out of action, "raging," in William Howard Russell's phrase, against him all over the camp. Irish-Italian, excitable, headstrong, recklessly courageous, Nolan was beside himself with irritation and anger as he swooped like an avenging angel from the heights, bearing the order which would force the man he detested and despised to attack at last.

With a sigh of relief the watchers saw him arrive safely, gallop furiously across the plain, and, with his horse trembling, sweating, and blown from the wild descent, hand the order to Lord Lucan sitting in the saddle between his two brigades. Lucan opened and read it.

The order appeared to him to be utterly obscure. Lord Raglan and General Airey had forgotten that they were looking down from six hundred feet. Not only could they survey the whole action, but the inequalities of the plain disappeared when viewed from above. Lucan from his position could see nothing; inequalities of the ground concealed the activity round the redoubts, no single enemy soldier was in sight; nor had he any picture of the movements of the enemy in his mind's eye, because he had unaccountably neglected to take any steps to acquaint himself with the Russian dispositions. He should, after receiving the third order, have made it his business to make some form of reconnaissance; he should, when he found he could see nothing from his position, have shifted his ground—but he did not.

He read the order "carefully," with the fussy deliberateness which maddened his staff, while Nolan quivered with impatience at his side. It seemed to Lord Lucan that the order was not only obscure but absurd: artillery was to be attacked by cavalry; infantry support was not mentioned; it was elementary that cavalry charging artillery in such circumstances must be annihilated. In his own account of these fatal moments Lucan says that he "hesitated and urged the uselessness of such an attack and the dangers attending it"; but Nolan, almost insane with impatience, cut him short and "in a most authoritative tone" repeated the final message he had been given on the heights: "Lord Raglan's orders are that the cavalry are to attack immediately."

For such a tone to be used by an aide-de-camp to a lieutenant-general was unheard of; moreover, Lord Lucan was perfectly aware that Nolan detested him and habitually abused him. It would have been asking a very great deal of any man to keep his temper in such circumstances, and Lord Lucan's temper was violent. He could see nothing, "neither enemy nor guns being in sight," he wrote, nor did he in the least understand what the order meant. It was said later that Lord Raglan intended the third and fourth orders to be read together, and that the instruction in the third order to advance and recover the heights made it clear that the guns mentioned in the fourth order must be on those heights. Lord Lucan, however, read the two orders separately. He turned angrily on Nolan, "Attack, sir? Attack what? What guns, sir?"

The crucial moment had arrived. Nolan threw back his head, and, "in a most disrespectful and significant manner," flung out his arm and, with a furious gesture, pointed, not to the Causeway Heights and the redoubts with the captured British guns, but to the end of the North Valley, where the Russian cavalry routed by the Heavy Brigade were now established with their guns in front of them. "There, my lord, is your enemy, there are your guns," he said, and with those words and that gesture the doom of the Light Brigade was sealed.

What did Nolan mean? It has been maintained that his gesture was merely a taunt, that he had no intention of indicating any direction, and that Lord Lucan, carried away by rage, read a meaning into his outflung arm which was never there.

The truth will never be known, because a few minutes later Nolan was killed, but his behaviour in that short interval indicates that he did believe the attack was to be down the North Valley and on those guns with which the Russian cavalry routed by the Heavy Brigade had been allowed to retire.

It is not difficult to account for such a mistake. Nolan, the cavalry enthusiast and a cavalry commander of talent, was well aware that a magnificent opportunity had been lost when the Light Brigade failed to pursue after the charge of the Heavies. It was, indeed, the outstanding, the flagrant error of the day, and he must have watched with fury and despair as the routed Russians were suffered to withdraw in safety with the much-desired trophies, their guns. When he received the fourth order, he was

The order which resulted in the Charge

*Lord Raglan wishes the cavalry to advance rapidly to the front,
follow the enemy and try to prevent the enemy carrying away the
guns. Troop Horse Artillery may accompany. French cavalry is
on your left. Immediate.   R. Airey*

almost off his head with excitement and impatience, and he misread it. He leapt to the joyful conclusion that at last vengeance was to be taken on those Russians who had been suffered to escape. He had not carried the third order, and read by itself the wording of the fourth order was ambiguous. Moreover, Lord Raglan's last words to him, "Tell Lord Lucan that the cavalry is to attack immediately," were fatally lacking precision.

And so he plunged down the heights and with a contemptuous gesture, scorning the man who in his opinion was responsible for the wretched mishandling of the cavalry, he pointed down the North Valley. "There, my lord, is your enemy; there are your guns."

Lord Lucan felt himself to be in a hideous dilemma. His resentment against Lord Raglan was indescribable; the orders he had received during the battle had been, in his opinion, not only idiotic and ambiguous, but insulting. He had been treated, he wrote later, like a subaltern. He had been peremptorily ordered out of his first position—the excellent position chosen in conjunction with Sir Colin Campbell—consequently after the charge of the Heavies there had been no pursuit. He had received without explanation a vague order to wait for infantry. What infantry? Now came this latest order to take his division and charge to certain death. Throughout the campaign he had had bitter experience of orders from Lord Raglan, and now he foresaw ruin; but he was helpless. The Queen's Regulations laid down that "all orders sent by aides-de-camp . . . are to be obeyed with the same readiness, as if delivered personally by the general officers to whom such aides are attached." The Duke of Wellington himself had laid this down. Had Lord Lucan refused to execute an order brought by a member of the headquarters staff and delivered with every assumption of authority he would, in his own words, have had no choice but "to blow his brains out."

Nolan's manner had been so obviously insolent that observers thought he would be placed under arrest. Lord Lucan, however, merely shrugged his shoulders, and turning his back on Nolan, trotted off, alone, to where Lord Cardigan was sitting in front of the Light Brigade.

Nolan then rode over to his friend Captain Morris, who was sitting in his saddle in front of the 17th Lancers—the same Captain Morris who had urged Lord Cardigan to pursue earlier in the day—and received permission to ride beside him in the charge.

There was now a pause of several minutes, and it is almost impossible to believe that Nolan, sitting beside his close friend and sympathiser, did not disclose the objective of the charge. If Nolan had believed the attack was to be on the Causeway Heights and the redoubts, he must surely have told Captain Morris. Morris, however, who survived the charge though desperately wounded, believed the attack was to be on the guns at the end of the North Valley.

Meanwhile Lord Lucan, almost for the first time, was speaking directly and personally to Lord Cardigan. Had the two men not detested each other so bitterly, had they been able to examine the order together and discuss its meaning, the Light Brigade might have been saved. Alas, thirty years of hatred could not be bridged; each, however, observed perfect military courtesy. Holding the order in his hand, Lord Lucan informed Lord Cardigan of the contents and ordered him to advance down the North Valley with the Light Brigade, while he himself followed in support with the Heavy Brigade.

Lord Cardigan now took an astonishing step. Much as he hated the man before him, rigid as were his ideas of military etiquette, he remonstrated with his superior officer. Bringing down his sword in salute, he said, "Certainly, sir; but allow me to point out to you that the Russians have a battery in the valley on our front, and batteries and riflemen on both sides."

Lord Lucan once more shrugged his shoulders. "I know it," he said, "but Lord Raglan will have it. We have no choice but to obey." Lord Cardigan made no further comment, but saluted again. Lord Lucan then instructed him to "advance very steadily and keep his men well in hand." Lord Cardigan saluted once more, wheeled his horse, and rode over to his second-in-command, Lord George Paget, remarking aloud to himself as he did so, "Well, here goes the last of the Brudenells."

Most of the officers and men of the Light Brigade were lounging by their horses, the officers eating biscuits and hard-boiled eggs and drinking rum and water from their flasks. One or two of the men had lighted pipes, and were told to put them out at once, and not disgrace their regiments by smoking in the presence of the enemy. Lord George Paget, who had just lighted a cigar, felt embarrassed. Was he setting a bad example? Ought he to throw away his excellent cigar, a rarity in Balaclava? While he was debating the point, Lord Cardigan rode up and said, "Lord George, we are ordered to make an attack to the front. You will take command of the second line, and I expect your best support—mind, your best support." Cardigan, who was very much excited, repeated the last sentence twice very loudly, and Lord George, rather irritated, replied as loudly, "You shall have it, my lord." It was the first intimation Lord George had had of an intended attack; he thought it was permissible to keep his cigar, and noticed that it lasted him until he got to the guns.

Lord Cardigan now hastened at a gallop back to his troops and drew the brigade up in two lines: the first the 13th Light Dragoons, 11th Hussars, and the 17th Lancers; the second the 4th Light Dragoons and the main body of the 8th Hussars. A troop of the 8th Hussars, under Captain Duberly, had been detached to act as escort to Lord Raglan.

At the last moment Lord Lucan irritatingly interfered and ordered the 11th Hussars to fall back in support of the first line, so that there were now three lines, with the 13th Light Dragoons and the 17th Lancers leading. Lord Lucan's interference was made more annoying by the fact that he gave the order, not to Cardigan, but directly to Colonel Douglas, who commanded the 11th. Moreover, the 11th was Cardigan's own regiment, of which he was inordinately proud, and the 11th was taken out of the first line, while the 17th Lancers, Lucan's old regiment, remained.

Lord Cardigan meanwhile had placed himself quite alone, about two lengths in front of his staff and five lengths in advance of his front line. He now drew his sword and raised it, a single trumpet sounded, and without any signs of excitement and in a quiet voice he gave the orders, "The Brigade will advance. Walk, march, trot," and the three lines of the Light Brigade began to move, followed after a few minutes' interval by the Heavy Brigade, led by Lord Lucan. The troop of Horse Artillery was left behind because part of the valley was ploughed.

The North Valley was about a mile and a quarter long and a little less than a mile wide. On the Fedioukine Hills, which enclosed the valley to the north, were drawn up eight battalions of infantry, four squadrons of cavalry, and fourteen guns; on the Causeway Heights to the south were the bulk of the eleven battalions, with thirty guns and a field battery which had captured the redoubts earlier in the day; at the end of the valley, facing the Light Brigade, the mass of the Russian cavalry which had been defeated by the Heavy Brigade was drawn up in three lines, with twelve guns unlimbered before them, strengthened by six additional squadrons of Lancers, three on each flank. The Light Brigade was not merely to run a gauntlet of fire: it was advancing into a deadly three-sided trap, from which there was no escape.

The Brigade was not up to strength, cholera and dysentery having taken their toll—the five regiments present could muster only about seven hundred of all ranks, and both regiments in the first line, the 17th Lancers and the 13th Light Dragoons, were led by captains, Captain Morris and Captain Oldham respectively.

Nevertheless, the Brigade made a brave show as they trotted across the short turf. They were the finest light horsemen in Europe, drilled and disciplined to perfection, bold by nature, filled with British self-confidence, burning to show the "damned Heavies" what the Light Brigade could do.

As the Brigade moved, a sudden silence fell over the battlefield: by chance for a moment gun and rifle fire ceased, and the watchers on the heights felt the pause was sinister. More than half a century afterwards old men recalled that as the Light Brigade moved to its doom a strange hush fell, and it became so quiet that the jingle of bits and accoutrements could be clearly heard.

The Brigade advanced with beautiful precision, Lord Cardigan riding alone at their head, a brilliant and gallant figure. It was his great day: he was performing the task for which he was supremely well fitted, no power of reflection or intelligence was asked of him, dauntless physical courage was the only requirement, and he had, as Lord Raglan said truly, "the heart of a lion." He rode quietly at a trot, stiff and upright in the saddle, never once looking back: a cavalry commander about to lead a charge must keep strictly looking forward; if he looks back, his men will receive an impression of uncertainty.

He wore the gorgeous uniform of the 11th Hussars and, living as he did on his yacht, he had been able to preserve it in pristine splendour. The bright sunlight lit up the brilliance of cherry colour and royal blue, the richness of fur and plume and lace; instead of wearing his gold-laced pelisse dangling from his shoulders, he had put it on as a coat, and his figure, slender as a young man's, in spite of his fifty-seven years, was outlined in a blaze of gold. He rode his favourite charger, Ronald, "a thoroughbred chestnut of great beauty," and as he led his Brigade steadily down the valley towards the guns, he was, as his aide-de-camp Sir George Wombwell wrote, "the very incarnation of bravery."

Before the Light Brigade had advanced fifty yards, the hush came to an end: the Russian guns crashed out, and great clouds of smoke rose at the end of the valley. A moment later an extraordinary and inexplicable incident took place. The advance was proceeding at a steady trot when suddenly Nolan, riding beside his friend Captain Morris in the first line, urged on his horse and began to gallop diagonally across the front. Morris thought that Nolan was losing his head with excitement, and, knowing that a mile and a quarter must be traversed before the guns were reached, shouted, "That won't do, Nolan! We've a long way to go and must be steady." Nolan took no notice; galloping madly ahead and to the right, he crossed in front of Lord Cardigan— an unprecedented breach of military etiquette—and, turning in his saddle, shouted and waved his sword as if he would address the Brigade, but the guns were firing with great crashes, and not a word could be heard. Had he suddenly realised that his interpretation of the order had been wrong, and that in his impetuosity he had directed the Light Brigade to certain death? No one will ever know, because at that moment a Russian shell burst on the right of Lord Cardigan. and a fragment tore its way into Nolan's breast, exposing his heart. The sword fell from his hand, but his right arm was still erect, and his body remained rigid in the saddle. His horse wheeled and began to gallop back through the advancing Brigade, and then from the body there burst a strange and appalling cry, a shriek so unearthly as to freeze the blood of all who heard him. The terrified horse carried the body, still shrieking, through the 4th Light Dragoons, and then at last Nolan fell from the saddle, dead.

Lord Cardigan, looking strictly straight ahead and not aware of Nolan's death, was transported with fury. It was his impression that Nolan had been trying to take the command of the Brigade away from him, to lead the charge himself; and so intense was his rage that when he was asked what he thought about as he advanced towards the guns, he replied that his mind was entirely occupied with anger against Nolan.

The first few hundred yards of the advance of the Light Brigade covered the same ground, whether the attack was to be on the guns on the Causeway Heights or the guns at the end of the valley. The Russians assumed that the redoubts were to be charged, and the watchers on the heights saw the Russian infantry retire first from Redoubt No. 3 and then from No. 2 and form hollow squares to receive the expected charge; but the Light Brigade, incredibly, made no attempt to wheel. With a gasp of horror, the watchers saw the lines of horsemen continue straight on down the North Valley.

The Russian artillery and riflemen on the Fedioukine Hills and the slopes of the Causeway Heights were absolutely taken by surprise; it was not possible to believe that this small force trotting down the North Valley in such beautiful order intended to attempt an attack on the battery at the end of the valley, intended, utterly helpless as it was, to expose itself to a cross-fire, of the most frightful and deadly kind, to which it had no possibility of replying. There was again a moment's pause, and then from the Fedioukine Hills on one side and the Causeway Heights on the other, battalion upon battalion of riflemen, battery upon battery of guns, poured down fire on the Light Brigade.

When advancing cavalry are caught in a withering fire and are too courageous to think of retreat, it is their instinct to quicken their pace, to gallop forward as fast as individual horses will carry them and get to grips with the enemy as soon as possible. But Lord Cardigan tightly restrained the pace of the Light Brigade: the line was to advance with parade-ground perfection. The inner squadron of the 17th Lancers broke into a canter, Captain White, its leader, being, he said, "frankly anxious to get out of such a murderous fire and into the guns as being the lesser of two evils," and he shot forward, level with his brigadier. Lord Cardigan checked him instantly; lowering his sword and laying it across Captain White's breast, he told him sharply not to ride level with his commanding officer and not to force the pace. Private Wightman of the 17th Lancers, riding behind, heard his stern, hoarse voice rising above the din of the guns, "Steady, steady, the 17th Lancers." Otherwise during the whole course of the charge Lord Cardigan neither spoke nor made any sign.

All he could see at the end of the valley as he rode was a

white bank of smoke, through which from time to time flashed great tongues of flame marking the position of the guns. He chose one which seemed to be about the centre of the battery and rode steadily for it, neither turning in his saddle nor moving his head. Erect, rigid, and dauntless, his bearing contributed enormously to the steadiness, the astonishing discipline which earned the Charge of the Light Brigade immortality.

And now the watchers on the heights saw that the lines of horsemen, like toys down on the plain, were expanding and contracting with strange mechanical precision. Death was coming fast, and the Light Brigade was meeting death in perfect order; as a man or horse dropped, the riders on each side of him opened out; as soon as they had ridden clear, the ranks closed again. Orderly, as if on the parade ground, the Light Brigade rode on, but its numbers grew every moment smaller and smaller as they moved down the valley. Those on the heights who could understand what that regular mechanical movement meant in terms of discipline and courage were intolerably moved, and one old soldier burst into tears. It was at this moment that Bosquet, the French general, observed, *"C'est magnifique mais ce n'est pas la guerre."*

The fire grew fiercer; the first line was now within range of the guns at the end of the valley, as well as the fire pouring from both flanks. Round shot, grape, and shells began to mow men down not singly, but by groups; the pace quickened and quickened again—the men could no longer be restrained, and the trot became a canter.

The Heavy Brigade were being left behind; slower in any case than the Light Cavalry, they were wearied by their earlier action, and as the pace of the Light Brigade quickened, the gap began to widen rapidly. At this moment the Heavy Brigade came under the withering cross-fire which had just torn the Light Brigade to pieces. Lord Lucan, leading the Brigade, was wounded in the leg and his horse hit in two places; one of his aides was killed, and two of his staff wounded. Looking back, he saw that his two leading regiments—the Greys and the Royals—were sustaining heavy casualties. In the Royals twenty-one men had already fallen. Lord Lucan's indifference under fire was remarkable: it was on this occasion that an officer described as "one of his most steady haters" admitted, "Yes, damn him, he's brave," but he felt himself once more in a dilemma. Should he continue to advance and destroy the Heavy Brigade, or should he halt and leave the Light Brigade to its fate without support? He turned to Lord William Paulet, who was riding at his side and had just had his forage cap torn off his head by a musket ball. "They have sacrificed the Light Brigade: they shall not the Heavy, if I can help it," he said. Ordering the halt to be sounded, he retired the brigade out of range and waited, having decided in his own words that "the only use to which the Heavy Brigade could be turned was to protect the Light Cavalry against pursuit on their return."

With sadness and horror the Heavy Brigade watched the Light Brigade go on alone down the valley and vanish in smoke. Help now came from the French. As a result of General Canrobert's earlier order the Chasseurs d'Afrique were drawn up beneath the heights. Originally raised as irregular cavalry, this force, which had a record of extraordinary distinction, now consisted of French troopers, mounted on Algerian horses.

Their commander, General Morris, had seen the Light Brigade fail to wheel, and advance down the valley to certain doom with stupefied horror. Nothing could be done for them, but he determined to aid the survivors. He ordered the Chasseurs d'Afrique to charge the batteries and infantry battalions on the Fedioukine Hills. Galloping as if by a miracle over broken and scrubby ground in a loose formation learned in their campaigns in the Atlas mountains of Morocco, they attacked with brilliant success. Both Russian artillery and infantry were forced to retreat, and at a cost of only thirty-eight casualties—ten killed and twenty-eight wounded—the fire from the Fedioukine Hills was silenced. Such remnants of the Light Brigade as might return would now endure fire only on one flank, from the Causeway Heights.

The first line of the Light Brigade was now more than half-way down the valley, and casualties were so heavy that the squadrons could no longer keep their entity: formation was lost and the front line broke into a gallop, the regiments racing each other as they rode down to death. "Come on," yelled a trooper of the 13th to his comrades, "come on. Don't let those b——s of the 17th get in front of us." The men, no longer to be restrained, began to shoot forward in front of their officers, and Lord Cardigan was forced to increase his pace or be overwhelmed. The gallop became headlong, the troopers cheering and yelling; their blood was up, and they were on fire to get at the enemy. Hell for leather, with whistling bullets and crashing shells taking their toll every moment, cheers changing to death cries, horses falling with a scream, the first line of the Light Brigade—17th Lancers and 13th Light Dragoons—raced down the valley to the guns. Close behind them came the second line. Lord George Paget, remembering Lord Cardigan's stern admonition, "Your best support, mind, your best support," had increased the pace of his regiment, the 4th Light Dragoons, and caught up the 11th Hussars. The 8th Hussars, sternly kept in hand by their commanding officer, Colonel Shewell, advanced at a steady trot, and refused to increase their pace. The second line therefore consisted of the 4th Light Dragoons and the 11th Hussars, with the 8th Hussars to the right rear.

As they, too, plunged into the inferno of fire, and as batteries and massed riflemen on each flank began to tear gaps in their ranks and trooper after trooper came crashing to the ground, they had a new and horrible difficulty to face. The ground was strewn with casualties of the first line—not only dead men and dead horses, but horses and men not yet dead, able to crawl, to scream, to writhe. They had perpetually to avoid riding over men they knew, while riderless horses, some unhurt, some horribly injured, tried to force their way into the ranks. Troop horses in battle, as long as they feel the hand of their rider and his weight on their backs, are, even when wounded, singularly free from fear. When Lord George Paget's charger was hit, he was astonished to find the horse showed no sign of panic. But, once deprived of his rider, the troop horse becomes crazed with terror. He does not gallop out of the action and seek safety: trained to range himself in line, he seeks the companionship of other horses, and, mad with fear, eyeballs protruding, he attempts to attach himself to some leader or to force himself into the ranks of the nearest squadrons. Lord George, riding in advance of the second line, found himself actually in danger. The poor brutes made dashes at him, trying to gallop with him. At one moment he was riding in the midst of seven riderless horses, who cringed and pushed against him as round shot and bullets came by, covering him with blood from their wounds, and so nearly unhorsing him that he was forced to use his sword to free himself.

And all the time, through the cheers, the groans, the ping of bullets whizzing through the air, the whirr and crash of shells, the earth-shaking thunder of galloping horses' hooves, when men were not merely falling one by one but being swept away in groups, words of command rang out as on the parade ground, "Close in to your centre. Back the right flank! Keep up, Private Smith. Left squadron, keep back. Look to your dressing." Until at last, as the ranks grew thinner and thinner, only one command was heard: "Close in! Close in! Close in to the centre! Close in! Close in!"

Eight minutes had now passed since the advance began, and Lord Cardigan, with the survivors of the first line hard on his heels, galloping furiously but steadily, was within a few yards of the battery. The troopers could see the faces of the gunners, and Lord Cardigan selected the particular space between two guns where he intended to enter. One thought, wrote a survivor, was in all their minds: they were nearly out of it at last, and close on the accursed guns, and Lord Cardigan, still sitting rigid in his saddle, "steady as a church," waved his sword over his head. At that moment there was a roar, the earth trembled, huge flashes of flame shot out, and the smoke became so dense that darkness seemed to fall. The Russian gunners had fired a salvo from their twelve guns into the first line of the Light Brigade at a distance of eighty yards. The first line ceased to exist. To the second line, riding behind, it was as if the line had simply dissolved. Lord Cardigan's charger Ronald was blown sideways by the blast, a torrent of flame seemed to belch down his right side, and for a moment he thought he had lost a leg. He was, he estimated, only two or three lengths from the mouths of the guns. Then, wrenching Ronald's head round, he drove into the smoke and, charging into the space he had previously selected, was the first man into the battery. And now the Heavy Brigade, watching in an agony of anxiety and impatience, became aware of a sudden and sinister silence. No roars, no great flashes of flame came from the guns—all was strangely, menacingly quiet. Nothing could be seen: the pall of smoke hung like a curtain over the end of the valley; only from time to time through their glasses the watchers saw riderless horses gallop out and men stagger into sight to fall prostrate among the corpses of their comrades littering the ground.

Fifty men only, blinded and stunned, had survived from the first line. Private Wightman of the 17th Lancers felt the frightful crash, saw his captain fall dead; then his horse made a "tremendous leap into the air," though what he jumped at Wightman never knew—the pall of smoke was so dense that he could not see his arm before him—but suddenly he was in the battery, and in the darkness there were sounds of fighting and slaughter. The scene was extraordinary: smoke so obscured the sun that it was barely twilight, and in the gloom the British troopers, maddened with excitement, cut and thrust and hacked like demons, while the Russian gunners with superb courage fought to remove the guns.

While the struggle went on in the battery, another action was taking place outside. Twenty survivors of the 17th Lancers—the regiment was reduced to thirty-seven men—riding behind Captain Morris had outflanked the battery on the left, and, emerging from the smoke, suddenly found themselves confronted with a solid mass of Russian cavalry drawn up behind the guns. Turning in his saddle, Morris shouted, "Now, remember what I have told you, men, and keep together," and without a moment's hesitation charged. Rushing himself upon the Russian officer in command, he engaged him in single combat and ran him through the body. The Russians again received the charge halted, allowed the handful of British to penetrate their ranks, broke, and retreated in disorder, pursued by the 17th. Within a few seconds an overwhelming body of Cossacks came up, the 17th were forced to retreat in their turn, and, fighting like madmen, every trooper encircled by a swarm of Cossacks, they tumbled back in confusion towards the guns. Morris was left behind unconscious with his skull cut open in two places.

Meanwhile in those few minutes the situation in the battery had completely changed. In the midst of the struggle for the guns, Colonel Mayow, the brigade major, looked up and saw a body of Russian cavalry preparing to descend in such force that the men fighting in the battery must inevitably be overwhelmed. Shouting, "Seventeenth! Seventeenth! this way! this way!" he collected the remaining survivors of the 17th and all that was left of the 13th Light Dragoons—some twelve men—and, placing himself at their head, charged out of the battery, driving the Russians before him until he was some five hundred yards away.

At this moment the second line swept down. The 11th Hussars outflanked the battery, as the 17th had done; the 8th Hussars had not yet come up, but the 4th Light Dragoons under Lord George Paget crashed into the battery. So great was the smoke and the confusion that Lord George did not see the battery until his regiment was on top of it. As they rode headlong down, one of his officers gave a "View halloo," and suddenly they were in and fighting among the guns. The Russian gunners, with great courage, persisted in their attempt to take the guns away, and the 4th Light Dragoons, mad with excitement, fell on them with savage frenzy. A cut-and-thrust, hand-to-hand combat raged, in which the British fought like tigers, one officer tearing at the Russians with his bare hands and wielding his sword in a delirium of slaughter. After the battle this officer's reaction was so great that he sat down and burst into tears. Brave as the Russians were, they were forced to give way; the Russian gunners were slaughtered, and the 4th Light Dragoons secured absolute mastery of every gun.

While this fierce and bloody combat was being waged, Colonel Douglas, outflanking the battery with the 11th Hussars, had charged a body of Lancers on the left with considerable success, only to find himself confronted with the main body of the Russian cavalry, and infantry in such strength that he felt he was confronted by the whole Russian army. He had hastily to retreat with a large Russian force following in pursuit.

Meanwhile the 4th Light Dragoons, having silenced the guns, had pressed on out of the battery and beyond it. Lord George had, he said, an idea that somewhere ahead was Lord Cardigan, and Lord Cardigan's admonition enjoining his best support was "always ringing in his ears." As they advanced, they collided with the 11th in their retreat, and the two groups, numbering not more than seventy men, joined together. Their situation was desperate. Advancing on them were enormous masses of Russian cavalry—the leading horsemen were actually within a few hundred yards; but Lord George noticed the great mass was strangely disorderly in its movements and displayed the hesitation and bewilderment the Russian cavalry had shown when advancing on the Heavy Brigade in the morning. Reining in his horse, Lord George shouted at the top of his voice, "Halt front; if you don't front, my boys, we are done." The 11th checked, and, with admirable steadiness, the whole group "halted and fronted as if they had been on parade." So for a few minutes the handful of British cavalry faced the advancing army. The movement had barely been completed when a trooper shouted, "They are attacking us, my lord, in our rear," and, looking round, Lord George saw, only five hundred yards away, a formidable body of Russian Lancers formed up in the direct line of retreat. Lord George turned to his major: "We are in a desperate scrape; what the devil shall we do? Has anyone seen Lord Cardigan?"

When Lord Cardigan dashed into the battery he had, by a miracle, passed through the gap between the two guns unhurt, and in a few seconds was clear—the first man into the battery and the first man out. Behind him, under the pall of smoke, in murk and gloom, a savage combat was taking place, but Lord Cardigan neither turned back nor paused. In his opinion, he said later, it was "no part of a general's duty to fight the enemy among private soldiers"; he galloped on, until suddenly he was clear of the smoke, and before him, less than one hundred yards away, he saw halted a great mass of Russian cavalry. His charger was wild with excitement, and before he could be checked Lord Cardigan had been carried to within twenty yards of the Russians. For a moment they stared at each other, the Russians utterly astonished by the sudden apparition of this solitary horseman, gorgeous and glittering with gold. By an amazing coincidence, one of the officers, Prince Radzivil, recognized Lord Cardigan—they had met in London at dinners and balls—and the Prince detached a troop of Cossacks with instructions to capture him alive. To this coincidence Lord Cardigan probably owed his life. The Cossacks approached him, but did not attempt to cut him down; and after a short encounter in which he received a slight wound on the thigh, he evaded them by wheeling his horse, galloped back through the guns again, and came out almost where, only a few minutes earlier, he had dashed in.

By this time the fight in the guns was over, and the battery, still veiled with smoke, was a hideous, confused mass of dead and dying. The second line had swept on, and Lord George Paget and Colonel Douglas, with their handful of survivors, were now halted, with the Russian army both in front of them and behind them, asking, "Where is Lord Cardigan?"

Lord Cardigan, however, looking up the valley over the scene of the charge, could see no sign of his brigade. The valley was strewn with dead and dying; small groups of men wounded or unhorsed were struggling towards the British lines; both his aides-de-camp had vanished; he had ridden never once looking back, and had no idea of what the fate of his brigade had been. Nor had he any feeling of responsibility—in his own words, having "led the Brigade and launched them with due impetus, he considered his duty was done." The idea of trying to find out what had happened to his men or of rallying the survivors never crossed his mind. With extraordinary indifference to danger he had led the Light Brigade down the valley as if he were leading a charge in a review in Hyde Park, and he now continued to behave as if he were in a review in Hyde Park. He had, however, he wrote, some apprehension that for a general his isolated position was unusual, and he avoided any undignified appearance of haste by riding back very slowly, most of the time at a walk. By another miracle he was untouched by the fire from the Causeway Heights, which, although the batteries on the Fedioukine Hills had been silenced by the French, was still raking the unfortunate survivors of the charge in the valley. As he rode he continued to brood on Nolan's behaviour, and on nothing else. The marvellous ride, the dauntless valour of the Light Brigade and their frightful destruction, his own miraculous escape from death, made no impression on his mind; Nolan's insubordination occupied him exclusively, and when he reached the point where the Heavy Brigade was halted, he rode up to General Scarlett and immediately broke into accusations of Nolan, furiously complaining of Nolan's insubordination, his ride across the front of the Brigade, his attempt to assume command, and, Lord Cardigan finished contemptuously, "Imagine the fellow screaming like a woman when he was hit." General Scarlett checked him: "Say no more, my lord; you have just ridden over Captain Nolan's dead body."

Meanwhile the seventy survivors of the 4th Light Dragoons and 11th Hussars under Lord George Paget, unaware that their general had retired from the field, were preparing to sell their lives dearly. There seemed little hope for them: they were a rabble, their horses worn out, many men wounded. Nevertheless, wheeling about, and jamming spurs into the exhausted horses, they charged the body of Russian Lancers who barred their retreat, "as fast," wrote Lord George Paget, "as our poor tired horses could carry us." As the British approached, the Russians, who had been in close column across their path, threw back their right, thus presenting a sloping front, and, with the air of uncertainty Lord George had noticed earlier, stopped—did nothing. The British, at a distance of a horse's length only, were allowed to "shuffle and edge away," brushing along the Russian front and parrying thrusts from Russian lances. Lord George said his sword crossed the end of lances three or four times, but all the Russians did was to jab at him. It seems probable that the Russians, having witnessed the destruction of the main body of the Light Brigade, were not greatly concerned with the handfuls of survivors. So, without the loss of a single man, "and how I know not," wrote Lord George, the survivors of the 4th Light Dragoons and the 11th Hussars escaped once more, and began the painful retreat back up the valley.

One other small body of survivors had also been fighting beyond the guns. The 8th Hussars, restrained with an iron hand by their commanding officer, Colonel Shewell, had reached the battery in beautiful formation to find the 4th Light Dragoons had done their work and the guns were silenced. Colonel Shewell then led his men through the battery and halted on the other side, enquiring, like Lord George Paget, "Where is Lord Cardigan?" For about three minutes the 8th Hussars waited, then on the skyline appeared lances. The fifteen men of the 17th Lancers, who with the few survivors of the 13th Light Dragoons had charged out of the battery before the second line attacked, were now retreating, with a large Russian force in pursuit. Colonel Mayow, their leader, galloped up to Colonel Shewell. "Where is Lord Cardigan?" he asked. At that moment Colonel Shewell turned his head and saw that he, too, was not only menaced in front: at his rear a large force of Russian cavalry had suddenly come up, and was preparing to cut off his retreat and the retreat of any other survivors of the Light Brigade who might still be alive beyond the guns. A stern, pious man, by no means popular with his troops, Colonel Shewell had the harsh courage of Cromwell's Bible soldiers. Assuming command, he wheeled the little force into line and gave the order to charge. He himself, discarding his sword—he was a poor swordsman—gripped his reins in both hands, put down his head, and rushed like a thunderbolt at the Russian commanding officer. The Russian stood his ground, but his horse flinched. Shewell burst through the gap and was carried through the ranks to the other side. Riding for their lives, his seventy-odd troopers dashed after him. The Russians were thrown into confusion and withdrew, and the way was clear.

But what was to be done next? Colonel Shewell paused. No supports were coming up, Lord Cardigan was not to be seen; there was nothing for it but retreat, and, just ahead of Lord George Paget and Colonel Douglas with the 4th Light Dragoons and the 11th Hussars, the other survivors of the Light Brigade began slowly and painfully to trail back up the valley.

Confusion was utter. No one knew what had taken place, who was alive, or who was dead; no control existed; no one gave orders; no one knew what to do next. At the time when the survivors of the Light Brigade had begun to trail up the valley, Captain Lockwood, one of Lord Cardigan's three aides-de-camp, suddenly rode up to Lord Lucan.

"My lord, can you tell me where is Lord Cardigan?" he asked. Lord Lucan replied that Lord Cardigan had gone by some time ago, upon which Captain Lockwood, misunderstanding him, turned his horse's head, rode down into the valley, and was never seen again.

The retreat, wrote Robert Portal, was worse than the advance. Men and horses were utterly exhausted and almost none was unhurt. Troopers who had become attached to their horses refused to leave them behind, and wounded and bleeding men staggered along, dragging with them wounded and bleeding beasts. Horses able to move were given up to wounded men; Major de Salis of the 8th Hussars retreated on foot, leading his horse with a wounded trooper in the saddle. All formation had been lost, and it was a rabble who limped painfully along. Mrs. Duberly on the heights saw scattered groups of men appearing at the end of the valley. "What can those skirmishers be doing?" she asked. "Good God! It is the Light Brigade!" The pace was heartbreakingly slow; most survivors were on foot; little groups of men dragged along step by step, leaning on each other. At first Russian Lancers made harassing attacks, swooping down, cutting off stragglers, and taking prisoners, but when the retreating force came under fire from the Causeway Heights the Russians sustained casualties from their own guns and were withdrawn. Nearly a mile had to be covered, every step under fire; but the fire came from one side only, and the straggling trail of men offered no such target as the brilliant squadrons in parade order which had earlier swept down the valley. The wreckage of men and horses was piteous. "What a scene of havoc was this last mile—strewn with the dead and dying and all friends!" wrote Lord George Paget. Men recognised their comrades, "some running, some limping, some crawling," saw horses in the trappings of their regiments "in every position of agony struggling to get up, then floundering back again on their mutilated riders." So, painfully, step by step, under heavy fire, the exhausted, bleeding remnants of the Light Brigade dragged themselves back to safety. As each group stumbled in, it was greeted with ringing cheers. Men ran down to meet their comrades and wrung them by the hand, as if they had struggled back from the depths of hell itself.

One of the last to return was Lord George Paget, and as he

toiled up the slope he was greeted by Lord Cardigan, "riding composedly from the opposite direction." Lord George was extremely angry with Lord Cardigan; later he wrote an official complaint of his conduct. He considered it was Lord Cardigan's "bounden duty," after strictly enjoining that Lord George should give his best support—"your best support, mind"—to "see him out of it"; instead of which Lord Cardigan had disappeared, leaving his brigade to its fate. "Halloa, Lord Cardigan! were you not there?" he said. "Oh, wasn't I, though!" replied Lord Cardigan. "Here, Jenyns, did you not see me at the guns?" Captain Jenyns, one of the few survivors of the 13th Light Dragoons, answered that he had: he had been very near Lord Cardigan at the time when he entered the battery.

Out of this conversation, and a feeling that Lord Cardigan's desertion of his brigade could not be reconciled with heroism, grew a legend that Lord Cardigan never had taken part in the charge. During his lifetime he was haunted by the whisper, and as late as 1909 Wilfrid Scawen Blunt was told positively that "Cardigan was not in the charge at all, being all the time on board his yacht, and only arrived on the field of battle as his regiment was on its way back from the Valley of Death."

When the last survivors had trailed in, the remnants of the Light Brigade re-formed on a slope looking southward over Balaclava. The charge had lasted twenty minutes from the moment the trumpet sounded the advance to the return of the last survivor. Lord Cardigan rode forward. "Men, it is a mad-brained trick, but it is no fault of mine," he said in his loud, hoarse voice. A voice answered, "Never mind, my lord; we are ready to go again," and the roll call began, punctuated by the melancholy sound of pistol shots as the farriers went round despatching ruined horses.

Some 700 horsemen had charged down the valley, and 195 had returned. The 17th Lancers were reduced to thirty-seven troopers, the 13th Light Dragoons could muster only two officers and eight mounted men; 500 horses had been killed.

13

While the shattered remnants of the Light Brigade trailed back, Lord Raglan with his staff and his little crowd of onlookers descended from the heights, and he was now in the plain at the end of the valley. As soon as the roll call was over, Lord Cardigan rode up to him. For once Lord Raglan had lost control of himself; he was quivering with anger, and William Howard Russell noticed how his head shook and how he gesticulated, waving the stump of his amputated arm. He challenged Lord Cardigan furiously. "What did you mean, sir, by attacking a battery in front, contrary to all the usages of war and the customs of service?" Lord Cardigan's demeanour was noticeably serene; indeed, neither now, or ever did any part of his conduct on the day of Balaclava cause him a moment's concern, convinced as he was that he had done his duty in accordance with the best precedents. "My lord," he replied, "I hope you will not blame me, for I received the order to attack from my superior officer in front of the troops." A few minutes later he was seen to canter off, bearing himself proudly and in no way depressed.

Both divisions of infantry were now in the plain and ready for action. The British infantry force was strong enough to make an attempt on the redoubts and the Causeway Heights, and the order to attack was expected every minute. The Russians brought up reinforcements; the Heavy Brigade impatiently awaited the order to advance. "When are we going to begin? Surely we're not going to let those fellows stay there," said a subaltern.

The British troops, in spite of the disaster of the Light Brigade—indeed, even on account of it—felt they had a moral ascendancy. Bodies of Russian cavalry had been put to flight by handfuls of British horsemen at odds of twenty, fifty, even a hundred to one; a battery had been attacked in front by cavalry and silenced—a most extraordinary feat—above all, the charge of the Heavy Brigade had shown what British cavalry could do when they had the opportunity. After the war was over the Russians admitted that the British cavalry had inspired awe—"those terrible horsemen," one officer called them. Lord Raglan, divining the temper of his troops, wished to attack, but the inevitable difficulty arose: he was lamentably short of men. If Sebastopol were to be assaulted, troops could not be spared to occupy the redoubts on the Causeway Heights; on this ground General Canrobert, the French Commander-in-Chief, strongly opposed an attack. Neither commander appreciated the enormous importance of the Woronzoff Road.

No attack was made. The Russians were allowed to remain in possession of the three important redoubts to the east, and therefore of the Woronzoff Road; Turks were once more placed in the three redoubts to the west. The British army was thus left with no means of communication between its base and its camp but rough precipitous tracks, and the suffering and starvation of the coming winter became inevitable.

At four o'clock firing ceased, and the Russians in triumph carried to Sebastopol seven British naval guns which they had taken from the redoubts. As to the result—the battle was thought to be a draw. The Russians had captured the redoubts, but had not captured Balaclava; the British had lost the redoubts, but had not lost Balaclava. No one discerned that the fatal outcome of the battle was the loss of the Woronzoff Road.

About half-past five the survivors of the Light Brigade were allowed to return to their camp. The shattered regiments had been re-formed and kept on the ground for five hours less than half a mile from their camp. Many of the men and horses had had nothing to eat since the evening before. Hungry, miserable, utterly depressed, they had spent the five hours in silence—there was not a man, wrote a survivor, who had the heart to talk—and in silence the remnants returned to their camp. Meanwhile, General Liprandi, the Russian comander, was examining the prisoners, among them Private Wightman of the 17th Lancers, who had charged into the battery behind Lord Cardigan, received wounds in four places, including a shattered knee, and been captured when his horse was shot dead under him. "Come now, men," said General Liprandi genially, and in excellent English. "What did they give you to drink? Did they not prime you with spirits to come down and attack us in such a mad manner?" "You think we were drunk?" said a wounded trooper. "By God, I tell you that if we had so much as smelt the barrel we would have taken half Russia by this time." Liprandi smiled good-humouredly, and a private of the 4th Light Dragoons, lying mortally wounded in a corner, raised himself with difficulty on his elbow. "On my honour, sir, except for the vodka your men have given to some of us, there is not a man who has tasted food or drink this day. We left camp before daylight and were continuously in the field until we became prisoners of war. Our uncooked rations are still in our haversacks. Our daily issue of a mouthful of rum is made in the afternoon and, believe me, sir, we don't hoard it." Liprandi was moved. "You are noble fellows," he said, "and I am sincerely sorry for you. I will order you some vodka."

Meanwhile Lord Cardigan rode back to his yacht, had a bath and a bottle of champagne with his dinner, and went to bed.

Late that evening Lord Lucan went to see Lord Raglan. There were no conventional courtesies. As he entered, Lord Raglan flung at him a single sentence of searing bitterness: "You have lost the Light Brigade," he said.

It was precisely what Lord Lucan had anticipated: he was

to be blamed for the disaster; he was to be made the scapegoat for Lord Raglan's mistake, for General Airey's mistake. He furiously denied that he had lost the Light Brigade. All he had done was to carry out the orders conveyed to him by Captain Nolan, pressed on him by Captain Nolan, indeed absolutely forced on him in such a manner that he could not refuse. Lord Raglan now advanced a most extraordinary argument. Lord Lucan had unquestionably made grave errors, and those errors, in Lord Raglan's opinion, had largely caused the disaster. Three days later, in a private letter to the Duke of Newcastle, he pointed out that Lord Lucan had not taken any steps to ascertain the Russian dispositions, had not asked the assistance of the French cavalry, had not brought up his Horse Artillery, or made use of the Heavy Brigade. But now, on the evening of the battle, Lord Raglan said, "Lord Lucan, you were a lieutenant-general and should therefore have exercised your discretion, and, not approving of the charge, should not have caused it to be made." It was too much. A great rage seized Lord Lucan. What had he not endured from Lord Raglan? What neglects, what restraints, what misrepresentations? Had he not complained that he was given orders and told to execute them like a subaltern? Had he not begged again and again to be allowed a little latitude? He fiercely defended himself. What! Disobey an order sent from the Comander-in-Chief! Did not the Queen's Regulations lay down that all orders brought by aides-de-camp were to be obeyed with the same readiness as if brought personally by the general officers to whom those aides-de-camp were attached? Had not the Duke of Wellington, that great man, laid this down himself? What would be the fate of a general who took it upon himself to disobey such an order? He would risk the loss of his commission, and do better to put a bullet through his head. Lord Raglan had been in a superior position—he had been up on the heights, able to survey the battlefield as no one could survey it from the plain below. He, Lord Lucan, had been able to see nothing, and Lord Raglan had known he could see nothing because, in his order, he had informed him that French cavalry were on his left. Etiquette and respect were finally forgotten as Lord Lucan furiously adjured Lord Raglan to mind what he did. He would accept no blame in this Light Cavalry affair; be careful none was placed on him—he would not bear it. And so they parted.

Night fell on the camp—a miserable night. An order had been issued that no fires were to be lit and no noise made, since a further attack by the Russians was feared. The survivors of the Light Brigade stood about in groups talking of their dead comrades and the disasters of the day. The men were exhausted and over-wrought, the night was bitterly cold. Without fires nothing could be cooked, and most of them had still had nothing to eat beyond the dry biscuit in their haversacks and the afternoon dram of rum. They especially mourned their horses. Sergeant-Major Loy Smith of the 11th Hussars was "moved to tears when I thought of my beautiful horse; she was a light bay, nearly thoroughbred, I became her master nearly three years before."

Lord Lucan sat in his tent. Mud seeped through the floor boards, the Crimean wind, presage of winter hastening on, moaned outside, and deep depression weighed him down. Troublesome, unpopular, and out of date, he nevertheless had a genuine passion for the Army. He had worked, he had striven to let no detail escape his eye; he had spared himself nothing—and a mile away the ground was littered with the corpses of the men and horses of the Light Brigade, "the finest brigade that ever left the shores of England"; and his own regiment, the 17th Lancers—"Bingham's Dandies"—had been wiped out. What had he not hoped, what dreams of glory had not whirled in his brain as he embarked on this war? His belief in his capacities had been complete, his faith in himself enormous; but beneath the agony of disappointment and grief burned white-hot anger. "I do not intend," he wrote, "to bear the smallest particle of responsibility. I gave the order to charge under what I considered a most imperious necessity, and I will not bear one particle of the blame."

Who indeed was to blame? Many of the causes of the disaster

lay far far back, in the old hatred between Lord Cardigan and Lord Lucan, in events nearly ten years old in Ireland, in Lord Raglan's character, that extraordinary blend of suavity, charm, aristocratic prejudice, and marble indifference. Above all the disaster was the fruit of the system under which the British Army was commanded. Untrained, untried officers were in charge of divisions and brigades in the field, the staff were ignorant of their duties and quite unable to translate the Commander-in-Chief's wishes into clear language, the Commander-in-Chief himself, Lord Raglan, unpractised and inexperienced in active command, was fatally ambiguous. To the trained staff officer of today the famous four orders of Balaclava are vague, obscure, the work of an amateur, and an invitation to disaster.

Meanwhile at headquarters Lord Lucan had left considerable uneasiness behind him. If Lord Lucan was determined to make trouble—and he was well known to stop at nothing—enormous unpleasantness and awkwardness would result. The situation which must always at all costs be avoided would inevitably arise: there would be publicity, questions in the House, articles in the press, Army affairs would be discussed by outsiders, and something closely resembling military dirty linen would be washed in public.

It began to be felt that Lord Lucan was behaving in an unprofessional and unsoldier-like manner. War, after all, was war; the rough must be taken with the smooth; but civilians did not understand the facts of war, and to drag the details of an unfortunate occurrence like the Light Brigade charge into the open was detrimental to the good of the service.

Though Lord Lucan was to blame, Lord Raglan had no wish to pillory him. In his confidential account written privately to the Duke of Newcastle on October 25 Raglan stated plainly that: "Lord Lucan had made a fatal mistake. . . . The written order sent to him by the Quartermaster General did not exact that he should attack at all hazards, and contained no expression which could bear that construction."

In his official dispatch, however, Lord Raglan let Lucan off more lightly, merely remarking that "from some misconception of the order to advance, the Lieutenant-General [Lord Lucan] considered that he was bound to attack at all hazards." He could hardly, in his opinion, say less.

Lord Raglan had recovered his "marble calm," and with it the conviction that the best course was to persuade Lord Lucan to put the Light Brigade affair behind him and go on as usual. When a disaster occurred, the only thing to be done was to make the best of it. Disasters, after all, did quite frequently occur. Only five years ago there had been a frightful cavalry disaster in India, during a battle fought against the Sikhs at a place called Chillianwallah. No one knew precisely what had happened or where the blame lay, but when the cavalry were committed to a charge, the front ranks suddenly thought they had been ordered to retreat. They turned, collided with the men behind them, utter confusion was succeeded by wild panic, and a division of British cavalry stampeded to the rear, upsetting their own guns. The troops could not be rallied, and a rout of British by native troops took place, and three regiments lost their colours. At least the Light Brigade disaster had not been shameful: Lord Raglan in his official dispatch was able to write of "the brilliancy of the attack, and the gallantry, order and discipline which distinguished it." It was, he wrote, "the finest thing ever done."

Let Lord Lucan, for his own sake and for the good of the service, restrain himself and try to see the affair in proportion. He had made a mistake—very regrettably—but such mistakes did and would occur in war; other men had made similar blunders, and would make them again. Indeed, many worse mistakes had been made than the error which sent the Light Brigade down the North Valley to the guns. Lord Lucan should console himself with that reflection and keep quiet.

On the evening of October 27 General Airey came down from the heights to see Lord Lucan and found him sitting in his tent. It was part of Lucan's conscientiousness and his stiff-necked pride to share the hardships of his troops. Lord Cardigan might live in luxury, sleeping late in his yacht; but Lord Lucan stayed on the spot, rising at dawn and sharing the mud, the cold, the icy winds, and the lice. "Hullo, Russell," he had called out to William Howard Russell. "Are you lousy? Bingham and I are."

General Airey had come on a mission: he was deputed to talk Lord Lucan round, to make the glowering, furious, miserable man before him see reason and behave sensibly. It was a kind of undertaking in which General Airey particularly excelled. On this occasion, however, he was not to succeed. But his method of approach cast an extraordinary illumination on the minds of the men who commanded the British Army. The scene was long, but Airey's first words disclosed the nature of the reflections which were thought likely to console Lord Lucan. As he came into the tent Lucan said to him, "General Airey, this is a most serious matter." With remarkable light-heartedness Airey replied: "These sort of things will happen in war," and then he pronounced what might well serve as the official epitaph on the Charge of the Light Brigade. "It is nothing," he said, "to Chillianwallah."

14

The drama was over, the tragedy had occurred, the Charge of the Light Brigade was a matter of history. But the two chief personages in the drama remained, and it was beyond the power of tragedy or disaster to chasten or change them. There was to be a long, a painfully characteristic, aftermath.

Calamity was inevitable for Lord Lucan. He could not see that he was demanding the impossible, that either he or Lord Raglan must be responsible for the Light Brigade charge, and it was beyond the bounds of reason that Lord Raglan, the Commander-in-Chief, should take the blame on himself. Nevertheless, blinded by the most fatal and ill-omened of all grievances, a grievance against a superior officer, Lord Lucan pressed on to his own undoing.

At the interview of October 27, General Airey, finding Lord Lucan could not be reasoned with, became soothing. He was, as Lucan himself said, no unskilful diplomatist. There was no question of blame, he said reassuringly. Lord Raglan's report on the battle, which went out that day, dealt with Lord Lucan's part in the Light Brigade charge fully and fairly. "You may rest satisfied, Lord Lucan," said General Airey, "you will be pleased with Lord Raglan's report." Lucan allowed himself to accept this assurance, and a month passed before Lord Raglan's dispatch on

Balaclava reached the Crimea. He was then transported with fury to read, in the section devoted to the Charge of the Light Brigade, the statement that "from some misconception of the instruction to attack, the Lieutenant-General considered he was bound to attack at all hazards."

The blame was to be put on him, after all; in spite of General Airey's promises, Lord Raglan was making him responsible for the disaster. An extra cause for anger was Lord Raglan's warm commendation of Lord Cardigan, who had "obeyed the order in the most spirited and gallant manner" and had "charged with the utmost vigour."

White-hot with anger Lord Lucan devised a scheme. He would write a letter "so that the English public should know the facts of the case." This letter should go to the Secretary for War, the Duke of Newcastle, and be published with Lord Raglan's dispatch. The rules of the service laid down that such a letter must be transmitted through the Commander-in-Chief, and on November 30 Lord Lucan addressed a letter to Lord Raglan. It was an excellent letter. He stressed the ambiguous wording of Lord Raglan's two last orders, the authoritative behaviour of Captain Nolan, and the impossibility of disobeying an order brought by an aide-de-camp from headquarters. "I cannot remain silent," he wrote finally; "it is, I feel, incumbent on me to state those facts which, I cannot doubt, must clear me from what, I respectfully submit, is altogether unmerited."

Lord Raglan did his best to dissuade Lord Lucan from sending the letter, and on three occasions sent General Airey to remonstrate with him. No doubt his motives were mixed, but magnanimity was among them; he was aware that he held all the cards in his hand. However, Lord Lucan insisted, and on December 18 the letter was sent off with a letter from Lord Raglan covering Lucan's points. He had, he wrote, "asked General Airey to suggest to Lord Lucan that he should withdraw the letter, considering that it would not lead to his advantage to the slightest degree, but Lord Lucan refused."

On January 12 the Duke of Newcastle, having received the letter, wrote privately to Lord Raglan that he was "very sorry for the unfortunate course taken by Lord Lucan. I may tell you that I had already seen his letter to you, for he had sent it to this country to be published if you did not send it to me. I presume he is under the impression that I shall publish it with the dispatch from you. Of course I shall do nothing of the kind."

On January 27 the Duke of Newcastle officially communicated to Lord Raglan what Lucan might have known would be the inevitable consequence of his letter—the Earl of Lucan was to be recalled. After reading Lord Lucan's letter, the Duke "felt that the public service and the general discipline of the army, must be greatly prejudiced by any misunderstanding between your lordship, as the general commanding Her Majesty's forces in the field, and the Lieutenant-General commanding the Division of Cavalry. Apart from any consideration of the merits of the question raised by Lord Lucan, the position in which he has now placed himself towards your lordship, renders his withdrawal from the army under your command in all respects advisable." Lord Hardinge, the Commander-in-Chief in England, had been consulted, and the Queen had approved. Lord Raglan was to inform Lord Lucan that "it is Her Majesty's pleasure that he should resign the command of the Cavalry Division and return forthwith to England."

In a private note the Duke added, "Spare his feelings as much as you can, but I despair of his ever seeing the justice and propriety of this decision."

The intimation of his recall reached Lord Lucan on February 12, and it came on him like a thunderbolt. "No one," wrote William Forrest, "is so astonished as Lord Lucan himself." It had never crossed his mind that his letter, so admirable in its advocacy, could have this fatal result. On the whole the army thought he was ill used, though no one wished him back. One of his very young officers wrote that it was "quite a relief to get rid of him, poor old man; he was a horrible old fellow." William

Forrest attributed his downfall to his irritability and obstinacy "he could not bear to have any suggestion made to him by anybody, and by his manner and address made many enemies. He will though, I think, come out of any investigation better than our old friend Lord Cardigan."

On February 14 Lord Lucan left the Crimea. William Howard Russell went on board the transport to bid him good-bye. There had been a friendship between them, and Russell respected Lord Lucan's conscientiousness. There was a fire, said Russell, burning fiercely in Lord Lucan's eye, and in farewell he shook his fist at the heights where headquarters stood.

Lord Cardigan had preceded him some weeks earlier, but Lord Cardigan came home crowned with laurels—a hero.

After the battle of Balaclava Lord Cardigan had spent even more time on his yacht. He saw a good deal of Lord Raglan, who was, he wrote, "particularly kind to me about this time and asked me frequently to accompany him riding," and he exchanged some angry letters with Lucan on the subject of the orderlies who rode to and from his yacht, and the lateness of his returns.

On November 5 the Russians attacked again, and the battle of Inkerman was fought. It was, however, a battle in which the cavalry took no part, and it was therefore of no consequence that, though the battle began at five in the morning, Cardigan did not get up to his brigade until a quarter past ten.

After Inkerman the remnants of the Light Brigade were moved up near the scene of the attack, in case the enemy attempted a surprise. The camp of the Light Brigade was then more than six miles away from Cardigan's yacht, but still he did not relinquish command of the brigade.

Winter now set in, the worst winter for more than a century in the Crimea, and Lord Cardigan's health compelled him to stay on his yacht for four or five days at a time. Meanwhile the survivors of the Light Brigade, and especially the horses, were enduring fearful hardships. Sleet and snow borne on great gales of icy wind swept through their camp; the men had only tents, the horses had no shelter of any kind.

About November 7 the Commissariat notified Lord Cardigan that they no longer had transport to bring forage the six miles up to the camp, and suggested the horses should either be sent down to Balaclava together, or fetch their own forage. Lord Cardigan refused to allow either. The horses must remain where they had been posted in case of another attack.

On Saturday, November 11, the horses had one handful of barley each as their day's food and the same the next day. They were standing knee-deep in mud, with the bitter Crimean wind cutting their emaciated bodies. They ate their straps, saddle flaps, and blankets, and gnawed each other's tails to stumps. An order had been issued that no horse was to be destroyed except for a broken limb or glanders, and horses, dying of starvation, lay in the mud in their death agony for three days, while no one dared shoot them.

On November 14 a fearful hurricane blew, sealing the doom of the British army. Tents were blown away, horses bowled over, such stores as existed were destroyed, and in the harbour a number of vessels were wrecked.

On the 19th Lord Cardigan wrote to Lord Raglan, and after a few remarks about Lord Lucan (he had been collecting complaints about Lucan's conduct which he enclosed in two envelopes), he informed Lord Raglan that, much to his regret, he would be "obliged shortly to ask you for leave of absence on sick certificate. Were it not for bad health, I assure you I should have no wish to go, for you know you have no keener soldier in your army." He might, he suggested, get a certificate from the principal medical officer "without having to explain my ailments in detail before a Medical Board." His intention was to go for a time to a warm climate, perhaps Naples, and he would like to go as soon as possible. "But I will follow your wishes and advice, even to the detriment of my health." Lord Raglan replied curtly that if Lord Cardigan wished to go home he must go before a medical board in the usual way. The board was held on December 3, and Cardigan was pronounced unfit for duty. On December 8 with Mr. de Burgh he left the Crimea, pausing for a few days at Constantinople, whence on December 12 he wrote Lord Raglan a last farewell complaint of Lord Lucan. "I cannot leave the country without affording you an opportunity of knowing how the duties of the cavalry command are carried on." He and Lord Lucan had had a final and furious wrangle about the orderlies who plied to and from Lord Cardigan's yacht, and Lucan had "taken the opportunity of commenting on the permission I received from your lordship to live on my yacht." Lucan had apparently been extremely offensive. "Can it be believed," wrote Lord Cardigan, "that any other general officers commanding brigades can be so treated in this army except those who have the misfortune to serve in the Cavalry Division?" Having dispatched this final appeal, he sailed for Marseilles.

On January 13 Lord Cardigan landed at Dover to find himself a hero. As he came on to the pier a crowd gathered and gave "three cheers for Balaclava." In London he was mobbed by enthusiastic crowds, his picture was in every shop window, his biography in every newspaper. A woollen jacket, such as he had worn in the Crimea, was copied, christened a Cardigan, and has been sold by the thousand. The jacket keeps the name to this day. *Punch* published a flattering cartoon entitled "A trump Card(-igan)." The Queen, immediately he arrived, asked him to Windsor from Tuesday to Thursday, and at Prince Albert's request he gave a description of the charge. The day he left Windsor he called at the Horse Guards and was told he was to be appointed Inspector-General of Cavalry. Unfortunately he did not keep his head. On February 5 a banquet was given in his honour at the Mansion House, and he made an egotistic and bombastic speech giving a highly coloured account of his own prowess in the Light Brigade charge. He arrived on horseback wearing the uniform he had worn at Balaclava, and was cheered by immense crowds, who plucked the hairs from his horse's tail to keep as souvenirs. *The Times* commented that there was a strong flavour of Madame Tussaud's wax-works about the whole affair.

All England, it seemed, panted to do him honour. The county of Northamptonshire presented him with a testimonial in the form of a roll forty yards long, Yorkshire gave him a sword, Leicester an illuminated address. Bands met him at the railway station playing "See the conquering hero comes"; women wept as he delivered his speech. As time went on, he spoke with more and more emotion and became "so overcome that he was unable to proceed" and had "to frequently pause and be revived."

When Lord Cardigan's glory was at its height, on March 1, Lord Lucan arrived in England, and at once sent his son, Lord Bingham, to the Commander-in-Chief, Lord Hardinge, to demand a court-martial. It was refused. On March 2 Lord Lucan addressed the House of Lords on the subject of his recall, and again on the 6th and 9th. On March 5 he sent another demand for a court martial. It, too, was refused. Lord Panmure, who had succeeded the Duke of Newcastle as Secretary for War, wrote to Lord Raglan on March 16 that he was absolutely against it. It would be a scandal to the Army. "We have so far prevented him and Lord Cardigan coming into collision," he added. On March 19 Lord Lucan once more addressed the House of Lords at great length on his recall and his being refused a court martial, and a debate followed. The House was against him. It was felt that he had acted improperly in exposing the intimate affairs of the high command of the Army to the public gaze. "It was regrettable," said the Duke of Richmond, "to hear particular acts, accusations and private conversations brought forward," nor should Lord Lucan, in his high military position, have publicly attacked Lord Raglan the Commander-in-Chief. No motion was brought forward to support his application for a court martial. He had failed.

He could do nothing more, and withdrew to Ireland to derive what satisfaction he could from seeing Castlebar illuminated in his honour and receiving an address of welcome from a body describing itself as his loyal and devoted tenantry.

He was, however, very shortly back in England. Not only his generalship but his personal courage was being impugned. Immediately after his speech in the House of Lords a pamphlet was published entitled "The British Cavalry at Balaclava. Remarks in reply to Lieut.-General Lord Lucan's speech in the House of Lords by a Cavalry Officer." The cavalry officer was no other than Lucan's old enemy, Anthony Bacon. He condemned Lord Lucan not only for being inefficient and out of date, but because he had not led the Charge of the Light Brigade himself. It was the practice both of the Duke of Wellington and of Napoleon when serious operations were in question and danger threatened to put themselves at the head of their troops. Murat, Ney, Massena, Hill, Crawford, Picton had all followed this practice; Lord Anglesey and Lord Combermere were to be found with their leading squadrons. "It was not their practice to . . . place a whole Brigade between the enemy and their own persons," wrote Anthony Bacon. In spite of entreaties from his friends, Lord Lucan would not keep silent. He published a pamphlet in reply, entitled "A Vindication of the Earl of Lucan from Lord Raglan's Reflections," and plunged into an abusive correspondence with Anthony Bacon, which was also published. Meanwhile Lord Cardigan went about London, speaking, wrote Henry Greville, "with great bitterness and asperity" of Lord Lucan's conduct in the charge and sneering at the "Look-on system of cavalry tactics."

Lord Lucan's unpopularity was now great, and when he was made K.C.B. and, in November, 1855, colonel of the 8th Hussars, *The Times* wrote scathingly of the appointments. Again he would not keep silent, and wrote angry letters, which *The Times* was delighted to publish.

It was the hour of triumph for Lord Cardigan, the hero of Balaclava, and in his new appointment as Inspector-General of Cavalry he revelled in military power. Officers hastily wrote to warn each other of the coming ordeal; nothing like it had been known before, no detail escaped the major-general's eye, and he was apt to be displeased with everything. "No very pleasant day was spent" when Lord Cardigan came down.

Meanwhile in June, 1855, Lord Raglan died in the Crimea, officially of Crimean fever; actually, it was said, of a broken heart. Fearful misfortunes had overtaken him. He had seen the British army perish before his eyes during the winter of 1854, starved and frozen to death on the heights, paying the price for the loss of the Woronzoff Road. "I could never return to England now," he said after the disasters of the winter. "They would stone me to death." Worse than the loss of an army was to follow. British casualties from sickness had been so great that the army before Sebastopol was now an army of inexperienced lads, raw recruits sent hastily out after a few weeks' drill. On June 18, the anniversary of Waterloo, an assault was at last made on Sebastopol. The task was exacting, there was a strong fortification to be stormed under deadly fire, casualties were high. But the men who had won the Alma by sheer fighting, the troops whose morale had carried them down the North Valley at Balaclava as if they were on parade, were dead. The raw British troops gave way, the assault failed, Lord Raglan's heart was broken, and a few days later he died.

The glory of Lord Cardigan did not long remain untarnished. He, too, had been made K.C.B. in the summer of 1855 as a reward for his distinguished services with the cavalry in the Crimea. But in January, 1856, Sir John McNeill and Colonel Tulloch published the results of their "Inquiry into the Supplies of the British Army in the Crimea." They baldly attributed the destruction of the cavalry to the inefficiency, indifference, and obstinacy of the Earl of Lucan and the Earl of Cardigan. A storm broke, Lord Cardigan and Lord Lucan were attacked in the press, columns described and deplored their conduct, leaders demanded their dismissal. Meanwhile the two noble Earls rushed into print to attack Sir John McNeill and Colonel Tulloch, and each other. In July, 1856, a board of general officers called the "White Washing Board" sat at Chelsea to examine the allegations. Both Lord Lucan and Lord Cardigan were handsomely exonerated, but Lord Lucan brought—and lost—a libel action against the *Daily News* for its comments on his want of self-command and bad temper.

Meanwhile peace had been signed in April, 1856, troops began to come home, and in December the Honourable Somerset Calthorpe, one of Lord Raglan's nephews and his aide-de-camp, published a book entitled *Letters from Headquarters*. After several highly uncomplimentary references to Lord Cardigan, he wrote that at Balaclava after the charge had taken place, "Lord Cardigan unfortunately was not present when wanted." This statement was taken to imply that Lord Cardigan had never reached the guns; indeed, many people who had been present at Balaclava believed that was the truth. Moreover, the cavalry left in the Crimea had raged as they read of Lord Cardigan's triumphs. Robert Portal wrote that he wished "someone at the public meetings, where he trumpets his own praises, would ask him a few home questions. Who was the first man out of action at Balaclava? Was he not asked if he had been in action at all on that occasion?" William Forrest told his wife that the cavalry were disgusted and Cardigan was by no means the hero people at home imagined. As the Balaclava veterans returned, it began to be whispered everywhere that Lord Cardigan was a fake. Meanwhile Cardigan behaved with great foolishness. Having demanded a retraction, which Colonel Calthorpe refused, and asked for a court martial on Colonel Calthorpe, which he did not obtain, he embarked on a campaign of persecution. He wrote to Lord Westmorland, on whose staff Colonel Calthorpe held an appointment, asking that he should be dismissed. When, in 1859, Cardigan became colonel of the 5th Dragoon Guards, he did his best to prevent Colonel Calthorpe from exchanging into the regiment; he even wrote a personal appeal to the Prince Consort asking him to interfere. It was not, however, until 1863 that Lord

Cardigan applied for a criminal information for libel against Colonel Calthorpe in the Queen's Bench.

In June, 1863, the battle of Balaclava was fought over again in the Queen's Bench. The result was most unhappy for Lord Cardigan. It was proved beyond a shadow of doubt that he had reached the guns, and the fact that he was non-suited on the ground that the action had been too long delayed was of no importance. But the story which did emerge, the facts of his indifference, his neglect of his brigade, his callous lack of responsibility for his men, created an impression his courage could not efface. "He was," it had been written, "the personification of all the men who rode that bloody course. His name transported us out of the common prosaic associations of our everyday life." He could be that personification no longer.

Lately, however, a great change had taken place in his life. In January, 1857, a certain Miss Adeline de Horsey had come with her father, Mr. Spencer Horsey de Horsey, to stay at Deene Park. Mr. de Horsey was an old friend, and Cardigan had known his daughter since she was a child—a considerable period, for she was thirty-three. Lord Cardigan was now nearly sixty years of age, but still remarkably handsome, and he would shortly be an eligible widower, since his wife, from whom he was separated, was known to be suffering from an incurable disease and her early death was inevitable. Miss de Horsey was extremely good-looking in a dashing Spanish style; she danced the cachucha after dinner wearing Spanish costume, rode superbly, and sparkled with vivacity. She was not, however, well thought of in the best society: her manners were free, she had been surrounded by too many admirers for too many years, and there had been an odd entanglement with a Count de Montemolin, who claimed to be a member of the Spanish royal family. Lord Cardigan, however, fell violently in love with her, and very soon she had quarrelled with her father, left home, and was established in a house off Park Lane, and visited by Cardigan every day. On July 12, 1858, at about half-past six in the morning, there came a loud banging at the door of the house off Park Lane; servants hurriedly withdrew the bolts, and Lord Cardigan, rushing upstairs into Miss de Horsey's bedroom, clasped her in his arms, "My dearest, she's dead . . . let's get married at once."

It was thought better to marry out of England, and in the course of a cruise in Lord Cardigan's magnificent yacht the marriage took place in September, 1858, at the Military Chapel, Gibraltar; Mr. de Burgh was a witness.

After the marriage Lord and Lady Cardigan lived in princely style. A private orchestra was set up at Deene Park supervised by a "master of music"; additions were made to the house and a great ballroom was built by Wyatt. There was the magnificent yacht, "of which the beauty and fittings caught every eye," at Cowes, and the mansion in Portman Square. Lord Cardigan also gave substantial presents to his wife. In 1864 she was "in ecstasies over the gift of a house in Scotland." Financial difficulties, however, were no longer unknown: in 1864 Lord Cardigan raised £150,000, and by the end of his life the estate was heavily mortgaged.

It was an unfortunate marriage. Lord Cardigan had been no wiser in the choice of his second wife than of his first. There were no children, and the second Lady Cardigan turned out to be a very strange person indeed.

She did not go much into society—the circumstances of her marriage had given Queen Victoria a prejudice against her—and she filled Deene Park with "a certain kind of racing society." The county was scandalised by her daring clothes, by her Spanish dancing, and the freedom of her conversation, and one at least of Lord Cardigan's sisters was forbidden by her husband to enter Deene Park. "It is an infamous house," he said. After Lord Cardigan's death her peculiarities became pronounced: she received visitors in the drawing-room at Deene Park dressed in Lord Cardigan's cuirass and cherry-coloured trousers—this, she said, was a bicycling costume—and in the summer she had herself rowed about the harbour at Cowes, reclining in the stern of a gig, dressed in Spanish costume, and singing to a guitar.

During Lord Cardigan's lifetime he was extremely jealous and for years refused to allow his wife to be taken down to dinner by any other man. She was equally jealous, and especially detested the memory of the first Lady Cardigan. One day Lady Cardigan was seen to snatch a miniature of her predecessor from a table and grind it to powder beneath her heel.

In 1860 Lord Cardigan realised a lifelong ambition: he was made colonel of the 11th Hussars. It was the one unalloyed satisfaction of his life. His last years were spent in declining health, and on March 28, 1868, at the age of seventy-one, he died from injuries resulting from a fall from his horse; it was thought that while riding he had had a stroke.

During the ten years of their marriage he never gave up the attempt to procure his wife social recognition: he would not speak to his friends unless they, and their wives, received her; he appealed to his sisters; he wrote round to his relatives reminding them it was their duty to acknowledge his wife by a formal call. "She is a very good little wife to me," he wrote to one of his sisters in 1866, "and no two people could be better suited."

However, the servants at Deene said the old man was frightened of her and that, when in a rage, she threw plates at him. Since the Earl of Cardigan had no son by either of his marriages, his distant cousin the Marquess of Ailesbury succeeded to his title; both the Earl and the Marquess being great-grandsons of the third Earl of Cardigan. After more than 130 years the descendants of Thomas Brudenell, the distinguished younger son of the third Earl, thus succeeded to the family title, and the Earldom is now the courtesy title of the eldest son of the Marquess.

Lord Lucan survived Lord Cardigan by twenty years. His undertakings in Ireland did not prosper. A very large scheme for rearing and fattening cattle to be sold as meat in England happened to coincide with the first introduction of frozen meat from the Argentine, a great deal of money was lost, and at the end of his life he felt himself to be financially straitened. He had the consolation of military honours: he was promoted general, made Gold Stick and colonel of the 1st Life Guards in 1865, made G.C.B. in 1869, and finally promoted field marshal in 1887. His most important act, however, was of a totally unexpected nature. In 1858 the House of Lords and the House of Commons disagreed over Lord John Russell's Bill to remove the disabilities of Jews in taking the Parliamentary oath. Practising Jews were unable to sit as Members of Parliament, as their religion precluded them from taking the oath, but Lords and Commons could not agree as to what the form of the oath for Jews was to be. Lord Lucan got up and proposed a simple and practical compromise—a clause was to be added to the Bill to enable each House to modify the form of oath required at will. The solution was hailed with universal relief, and the Bill with Lord Lucan's suggested clause added passed both Houses in July. The Jewish community, through Sir David Salomons, presented Lord Lucan with an official address of thanks.

In 1888, at eighty-eight years of age, Lord Lucan died, vigorous and alert to the last. "A marvellous survival," wrote William Howard Russell—"younger than most people's elder sons." He was succeeded by his son, Lord Bingham, one of the most lovable and universally beloved of men. The fourth Lord Lucan and his wife did a great deal for Mayo. Under the Land Acts of the end of the nineteenth century, Irish peasants had certain rights of purchasing land, and the fourth Earl of Lucan made it easy, at considerable cost to himself, for his tenants to buy their holdings. Much of the land his father had "consolidated" was thus restored, and the Mall in the centre of Castlebar was presented to the town. Lady Lucan started a tweed industry in Castlebar, to which she devoted a large part of her time, providing a warehouse for the tweed at Laleham. Most important of all, the fourth Earl of Lucan made friends among Catholics. In 1866, as Lord Bingham, he had added a clause to the Poor

Law Amendment Bill enabling Roman Catholic children in workhouse schools to be educated in their own faith; when he became Earl of Lucan, Canon Lyons, the parish priest of the Roman Catholic Church at Castlebar, was one of his intimate friends. Old people at Castlebar still like to recall how the Earl and the priest were to be seen almost every day walking up and down together under the trees in the Mall.

It is the memory of the fourth Earl which remains in Mayo. There are no longer Earls of Lucan at Castlebar, and the third Earl has passed from everyone's mind, but the recollection of his son is cherished. Today if anyone mentions the name of the Earl of Lucan in Castlebar, he will be told "Ah—he was a saint."

The sufferings, the courage, the endurance displayed in the Crimean War were not wasted. It had been a small war, an unsuccessful war, a horribly mismanaged war, but it proved to be of enormous importance. After the Crimean War, a change came in military affairs—even the incompetence of the Crimea bore fruit. A new age of army reform began not only in England but in Europe and the United States of America: staff colleges were set up, the conditions under which commissions and promotion were obtained were reformed, medical and hospital services, supply, clothing, cooking were all investigated and improved. Above all, the treatment of the private soldier was changed. The bravery, the stubborn endurance of private soldiers, reported in newspapers for the first time during the Crimea, had been a revelation. At the beginning of the campaign the private soldier was regarded as a dangerous brute; at the end he was a hero. Army welfare and army education, army recreation, sports, and physical training, the health services, all came into being as a result of the Crimea. The agony had been frightful, but it had not been useless.

It might, almost, be called a happy ending.

Principal Sources

MSS.

The Bingham Papers
The Brudenell Papers
The Ailesbury Papers
The Wellington Papers at Apsley House
The Military Papers of Lord FitzRoy James Henry Somerset, first Baron Raglan, Field Marshal
Correspondence of Sir Robert Peel
The letters and memoranda of Gen. William Charles Forrest, C.B.
The Crimean letters of Lt.-Gen. Edward Seager, C.B.
Letters from Capt. William Pechell, late 77th Regiment
Crimean Diary of Capt. A. W. Godfrey, Rifle Brigade
Letters of Gen. Sir George de Lacy Evans, G.C.B., D.C.L.
Letters from Turkey and the Crimea. Col. Sir Ashley Maude, K.C.B.
The War Office Files
The Records of the Judge Advocate General's Office
Affidavits in the action brought in the Queen's Bench against Lt. Col. the Hon. Somerset Calthorpe by James Thomas, Earl of Cardigan

PRIVATELY PRINTED WORKS

Letters from the Crimea. Capt. Robert Portal, 4th Light Dragoons
Letters written during the Crimean War by Cornet E. R. Fisher-Rowe, 4th Dragoon Guards
Eight Months on Active Service, by a General Officer
William Forster's visit to some of the distressed districts in Ireland 1846 and 1847

Recollections of the Light Brigade, by Albert Mitchell, Sergeant, 13th Hussars

English Cavalry in the Army of the East, 1854-1855

Memoranda and Observations on the Crimean War, from manuscripts by the late Gen. Sir George Brown, G.C.B., etc.

A Plea for Mercy in Mayo

NEWSPAPERS AND PERIODICALS

The Files of *The Times*

The Files of the *Morning Chronicle*

The Files of the *Globe*

The Files of the *Daily News*

The Files of the *Telegraph and Connaught Ranger*

The Files of the *United Services Gazette*

The Files of the *Army & Navy Gazette*

The Files of the *Gentleman's Magazine*

The Files of the *Annual Register*

The Files of *The Age*

The Files of the *Court Journal*

Official report of proceedings in Parliament

PRINCIPAL PRINTED AUTHORITIES

(Published in London unless otherwise stated)

The Army Purchase Question—Ridgway 1858

Queen Adelaide, by Mary Hopkirk—John Murray 1946

The Story of General Bacon, by Alnod J. Boger—Methuen 1903

British Cavalry at Balaclava, by a Cavalry Officer—T. Boone & Co. 1855

The British Expedition to the Crimea, by William Howard Russell, LL.D.—George Routledge & Sons 1877

"Balaclava and the Russian Captivity," by J. W. Wightman—*Nineteenth Century* May, 1892

Chit Chat, by Lady Augusta Fane—Thornton Butterworth 1925

Correspondence between Major General the Earl of Lucan, K.C.B., and General Bacon—G. I. Palmer 1855

The Creevey Papers, edited by Sir Herbert Maxwell, Bart., M.P., LL.D., F.R.S.—John Murray 1904

The Croker Papers, edited by Louis J. Jenning—John Murray 1884

The Crimea in Perspective, by Lt.-Gen. Sir George MacMunn, K.C.B., K.C.S.I., etc.—G. Bell & Sons 1933

The Crimea in 1854 and 1894, by Gen. Sir Evelyn Wood, V.C., G.C.B., etc.
—Chapman & Hall 1895

The Crimean Expedition, by The Baron de Bazancourt—Sampson Low 1856

Correspondence by Sarah Spencer Lady Lyttelton, 1787-1870, edited by
the Hon. Mrs. Hugh Wyndham—John Murray 1912

Diary of a Soldier's Life: Letters of General Beauchamp Walker—Chapman & Hall 1924

My Diaries 1888-1914, by Wilfred Scawen Blunt—Martin Secker 1919

Diary and Letters of Madame D'Arblay—Macmillan 1904

*Crimean Diary and letters of Lieut.-General Sir Charles Ash Windham,
K.C.B.*—Kegan Paul, Trench, Trubner & Co. 1897

A Fortnight in Ireland, by Sir Francis B. Head, Bart.—John Murray 1852

The Glenbervie Journals, edited by Walter Sichel—Constable & Co. 1910

*Granville Leveson Gower (first Earl Granville), Private Correspondence,
1781-1821,* edited by Castalia Countess Granville—John Murray 1916

The Greville Memoirs, 1814-1860, edited by Lytton Strachey and Roger
Fulford—Macmillan 1938

Galignani's New Paris Guide for 1858, The Great War with Russia, by
William Howard Russell, LL.D.—George Routledge & Sons 1895

The Great Famine in Ireland, by W. P. O'Brien, C.B.—Downey & Co. 1896

History of the Archdiocese of Tuam, by the Rt. Rev. Mgr. Alton—Phoenix
Publishing Co., Dublin 1928

A Personal History of the Horse-Guards, 1750-1832, by J. H. Stocqueler—
Hurst & Blackett 1873

Historical Manuscripts Commission Buccleuch MSS.

History of the 17th Lancers (Duke of Cambridge's Own), by the Hon. J. W.
Fortescue, LL.D., D.Litt.—Macmillan 1895

Historical Records of the Eleventh Hussars (Prince Albert's Own), by
Capt. Godfrey Trevelyan Williams—George Newnes 1908

A History of the British Army, by the Hon. J. W. Fortescue, LL.D.,
D.Litt., Vol. XIII—Macmillan 1930

The History of Ireland from the Treaty of Limerick to the Present Time,
by John Michel—James Duffy, Dublin 1869

The Invasion of the Crimea, by A. W. Kinglake—William Blackwood &
Sons 1877

Illustrated History of the War against Russia, by E. H. Nolan, Ph.D.,
LL.D.—James Virtue 1857

Ireland from 1798-1898, by William O'Connor Morris—A. D. Innes & Co.
1898

Irish Distress and its Remedies, by James H. Tuke—Ridgway 1880

Journal kept during the Russian War, by Mrs. Henry Duberly—Longman, Brown, Green & Longman 1855

Letters of Queen Victoria, 1837-1861, edited by Arthur Christopher Benson, M.A., and Viscount Esher, G.C.V.O., K.C.B., etc.—John Murray 1907

Life of His Royal Highness the Prince Consort, by Theodore Martin—Smith, Elder & Co. 1877

Letters from Head Quarters, by an Officer on the Staff—John Murray 1856

The Light Cavalry Brigade in the Crimea, by Gen. Lord George Paget, K.C.B.—John Murray 1881

The Letters of Charles Greville and Henry Reeve, 1836-1865, edited by the Rev. A. H. Johnson, M.A.—Fisher Unwin 1924

Leaves from the Diary of Henry Greville, edited by the Viscountess Enfield—Smith, Elder & Co. 1883

Letters of Harriet Countess Granville, 1810-1845, edited by the Hon. F. Leveson Gower—Longmans, Green & Co. 1894

Memoirs of an Ex-Minister, by the Right Hon. The Earl of Malmesbury, G.C.B.—Longmans, Green & Co. 1885

The Military Forces of the Crown, by Charles M. Clode—John Murray 1869

Money or Merit, by Edward Barrington de Fonblanque—Skeet 1857

Men of the Time—David Bogue 1856

Memoirs of the Binghams, by Rose E. Calmont—Spottiswoode & Co. 1915

On Chiltern Slopes, by A. H. Stanton, M.A.—Blackwell, Oxford 1927

Our Heroes of the Crimea, by George Ryan—George Routledge & Sons 1855

The Panmure Papers, edited by Sir George Douglas, Bart., and Sir George Dalhousie Ramsay—Hodder & Stoughton 1908

The Population of Ireland, 1750-1845, by K. H. Connell—The Clarendon Press, Oxford 1950

The Plantation Scheme of the West of Ireland, by James Caird—Blackwood & Sons 1850

Recollections of a Military Life, by Gen. Sir John Adye—Smith, Elder & Co. 1895

My Recollections, by the Countess of Cardigan and Lancastre—Eveleigh Nash 1909

Recommendations of the Oxford University Commissioners, by James Heywood, M.P.—Longman, Brown, Green & Longman 1853

Reminiscences and Recollections of Captain Gronow, 1810-1860—John C. Nimmo 1889

Recollections and Experiences, by Edmund Yates—Richard Bentley & Sons 1884

Report from Her Majesty's Commissioners of Inquiry into the State of the Law and Practice in Relation to the Occupation of Land in Ireland, 1845 (The Devon Commission)

Report of the Commission of Inquiry into the Supplies of the British Army in the Crimea, 1856 (The McNeill & Tulloch Commission)

Seventy-one Years of a Guardsman's Life, by Gen. Sir George Higginson, G.C.M., etc.—John Murray 1916

The Story of a Soldier's Life, by Field Marshal Viscount Wolseley, G.M., G.C.B., G.C.M.G., etc.—Constable & Co. 1903

Speech of Major-General the Earl of Lucan delivered in the House of Lords on March 19th, 1855—Hatchard 1855

The Tollemaches of Helmingham and Ham, by Maj.-Gen. E. D. H. Tollemache—Ipswich 1949

The Trial of James Thomas Earl of Cardigan before the Right Honourable the House of Peers in Full Parliament for Felony—Published by order of the House of Peers 1841

A Vindication of the Earl of Lucan from Lord Raglan's Reflections—Hatchard 1855

Under Five Reigns, by Lady Dorothy Nevill—Methuen 1910

A Twelve Months Residence in Ireland during the Famine and the Public Works, 1846-1847, by William Henry Smith—Longman, Brown, Green & Longman 1848

The War in the Crimea, by Gen. Sir Edward Hamley, K.C.B.—Seeley & Co. 1896

With the Guards We Shall Go, compiled from letters of Capt. the Hon. Sturge Jocelyn by Mabell Countess of Airlie—Hodder & Stoughton 1933

The War: the letters of *The Times* correspondent from the seat of War in the East—George Routledge & Sons 1855

The West of Ireland, by Henry Coulter—Hurst & Blackett 1862

The Wardens of Savenake Forest, by the Earl of Cardigan—Routledge & Kegan Paul 1949

Index

309

Library of Congress Cataloguing in Publication Data

Woodham-Smith, Cecil Blanche Fitz Gerald, 1896–
        The reason why.
Reprint. Originally published: New York: Time Inc., c1953.
   (Time reading program special edition)
   1. Cardigan, James Thomas Brudenell, 1797–1868.
   2. Lucan, George Charles Bingham, Earl, 1800–1888.
3. Balaklava, Battle of, 1854. 4. Great Britain. Army—Biography.
       5. Generals—Great Britain—Biography.
  I. Title. II. Series: Time reading program special edition.
  DA536.C3W6 1982b   941.081′092′4 [B]   82-742 AACR2
         ISBN 0-8094-3719-8 (pbk.)
         ISBN 0-8094-3718-X (deluxe)